UNBUILT TORONTO 2

UNBUILT TORONTO 2

More of the City That Might Have Been

Mark Osbaldeston

DUNDURN
TORONTO

Editor: Shannon Whibbs
Design: Courtney Horner
Printer: Friesens

Library and Archives Canada Cataloguing in Publication

Osbaldeston, Mark, 1966-
    Unbuilt Toronto 2 : more of the city that might have been / Mark Osbaldeston.

Includes index.
Issued also in electronic formats.
ISBN 978-1-55488-975-4

    1. Toronto (Ont.)--History. 2. Toronto (Ont.)--Buildings, structures, etc.--History. 3. City planning--Ontario--Toronto--History. I. Title.

FC3097.3.O723 2011   971.3'541   C2011-902587-6

1   2   3   4   5   15   14   13   12   11

We acknowledge the support of the **Canada Council for the Arts** and the **Ontario Arts Council** for our publishing program. We also acknowledge the financial support of the **Government of Canada** through the **Canada Book Fund** and **Livres Canada Books**, and the **Government of Ontario** through the **Ontario Book Publishing Tax Credit** and the **Ontario Media Development Corporation**.

Care has been taken to trace the ownership of copyright material used in this book. The author and the publisher welcome any information enabling them to rectify any references or credits in subsequent editions.

                                                                        J. Kirk Howard, President

Printed and bound in Canada.
www.dundurn.com

Dundurn
3 Church Street, Suite 500
Toronto, Ontario, Canada
M5E 1M2

Gazelle Book Services Limited
White Cross Mills
High Town, Lancaster, England
LA1 4XS

Dundurn
2250 Military Road
Tonawanda, NY
U.S.A. 14150

For my parents

CONTENTS

Commercial Buildings

Arts, Letters, and Leisure

INTRODUCTION

YOU CAN TELL A LOT ABOUT A PLACE by what its people build. But what they fail to build is often just as telling. It can tell you about their history, priorities, economy, even their luck. But if you want to see these monuments, you can't just follow the advice inscribed on Sir Christopher Wren's crypt and "look around you." Instead, you have to look in archives, or in the pages of old journals and periodicals, or, if it's still possible, draw on the records and memories of the people who were there when it was all being dreamed up.

That's what I did in researching *Unbuilt Toronto: A History of the City That Might Have Been.* In conjunction with its release at the end of 2008, the Toronto Society of Architects organized a show at the Royal Ontario Museum, augmenting images from the book with juried selections submitted by practising architects of their own, more recent, unbuilt projects. Opening night confirmed two things: I

was still interested in the topic, and other people were, too. I knew then that I was heading back to the archives.

A few of the projects in this book were selected from the "Unbuilt Toronto" exhibit. Others I discovered as I continued my research. Still others I learned about when someone who had read the first book or seen me speak came up and said, "Have you heard about …?" Though largely forgotten, these were all at one time real projects, with real sites, and a real chance of being constructed, as indeed some were, in altered or truncated form. At the end of each section, however, I look at more conceptual proposals. They may not have had a realistic chance of life beyond the drawing board, but they're fascinating nonetheless; the attempts of designers from different eras to urge their fellow Torontonians to dream a little or, in one case, to laugh a little.

I must express my gratitude to the architects, artists, and others who helped make this book possible by sharing their memories and knowledge, not to mention their artwork and photographs. I must also thank the archivists and librarians, at both private and public institutions, who offered their time and expertise, as well as the Ontario Arts Council for its assistance. Finally, my thanks to the following for their advice and help: Bert Archer, James Dawson, Robert Hill, Brian Hilligoss, Scott James, Loren Kolar, Leslie Jen, Rollo Myers, Stephen Otto, Douglas Richardson, Eric Shelton, and Steven Vieira. All of this generous support has helped me give an alternate life to the projects in the pages that follow.

Mark Osbaldeston
Toronto, April 2011

PUBLIC WORKS

Chapter 1

University Avenue Monuments
1871–1951/Unbuilt — Built to different plans

IN THE SUMMER OF 2010, ON THE LAST day of her twenty-second visit to Canada, the tireless Queen Elizabeth II unveiled a plaque commemorating the 150th anniversary of Queen's Park. It was a fitting bit of remembrance, since the park had been opened by her great-grandfather, the future Edward VII. But there was part of the story that didn't get mentioned: while he was there on that torrential afternoon of September 11, 1860, he laid the cornerstone for the base of a statue, at the head of what is now University Avenue. It was to be of his mother, Queen Victoria, and would serve, according to the *Globe*, "perpetually to remind the citizens of Toronto of the visit of the Royal youth, and his assisting them to show their loyalty and devoted attachment to the Crown and person of his exalted mother." A statue of the queen *was* eventually placed there — temporarily — but Sir John A. Macdonald has occupied that spot for more than a

century. So what ever happened to the statue of Edward's exalted mother? Quite a lot, it would seem …

In the second half of the nineteenth century, English sculptor Marshall Wood did a solid business selling statues of the queen across the empire. His first Canadian commission was for Victoria Square in Montreal. Heading to Canada in 1871 for the unveiling, Wood determined to make the voyage even more lucrative by bringing additional works to sell "on spec." He exhibited a marble statue of the monarch in the Senate in Ottawa and, as he had hoped, quickly sold it to the federal government (it's the centrepiece of the parliamentary library to this day). For Toronto, he brought a monumental bronze which, despite his assertions to the contrary, appeared to be a duplicate of Montreal's. True to plan, soon after its arrival in the city in April 1871, council let Wood erect it on a temporary wooden pedestal in Queen's Park, which still had no likeness of its namesake (Fig. 1-1).

Fig. 1-1. The statue that got away: Marshall Wood's monumental bronze of Queen Victoria reigned from Queen's Park between 1871 and 1874. The sculptor had brought it to Toronto "on spec." [Archives of Ontario, F 4436-0-0-0-31.]

What could be more perfect? Toronto needed a Victoria statue, and along comes Wood with one to spare. It looked like he had another sale after the city's committee on walks and gardens recommended that council approve $3,000 toward the purchase. When the issue was debated that fall, however, some aldermen balked at the expense. Several questioned whether Wood's statue even looked like the queen. In the end, council took no action one way or the other. Oblivious, Toronto's on-consignment sovereign continued to reign from her makeshift base.

In August 1873, the Halifax *Morning Chronicle* reported that Wood was trying to interest Haligonians in a statue of Queen Victoria "similar to those erected by him in Montreal and Toronto." Since, four months earlier, Toronto council had finally got around to voting against purchasing Wood's statue, it seems likely that the Victoria he was hawking in Halifax was more than "similar" to the Toronto property. In any event, Halifax took a pass. The next year, Toronto's city fathers asked Wood to remove his statue from Queen's Park.

To find out what happened to it next, you have to connect some dots. In 1879, a statue of Victoria by Wood was exhibited in Sydney, Australia. It looked like Toronto's, but it seems more likely that Toronto's cast-off had never left the country. In 1880, the *Daily Telegraph* in Quebec City reported that a bronze statue of the queen was being temporarily housed in the city's skating rink — for how long at that point is unclear. It was by Marshall Wood. Using his signature sales technique, Wood had erected it in the city with the hope that the provincial government would buy it, but it wasn't interested. Wood died in 1882, and in the years that followed, his statue popped up at various locations around Quebec City, looking worse for the wear. When Victoria's son, Prince Arthur, the Duke of Connaught, spotted it on a visit in

1890, he commented on its "neglected condition." Having become a rundown embarrassment, it was apparently put into storage in 1893. The *Daily Telegraph* noted its disappearance: "Perhaps it has committed suicide. The poor thing has been a tramp among statues … it has been hustled about from one place to another, and when it went to sleep at night, was never certain where it would wake up the next morning."

Its itinerating days ended in 1897 when Quebec City finally bought it from Wood's son — for pennies on the dollar — for the new Victoria Park. On June 22, 1897, the governor general, Lord Aberdeen, unveiled it in front of a crowd of twenty thousand people. Photographs show that it was identical to the Toronto statue, with one exception: the Toronto work had had a delicate sceptre that extended up past the crook of the queen's arm; the statue unveiled a quarter-century later had a sturdier sceptre that extended down past her hand. A little restorative work for a gal that had led a tough life? If it was, in fact, the Toronto statue, there was a nice symmetry when, in 1908, the future King George V dedicated a new base for it, just as his father had done forty-eight years earlier in Queen's Park (Fig. 1-2).

It was all too good to last. At 2:57 a.m., on July 12, 1963, people across Quebec City were wrenched awake by an explosion that rocked Victoria Park. Wood's statue had been knocked clear off its pedestal. The head, separated from the body, had been rocketed sixty feet away. It was a bombing, the work of the Front de libération du Québec. As it happened, they were even less keen on Wood's Victoriana than the citizens of nineteenth-century Toronto.

———

Fig. 1-2. Toronto's statue? Prior to its unveiling by Lord Aberdeen in Quebec City in 1897, this work by Marshall Wood was described as "a tramp among statues." It is seen here in an undated photograph.[Library and Archives Canada, PA-024005 (photograph by Jules-Ernest Livernois).]

Oddly enough, it wouldn't be the last time that an off-the-rack statue proposed for University Avenue ended up somewhere else. In 1951, John J. Cunningham, the educational director of the National Sculpture Society in New York, approached Toronto officials about buying a statue of Major-General James Wolfe by the sculptor J. Massey Rhind. It was one of four bronzes that had been removed from the Exchange Court, an office building in lower Manhattan.

The reason for their removal (sometime after 1944) is unknown. In fact, why Wolfe was there in the first place is a mystery. Three of the figures were associated with early New York: the explorer Henry Hudson; Peter Stuyvesant, the area's last Dutch governor; and George Clinton, an English colonial governor. That grouping made sense. Then there was Wolfe, immortalized for defeating the French forces — under the command of the Marquis de Montcalm — at Quebec City in 1759. Perhaps Wolfe was specified by the Exchange Court's builder, the deeply anglophilic William Waldorf Astor. Or perhaps it was the idea of the Scottish-born Rhind. Whatever the statue's origins, Hudson, Stuyvesant, and Clinton quickly found a new home in a park in Kingston, New York. But Wolfe was a tough sell in the United States. That's when Cunningham tried his luck in Canada. Intrigued by his offer, Mayor Hiram McCallum sent the city's building and planning commissioners to Gotham to inspect the work. Even though it was stashed in a Brooklyn junkyard, they reported that the two-ton, ten-foot-two-inch monument was in excellent shape.

The way Mayor McCallum saw it, the statue was a bargain at $5,000. He figured it was worth almost that much as scrap alone. And he already had a spot in mind for it: University Avenue, on the south side of College Street. On August 15, 1951, the city's board of control approved the purchase.

Not everyone was as keen as the mayor. Some, like Ontario's deputy treasurer, Chester Walters, thought the subject matter was insensitive at a time when Canada was trying to "forget all the old animosities." Philanthropist Sigmund Samuel wondered why Toronto needed two Wolfe statues within sight of one another: that year, the Royal Ontario Museum's Canadiana Building — which Samuel had helped fund — had opened on Queen's Park Crescent West. Its facade featured a stone sculpture of General Wolfe by Jacobine Jones. Editorialists questioned the artistic merits of erecting a Victorian sculpture in 1950s Toronto. A *Globe* editorial called Rhind's work "exceptionally ugly.... It embodies the worst in Victorian portraiture — stiff, unimaginative and graceless." The *Star* conducted an informal poll of what average Torontonians thought, focusing on people named Wolfe and Montcalm. The statue had become a joke. The board of control, including Mayor McCallum, reversed its position on the purchase the following week. The spot on University is now occupied by the late-1950s monument to former mayor and Ontario Hydro chair Robert H. Saunders.

Rhind's misfit masterpiece sat in its Brooklyn scrapyard for fifteen more years, until Alberta philanthropist Eric Harvie bought it for the City of Calgary as a centennial gift. It was unveiled in front of the Calgary Planetarium on September 13, 1967 (Fig. 1-3). Removed for restoration for nearly a decade, it was rededicated on the 250th anniversary of the Battle of the Plains of Abraham in 2009. Its new home is Calgary's South Mount Royal Park, between Wolfe Street and Montcalm Crescent.

———

Fig. 1-3. The other statue that got away: J. Massey Rhind's sculpture of General James Wolfe is unveiled in Calgary, September 13, 1967. At one time, it was intended for Toronto's University Avenue. [Glenbow Archives, G-1-1249-243-3.]

At least one of the monuments actually planned for University Avenue, the 1934 memorial to Sir Adam Beck, got there only because of the sculptor's tenacity.

A former municipal politician and provincial cabinet minister, Beck (shown in Fig. 3-2) was the founder and longtime president of the Hydro-Electric Power Commission of Ontario, responsible for putting hydro into public hands. Four years after his death in 1925, council appointed a committee to consider how best to memorialize a man who was being lauded as Ontario's greatest public servant. It recommended the erection of a bronze statue on University Avenue. A call for designs went out on April 29, 1929. Competitors were given a little over a month to prepare their submissions.

First prize went to sculptor Emanuel Hahn for his bronze on a concrete base that incorporated a stylized watercourse. Second and third prizes were awarded to Alfred Howell and G.A. Bachman. A record of their entries does not appear to survive, although a photograph exists of architect Alfred Chapman's (Figs. 1-4, 1-5). The sculptor was likely Charles McKechnie. He collaborated with Chapman and Oxley on numerous projects during this period, including the Princes' Gates at the CNE, which had been dedicated two years earlier.

It had always been the plan to place the statue in front of the 1915 Hydro building (now part of Princess Margaret Hospital). That idea had to be abandoned when it was discovered that it would interfere with access to the Toronto General Hospital across the street. Moving on, council voted at the end of 1929 to put it in Queen's Park, but Hahn pushed for an alternate University Avenue site. Relenting, council directed staff to work with him to find one.

The extension of University Avenue to Front Street in 1931 expanded the possibilities, and in February 1932, Hahn convinced council to approve a spot in the median

Fig. 1-4. Emanuel Hahn in his studio, February 2, 1934, working on his monument to Adam Beck. [City of Toronto Archives, Fonds 1231, Item 4.]

Fig. 1-5. The unsuccessful entry of architect Alfred Chapman in the 1929 competition for a memorial to Sir Adam Beck. The sculptor was likely Chapman's frequent collaborator, Charles Mckechnie. [Archives of Ontario, C-18-2.]

of the extension, just south of Queen. Now that Hahn's statue would no longer be outside its offices, Ontario Hydro considered incorporating its own Beck statue into the front entrance of its new University Avenue headquarters, which would open in 1935 (Fig. 1-6). Two statues on the same street of the same man — even such a great man — must have seemed liked overkill, and Hydro sensibly dropped the idea. But Hydro had never been left out. Even from its distant location, Hahn created a connection between his statue and the Hydro buildings, purposely orienting it northward, so that Beck could keep a constant eye on his old stomping grounds.

———

Beck's vigil was interrupted in 1947. That year, the city reconfigured University Avenue, shifting the central median west. The reconstruction necessitated temporarily moving all the avenue's monuments, as well as destroying its mature trees.

In 1950, consulting planner E.G. Faludi was hired to work with assistant city planner Austin Floyd in preparing a landscaping scheme for the reconfigured street. Among other improvements, they recommended that linden trees be planted along the eastern and western boulevards. Where the planners saw in the linden a tree that was hardy and symmetrical, a lot of people in postwar Toronto saw a tree with German associations. Berlin's grand avenue, after all, was called *Unter den Linden*. Dozens of upset Torontonians sent letters and telegrams urging council to substitute a "Canadian" tree, preferably some form of maple (Fig. 1-7).

Council capitulated. At a ceremony on April 28, 1951, Mayor McCallum helped plant the first of 145 red

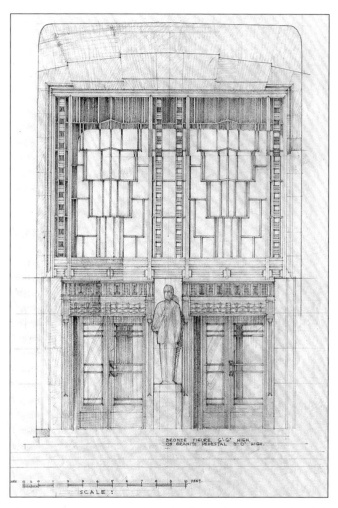

Fig. 1-6. A 1932 proposal by the firm of Sproatt and Rolph for a statue of Sir Adam Beck. It was meant for the new head office building of Ontario Hydro. [Archives of Ontario, C292-1-0-332.]

Fig. 1-7. A 1950 photomontage showing the "German" planting scheme proposed for University Avenue that riled many Torontonians. [Toronto Public Library.]

maples on the eastern and western boulevards. They may have been Canadian by association, but they weren't by origin: unable to find a Canadian supplier, city staff were forced to buy the "Canadian" trees from a nursery in the Netherlands.

Chapter 2

GOVERNMENT HOUSE
1910/BUILT TO DIFFERENT PLANS
WHITNEY BLOCK
1925/PARTIALLY BUILT

IT HAD BEEN A LONG TIME IN COMING. IN early 1910, the provincial government announced that it was closing government house. When the lieutenant governor's mansion had opened at the southwest corner of King and Simcoe Streets in 1870, Ontario's legislative buildings were a stone's throw away on Front Street. But now the politicians had moved up to Queen's Park, the railways were uncomfortably close to the south, and King Street West had become commercial. All in all, it was an unsuitable address for the Queen's representative.

To replace it, the province bought two adjacent residential lots from the Toronto Board of Education. They were on Bloor Street East, near Yonge. The school board had intended them as the site for what would become Central Technical School, before finding a larger and more central plot at Bathurst and Harbord. For the province, however, the five-acre parcel seemed adequately large and was well-located. Plus, it featured an attractive

setting on the Rosedale Ravine, and had the advantage of additional frontage on Bismarck Avenue (de-Germanized during the Great War to St. Paul's Square).

On May 12, 1910, J.O. Reaume, the minister of public works, put out a call to Canadian architects for competitive designs, receiving twelve entries by the July 15 deadline. When the results were announced in late October, first prize went to George W. King for his French Renaissance design; second prize went to George W. Gouinlock for his baronial Tudor-style entry (Figs. 2-1, 2-2, 2-3). And there was a further announcement: neither of them would be built. There was little explanation of why King and Gouinlock (and everyone else) had failed to make the grade. In his subsequent report to the legislature, Reaume said only that "neither of these designs was considered by the Government to fully comprehend or embody the requirements of a building suitable for an establishment of this kind…." The province instructed

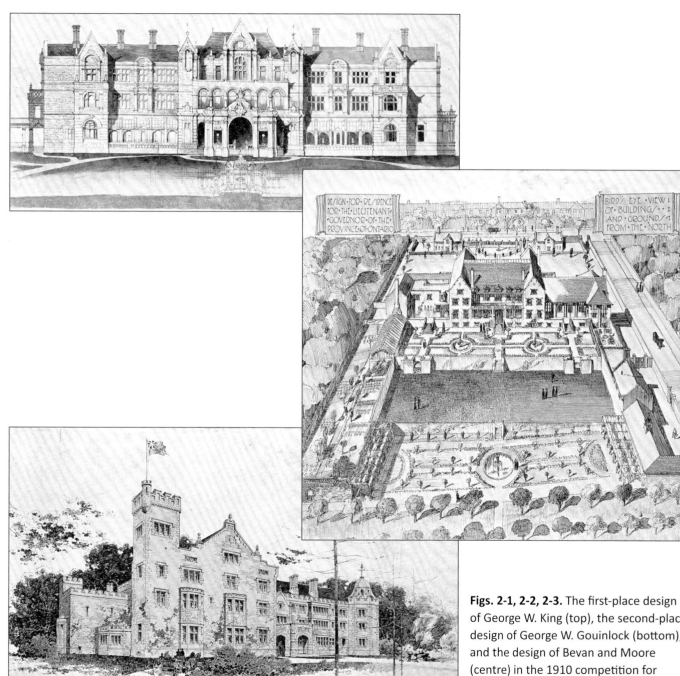

Figs. 2-1, 2-2, 2-3. The first-place design of George W. King (top), the second-place design of George W. Gouinlock (bottom), and the design of Bevan and Moore (centre) in the 1910 competition for Ontario's new government house. [Thomas Fisher Rare Books Library, University of Toronto.]

Fig. 2-4. (left) John Lyle's entry in the 1910 government house competition. Although unsuccessful, its interior layout appears to have been the basis for the plans later developed by the provincial architect. [Thomas Fisher Rare Books Library, University of Toronto.]

Fig. 2-5. (bottom) Chorley Park, shown here nearing completion, opened in 1915. It was Canada's grandest vice-regal mansion. [City of Toronto Archives, Fonds 1497, Series 387, Item 53.]

the provincial architect, Francis Riley Heakes, to come up with something better.

While there was undoubtedly some truth in Reaume's report, it doesn't seem to have been the full story. The Bloor Street site had been seen by many as a mistake from the beginning: too small, too narrow, and, just like the property it was replacing on King, in danger of becoming surrounded by commercial buildings (they were right, the site is now occupied by the Manufacturers Life Building, which has been dwarfed by nearby towers). The *Globe* had run frequent editorials urging the province to walk away from it.

They apparently had an effect. The first indication was that the announcement of the "winners" had come two months late. Declaring that none of the entries was worth building seems likely to have been a convenient way for the government to save face while also buying more time to figure out what its next step would be. In April 1911, it made its decision, abandoning Bloor Street in favour of Chorley Park, a fourteen-acre wooded site off Roxborough Drive in northeastern Rosedale. The *Globe* was even more critical of this site, judging it as too remote. It alleged that the government had only chosen it to increase the value of developers' landholdings in the area. This was a serious allegation, but it didn't stop the newspaper from collecting revenue on ads touting the proximity of two speculative subdivisions to the new vice-regal mansion.

Despite the *Globe*'s efforts, the province was committed to Chorley Park, convinced that Ontarians would embrace the location once they saw what could be done with it. It would take four years and a million dollars (quadruple the original budget) to test that hypothesis. Chorley Park officially opened at the end of 1915. Architectural historian William Dendy has noted

that the French château design that Francis Heakes came up with was clearly copied from George King's winning design for Bloor Street, with the interior plans taken from John Lyle's submission. Fair or not, the result was Canada's most opulent vice-regal mansion (Figs. 2-4, 2-5).

Perhaps on a main street, obviously looking like a public building, Chorley Park might have served as a source of provincial pride. But after the Depression hit, an opulent mansion tucked away in an exclusive enclave served mostly as a lightning rod for populist criticism. The Liberals, under Premier Mitchell Hepburn, made its closing part of their platform in their successful 1934 election bid. Out of respect, they delayed the actual deed until the term of the sitting lieutenant governor, Herbert Bruce, came to an end in December 1937. Future lieutenant governors would be given a suite in the legislative buildings.

The federal government acquired the property in 1940, using it for many years as a military hospital. In 1959, it sold the lease to the city for $100,000. In April of that year, while its fate was still being decided, Premier Leslie Frost announced that Ontario would be getting a proper vice-regal residence after all. It wasn't Chorley Park, but the thirty-room Forest Hill Road mansion of ninety-two-year-old philanthropist Sigmund Samuel, who intended to bequeath it to the province for that purpose on his death. When Samuel died in 1962, however, Lieutenant Governor J. Keiller Mackay declined to move in, as did his successor Earl Rowe. An era had passed; the property was sold. As for Chorley Park, the city demolished it in 1960. It had served as Ontario's government house for scarcely more than two decades.

———

Although Chorley Park is gone, another Toronto masterpiece designed by Francis Heakes still looms on Queen's Park Crescent, across from the legislative buildings. The Whitney Block was constructed in stages between 1925 and 1933, though never fully completed to Heakes's plans.

By the early twentieth century, Richard Waite's 1892 legislative buildings could no longer contain the growing provincial bureaucracy. In 1909, work began on a library wing on the building's north end, designed by the second-prize winner in the government house competition, George Gouinlock. It hadn't progressed beyond the foundation when fire ripped through the legislature's west wing. Making the most of a bad situation, architect E.J. Lennox added an additional floor in designing the replacement. But it still wasn't enough. In 1916, the government was looking at evening things out by adding a storey to the east wing, as well. By 1919, building two floors on the new north wing was being seriously considered, but Heakes advised the minister of public works that it would never produce satisfactory results: what was needed was a stand-alone office building.

In 1923, the province acquired land for the new building on the east side of Queen's Park Crescent. It was bounded by St. Alban's (now Wellesley) Street to the north, Grosvenor to the south, and to the east by the now-closed northern leg of Surrey Place. Mindful of the difficulty that adding on to the legislative buildings had posed, Heakes designed his complex so that it could be expanded in stages. The first would consist of three wings running east–west, connected by a north–south corridor. The wings were almost identical, save for a subtle seventh storey added to the centre wing, to house animals for the Department of Health. Ultimately, these three wings could be duplicated to the south, extending the building to four, five, and ultimately six wings, as necessary (Fig. 2-6).

George Henry, the minister of highways and public works, laid the cornerstone on July 30, 1925. Although the building had been called the East Block by the government from the beginning, it was popularly being referred to as the Whitney Block, after Sir James Whitney, Ontario's premier from 1905 until his death in 1914. The month before the building opened, rumours began to circulate that the government was thinking of naming the building after George Henry himself. Henry denied knowing anything about the "Henry Building" proposal, but, for reasons unexplained, said he was also opposed to naming the building after Whitney. On March 26, 1928, it formally opened as the East Block. Even so, the name Whitney Block never really went away, and in 1966 it finally became official.

There were more serious controversies over tendering irregularities and cost overruns. The government denied the former, but made no apologies for the latter, boasting that it had maximized job opportunities for Ontario workers. Day labourers dug the foundation by hand, and, to the greatest extent possible, the government used Ontario materials, often at increased expense. For example, Queenston blue dolomite limestone was used instead of the cheaper Indiana limestone for the exterior, and a defunct mine at Bancroft was specially reopened for the interior marble. All but $2,000 of the $2.5 million cost of the building was spent on Canadian materials, with over 90 percent of those being from Ontario.

At the building's opening, George Henry reiterated that what the public saw was merely half of what was to come, in about "two or three years." Right on schedule, a little over two years later, cabinet approved the building's expansion. In September 1930, however, Francis Heakes died, having served as provincial architect for thirty-five years. George White took over both the post and the

Fig. 2-6. Ninety percent of the materials used in the Whitney Block were produced in Ontario. The first phase, shown in this architectural perspective, officially opened in March 1928. As originally conceived, later additions would have seen these three wings duplicated to the south. [Archives of Ontario, RG 2-71.]

East Block project. The next phase of construction consisted of one new wing separated from the earlier building by a sixteen-storey tower. There had been no public mention of a tower when the project had been announced back in 1925. As preservation architect William Greer has written, it is likely that it wasn't conceived until later. If that was the case, White must be credited for skilfully integrating it into Heakes's design, creating an impressive landmark without overpowering what needed to remain the area's focus: the legislative buildings across the street (Fig. 2-7).

Twenty-five years later, the government turned its attention to finally completing the building down to Grosvenor, demolishing two Victorian houses in anticipation of the construction. Plans dated November 1958 show the missing two wings competed in a hybrid style. The first floor of the two new wings faithfully duplicated Heakes's work, with the top floor alluding to it after a fashion with its flattened peaks and restrained decorative treatment. The middle floors were, however, rooted in the postwar era, with the provincial architect, George N. Williams, specifying spandrels of fluted

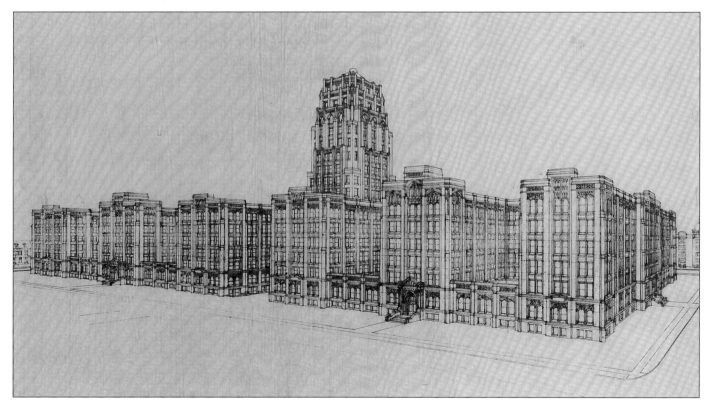

Fig. 2-7. The Whitney Block in its ultimate intended form, in a drawing likely dating from around 1930. A park now occupies the space reserved for the two southernmost wings. [Archives of Ontario, RG 15-13-2, L-240.]

stainless steel. The idea was to tie into the more modern architecture of the recently completed Treasury Building (now the Frost Building North) on the south side of Grosvenor, a structure that seems to have started the dialogue, its dimensions and siting taking their cue from the East Block's wings (Figs. 2-8, 2-9).

The connection between the buildings was made literal in conceptual sketches prepared earlier in 1958, in which the curved annex that would later be added to the Treasury Building on Queen's Park Crescent East (now the Frost Building South), spanned Grosvenor as a

seven-storey bridge, continuing on its north side as the East Block extension.

By December of 1959, the East Block plans had been modified to exactly recreate the two missing wings of Heakes's original plan. They would never be built. Two wings on a 1920s office complex were not going to address the province's space needs going into the 1960s. The construction of the massive Macdonald Block complex in that decade (see Fig. 2-9) saw the land reserved for the Whitney Block extension turned into the Whitney South Garden, integrated into an

Fig. 2-8. Plans prepared by the provincial government in 1958 to extend the Whitney Block south to Grosvenor Street show the building completed in a hybrid modern/Gothic style. [Archives of Ontario, RG 15-13-2, L-131]

Fig. 2-9. A photomontage from 1961 shows the area south of the Whitney Block depicted as a park. To the east of the Whitney Block, an early concept for the Macdonald Block has also been drawn in. The Treasury Building (now the Frost Building North) is across Grosvenor Street, to the south. Evidence of the continuing construction of the University subway line can be seen to the west.

[Archives of Ontario, C 30, ES16–311 A (photomontage by the Northway-Gestalt Corporation).]

extensive system of gardens and squares designed by Sasaki Strong and Associates.

Entering its ninth decade, the Whitney Block tower, with its allegorical exterior sculptures by Charles Adams, still serves as the monument to governmental authority that its builders intended. It's a brave front though: the tower has been empty since 1968, when the functionaries it was built to house condemned it for lacking a fire escape.

Chapter 3

1910 SUBWAY PLAN
1910/UNBUILT

RADIAL RAILWAYS PLAN
1915/UNBUILT

I N A LATER ERA, YOU WOULD HAVE CALLED the relationship dysfunctional. In 1891, the Toronto Railway Company signed a thirty-year exclusive franchise to operate streetcars in Toronto. Things went well at first, but by the end of the decade, the honeymoon was over. A suit brought by the city in 1899 alleging that the TRC was overcrowding its streetcars ignited a decade of litigation, on that matter and others, at tribunals and courts in two countries.

Things reached a low point (or high point, depending on your view), when the Judicial Committee of the Privy Council in London weighed in, ruling that the TRC had no obligation to provide service beyond Toronto's 1891 boundaries. It meant that the rapidly expanding city had to build and operate its own lines in areas annexed after that date, along routes such as St. Clair, Danforth, and Gerrard Street east of Greenwood.

Even as the city complained of the ludicrousness of having two streetcar systems in a single municipality, one private and one public, it forbade the privately run streetcar lines that connected Toronto to other towns — known as radial railways — from crossing the city limits. In Toronto, a northern radial line called the Metropolitan followed Yonge Street down from Lake Simcoe, but its passengers had to get off north of Summerhill. Similarly, cars on the eastern Scarborough line, the western Port Credit line, and northwestern lines along Dundas and Keele were forbidden to actually enter the city. The problem was, the radials were run by TRC affiliates, and the city refused to do anything that might give the hated company a further toehold in Toronto, even if it meant another point of transfer for travellers.

The TRC may have had the exclusive right to run transit *on* Toronto's streets, but that didn't prevent the city from building it *under* those streets. In the run-up to the municipal election held on January 1, 1910, controller

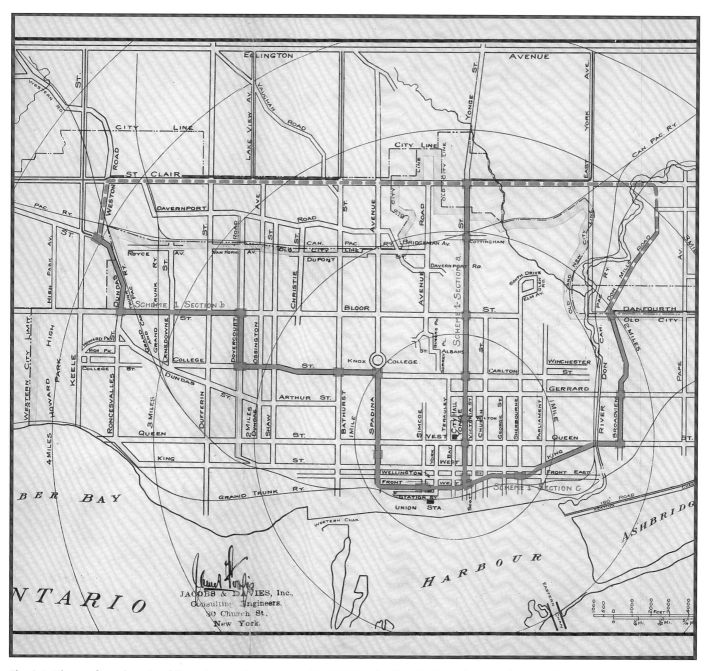

Fig. 3-1. The preferred route of the subway plan proposed in 1910 by the New York engineering firm Jacobs and Davies. [City of Toronto Archives, Series 60, Item 22.]

Horatio C. Hocken seized on this loophole, campaigning for mayor on a promise to bring "tubes" to Toronto. And in 1909, the future was underground. The year before, Boston had undertaken a third expansion of the streetcar subway system it had opened in 1898, New York's subway system had been up and running for five years, and across North America, cities large and small were considering subway proposals of their own. In Toronto, disenchantment with the TRC provided additional incentive.

Although the voters rejected Hocken, they didn't reject his vision, overwhelmingly approving a ballot question allowing the city to seek provincial approval for a subway system. The province responded swiftly, passing a bill in March 1910 that permitted Toronto to build and operate "a system of underground railways for the carriage and transportation of passengers and freight."

The next step was figuring out what it should look like. In May council commissioned the New York engineering firm Jacobs and Davies to prepare a report on the matter. Written by engineer James Forgie, it was released three months later. Despite the widespread dislike of the TRC locally, he concluded that streetcar service in Toronto was actually pretty good, and would adequately serve the city for several years to come. This didn't mean that Toronto shouldn't be thinking to the years beyond that, however. Or, in the report's words, "grasping time by the forelock."

Forgie proposed a subway scheme consisting of three parts: a line on Yonge Street from St. Clair to Wellington; a line from Broadview and Danforth to Front and Yonge; and a line from Front and Yonge to Dundas and Keele. Ultimately, these lines could form part of a circle route connected by a St. Clair line in the north. The system would be fed by an expanded streetcar and radial system. The entire tube portion could be built for just under $24 million (Fig. 3-1).

If economy dictated that the city build in stages, the report recommended starting on Yonge. As a cheaper overall alternative, the report suggested that the city could build the Yonge line, augmented with a line running east along Bloor Street and the Danforth. The report pointed out that this alternative would require the construction of a double-decker viaduct across the Don Valley — a suggestion that was realized eight years later with the completion of the Prince Edward Viaduct.

Tubes may have made a lot of sense, but in Jacobs and Davies's view, not if they were going to be operated in competition with the TRC's existing streetcar system as the city proposed. On that point, if council needed experts to tell it the obvious, it got its money's worth.

Undaunted, in 1911 the city actually sought bids for the construction of cement tubes for a north–south subway between Front Street and St. Clair Avenue. It followed the alignment of modern-day Bay Street, switching to a Yonge-Street alignment north of Davenport. E.L. Cousins, the assistant city engineer, planned it as part of a broader scheme that included a Bloor-Danforth line and a Queen line. In the municipal elections of 1912, however, voters rejected the $5.4-million expenditure needed to build the north–south line that was supposed to be the start of it all.

With no realistic prospect of subways any time soon, the city turned its attention to fixing its relationship with the TRC — by trying to get the company out of the picture altogether. In order to bolster its case that the TRC was in breach of its contract, the city hired Chicago-based transit consultant Bion J. Arnold to study the TRC's streetcar operations. Unlike Jacobs and Davies, he found them lacking. Subsequent meetings between the city and the TRC led to a tentative deal the

Fig. 3-2. Mayor Tommy Church (left) with Sir Adam Beck (centre). This picture was taken around 1916, a time when both men were deeply involved in proposals that would have seen Toronto as a hub for a system of intercity electrical railways. [City of Toronto Archives, Fonds 1244, Item 2465.]

next year, under which the city would pay the streetcar company $22 million to take over the system eight years early, and another $8 million to buy a hydroelectric company owned by the TRC.

Not everyone was happy. Tommy Church, a member of the city's board of control, considered it a boondoggle that gave the TRC a windfall. Even though the First World War had made financing the purchase impossible in the short term, Church made it a major issue in the 1915 mayoral race, taking his victory as an anti-TRC mandate. In his inaugural speech, Church called for the immediate creation of a special committee to consider the issue of radial railway access to the city and rapid transit generally (Fig. 3-2).

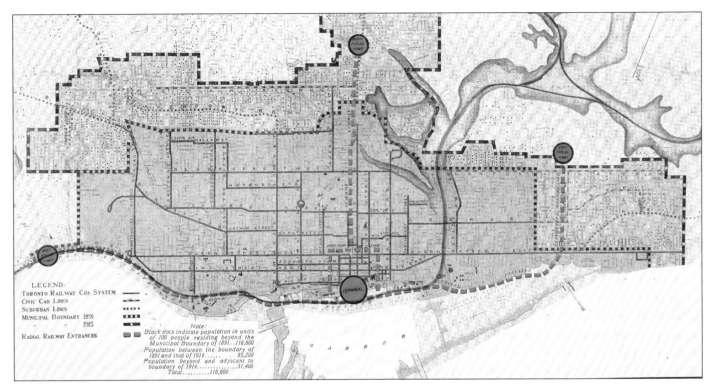

Fig. 3-3. In 1915, representatives of the city, the Hydro-Electric Power Commission of Ontario and the Toronto Harbour Commission prepared a report on radial railway entrances and rapid transit for Toronto. It recommended three "focal points" through which radial railways would enter the city, travelling in open cuts, on elevated tracks and in tunnels. [Toronto Public Library.]

It was formed the following month, appointing three men to prepare a report: R.C. Harris, the city's commissioner of works; E. L. Cousins, who was now the general manager and chief engineer of the Toronto Harbour Commission; and F.A. Gaby, chief engineer of the provincial hydro system. They released their findings at the end of 1915. They concluded that Toronto didn't need the kind of true rapid transit a subway network would provide; it could achieve much the same benefit by bringing the suburban radial lines into the city on their own rights-of-way, where they could also offer service within the city. The report called this approach "semi-rapid transit." The engineers' plan identified three "focal points" at which radial railways could enter the city. A new terminal south of the railway viaduct between Bay and Yonge would serve all three radials. After the TRC's franchise expired in 1921, a downtown loop could allow radial passengers access to the city's core via Richmond Street (Figs. 3-3, 3-4).

When the report was written, the future looked bright for radial railways generally. The provincial Hydro-Electric

Fig. 3-4. A perspective from the 1915 report on radial railways shows the proposed terminal that would have served lines coming in from the north, east, and west. Union Station, then under construction, is shown toward the left. [Toronto Public Library.]

Railway Act of 1914 allowed the Hydro-Electric Power Commission of Ontario to help municipalities finance inter-urban lines that Hydro would build and operate. It was part of a province-wide scheme of radials that Hydro chair and provincial minister without portfolio Sir Adam Beck had been pushing since 1912 (see Fig. 3-2). Since Hydro had the electricity to power the lines, as well as transmission rights-of-way on which to run them, the project was a perfect fit. Beck prioritized a first phase of three hundred miles of new lines, with Toronto's proposed waterfront radial terminal serving as a hub for many of them.

City council tabled the radial railway entrance report pending further action on Beck's scheme. That couldn't happen until after the war, but by then, the radial era had passed. Ontario's new premier, Charles Drury, wasn't supportive. He did, however, appoint a royal commission to look into the issue in July 1919. It released its exhaustive report in 1921. The report concluded that high-speed radials might be used as part of a rapid transit system between Toronto and its suburbs, but Beck's province-wide network couldn't be justified. Across North America, radial railways, and railways generally for that matter, were in financial trouble. The automobile age had arrived, and the provincial government's transportation budget was being taken up by building highways to accommodate it. The prime advantage that radials were seen to have over cars was their ability to speed through cities on exclusive rights-of-way, and in Toronto, those existed only on the pages of a six-year-old report.

A week after the royal commission's findings were released, Premier Drury announced that the provincial government would not help finance any new radial lines. Sir Adam Beck, who was still at the helm of Hydro, wasn't backing down yet. In 1916, Toronto voters had approved a line between Toronto and London, and Beck now wanted to complete it. Despite strong opposition to what was being characterized as "the waterfront grab," city council approved an exclusive six-track right-of-way for Beck's radial across the western lakeshore. The Drury government insisted that the new proposal was different from what had been approved in 1916, however. It was required to be put on the municipal ballot again as a result. In the elections of 1923, Torontonians voted it down. Sir Adam Beck died two years later, and with him the dream of publicly owned electrical railways linking communities throughout Ontario.

Chapter 4

WAR MEMORIALS

1920–2003/UNBUILT — BUILT TO DIFFERENT PLANS

IT'S DIFFICULT TO IMAGINE NOW THE meaning behind the numbers associated with Canada and the First World War. A country of less than 8 million people raised an expeditionary force of six hundred thousand soldiers, almost sixty thousand of whom lost their lives. In Ontario, 240,000 people enlisted, and more than 68,000 died or were injured. When the war ended, communities across the province built memorials to the sacrifice, and it was natural that the provincial government itself would also want to honour its citizens who had served.

In April 1920, the Ontario legislature created the Ontario War Memorial Committee to advise it on how to do just that. The next year, the committee recommended building two separate structures, a cenotaph to honour the dead, and a memorial hall to commemorate, through archives and art, all who had contributed to the war effort, from soldiers and nurses, to civilians from every

walk of life. At the same time, it would chronicle the war's effect on the home front. An architectural competition was to be held for both structures.

With the legislature's blessing, the committee got down to the business of making detailed plans. It conceived the memorial hall as the "Valhalla of the Province," a granite structure rising from the northernmost end of Queen's Park, embellished with stained glass, statues, and other commemorative art. The committee had gone so far as to draw up a notice of architectural competition for the building in 1922, but it was never issued. Even with free land, the memorial hall was going to cost over a million dollars, too much of an outlay in the postwar economy. In its final report to the legislature the following year, the committee recommended that the memorial hall be postponed, to be considered in the future in conjunction with the construction of a new provincial archives (the archives would ultimately take over several storeys in the new Whitney Block tower when it opened in 1933: see Fig. 2-9). The addition of the archives might necessitate a new site, but a new site would be needed, anyway. With the memorial hall stalled, the 48th Highlanders secured the Queen's Park location for their regimental memorial, which was dedicated on November 11, 1923.

As for the cenotaph, the committee dispensed with the original idea of a competition, concluding instead that the province should construct an exact replica of Sir Edwin Lutyens's cenotaph at Whitehall in London, even seeking Lutyens's permission to do so. The site would be one of honour, on the median of University Avenue, in front of the legislative buildings, just north of College Street. The cost would be a more palatable $50,000. The committee said that the city had already been approached and had no objections, provided the roadway was widened by ten feet

Figs. 4-1 (above), 4-2 (right). Sir Edwin Lutyens's cenotaph at Whitehall, London (above). In 1923, the province approved a plan to duplicate it in front of the legislative buildings on University Avenue, as shown on this 1922 site plan prepared for a special parliamentary committee (right). [Library and Archives Canada, R214-419-X-E; Archives of Ontario, RG 49-106]

on either side. The provincial cabinet approved this reduced commemorative program in May 1923 (Figs. 4-1, 4-2).

The city's commissioner of works, R.C. Harris, told the city's board of control that the cenotaph proposal was news to him. Further, he was personally opposed to the location: he felt that, at forty feet high and fifteen-and-a-half feet wide, the structure "would destroy the prospect looking north on University Avenue and dwarf the

Parliament Buildings…." Opinion varied on whether this was, in fact, a bad thing. Architect F.H. Marani, who had designed the memorial for the 48th Highlanders, his own regiment, recommended that a memorial arch be built instead of a cenotaph, specifically *because* it would better block out what he regarded as the unsightly legislative buildings. The board of control agreed with Harris, however, instructing him and the city's parks

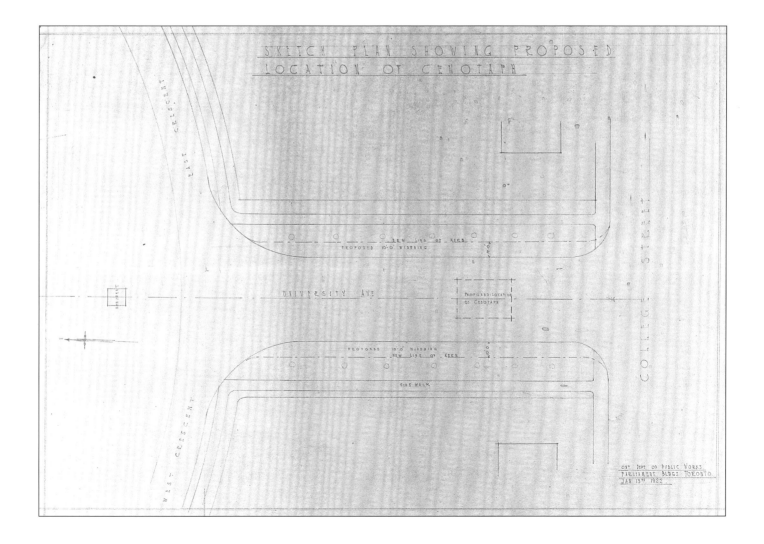

commissioner to meet with provincial officials. They found a sympathetic audience in the deputy minister of public works. In a memo written after their meeting, Harris noted that "further action on this matter was deferred, pending an inspection of further possible sites." There is no record that any such sites were inspected, or even considered, and nothing more seems to have been done about the provincial cenotaph — or the memorial hall — after the summer of 1923.

Economically, the years following the war were tough, and the city, like the province, felt it couldn't justify the funds needed to build the kind of monument it wanted. Each Armistice Day (it wouldn't become Remembrance Day until 1931), services were held at a temporary cenotaph set up outside City Hall. There was no shortage of grand ideas for something permanent, including the notion that a memorial square could be built when University Avenue was eventually extended south of Queen, a proposal that would become Vimy Circle in a

Fig. 4-3. Architect F.H. Marani proposed this memorial square in 1923, on the site of what would become Nathan Phillips Square. This view is looking southeast toward Queen Street. The building on the left is a proposed police and court building, joined to Old City Hall by a bridge across Bay Street. [Toronto Public Library.]

1929 city plan (see *Unbuilt Toronto*, Chapter 3).

In 1923, F.H. Marani took another idea that had been floating around for some time, a square between Osgoode Hall and City Hall (what would ultimately become Nathan Phillips Square), and suggested that it could be developed as a war memorial, part of a general scheme he had devised for new boulevards and squares in the downtown core (Fig. 4-3). Mayor Charles Maguire thought that cost put these types of ideas entirely out of the question. For reasons of economy, he had considered the city's joining in on the province's plans, but decided against it: "Personally, I favour a separate monument by the city. I don't see why we should not erect a splendid cenotaph right in front of the City Hall, where it can be seen by all the myriads who come down town. I don't much fancy a memorial in a park. I think this monument to the thousands of Toronto men who died should confront the eyes of the city."

Ultimately, that is what council decided, as well. On September 8, 1924, it announced a competition for a "Proposed Cenotaph or war memorial emblem." Competitors could design for two locations: in front of the main entrance to City Hall, or on City Hall's east lawn on Queen Street. The judges were Vaux Chadwick and Allan George, representing the Ontario Association of Architects, and J.E.H. MacDonald of the Ontario Society of Artists.

By the deadline of October 15, fifty designs had been submitted. Undoubtedly influenced by Lutyens's Whitehall cenotaph, most tended toward simple pylons. The *Toronto Daily Star* approved of this restraint, noting that "The general purity of style and graceful simplicity, together with the almost complete absence of the grotesque was striking evidence of the sound lines on which Canadian art is developing." The judges also favoured the simple approach. Both the second and third place entries, by J. Roxburgh Smith of Montreal, and the Thompson Monument Company, based in Toronto, were pylons. As shown in the *Journal of the Royal Architectural Institute of Canada*, the Thompson Monument entry did include a stylized human figure, however (Fig. 4-4).

Although unattributed, Thompson's design was likely by Emanuel Hahn (see Fig. 1-4). He was the company's chief designer, designing war memorials across the country for them. All but one were unsigned. Hahn had been born in Germany, and at a time when anti-German sentiment ran high, Thompson's competitors had been known to point that fact out to potential clients. They were right to think it might help: Hahn would go on to win the Winnipeg war memorial competition at the end of 1925 (with a design strikingly similar to the Thompson Monument Company's Toronto proposal), only to have the commission taken away from him when his ethnicity was discovered.

The winning team in the Toronto competition, Toronto architects William Ferguson and Thomas Pomphrey, could attract no such controversy. Ferguson and Pomphrey had been classmates in Glasgow, both eventually immigrating to Toronto, working in the architectural offices of John Lyle and Darling and Pearson. When hostilities broke out in 1914, they joined the 48th Highlanders, volunteering for overseas service. Each man suffered injuries in battle: Ferguson was wounded in the head by shell shrapnel in 1916, and Pomphrey suffered a permanent disability to his right arm the following year.

Their design was also a pylon, of grey granite, with its narrow end facing City Hall, so as not to obscure views of that building. At the base, facing Queen Street, was a symbolic sarcophagus (which was removed at the recommendation of the judges), and the inscription: "To the honour of all who served, 1914–1918."

Fig. 4-4. The runners-up in the city's 1924 war memorial competition. On the left is the second-place entry of J. Roxburgh Smith. On the right is the third-place entry, submitted by the Thompson Monument Company. *The Toronto Daily Star* lauded the "almost complete absence of the grotesque" in the fifty designs submitted to the competition. [Toronto Public Library.]

Fig. 4-5. The city's new cenotaph is unveiled on Armistace Day, 1925. Remedial work to change the monument's controversial inscription had been completed only days earlier. [City of Toronto Archives, Fonds 1266, Item 6585.]

The inscription became the source of controversy before the monument was formally dedicated. Based on its wording, Toronto had built a war memorial, honouring those who had served as well as those who had died. But a lot of Torontonians felt that a true cenotaph — a memorial only to those who had died — was what it should have got. With less than three weeks before the monument was set to be officially unveiled, council wrote to veterans' associations asking their views on whether the inscription should be changed. Given the timing, they asked the architects and contractor to cut replacement stones for the area where the inscription was, in case a change was needed. On November 2, 1925, based on the overwhelming public response on the issue, council voted unanimously to change the inscription on the monument to read "To Our Glorious Dead," an echo of the inscription on the Whitehall cenotaph, "The Glorious Dead." Scaffolding went up the next day, and the new wording was in place for the unveiling by Governor General Lord Byng on November 11, 1925 (Fig. 4-5).

In 1947, a memorial tablet and book of honour were dedicated on the landing of the City Hall's grand interior staircase, although the Great War cenotaph continued to be used at Remembrance Day services to honour the dead from all wars. With the construction of New City Hall, a new cenotaph was proposed, in a modern style, on the site that would later be used for Henry Moore's "The Archer." With that idea in mind, and in response to the complaints of veterans' groups about the flower beds surrounding the cenotaph being trampled at a Maple Leafs reception, in 1962 the board of control recommended moving the old cenotaph to the University Avenue median, in line with the polygonal underpass of the proposed new courthouse.

The unsuitability of this site for large gatherings was acknowledged, but dismissed, since it was expected that the cenotaph at New City Hall would basically render the old one defunct.

In the end, there was no new cenotaph, and the old one stayed where it was. Vaguely, the move was deemed "impracticable," but it seems likely that shunting the cenotaph off to a spot where no one was really expected to go seemed like breaking faith. In 1984, the queen rededicated the 1925 cenotaph, with the dates of the Second World War and the Korean War added to its base ("Peacekeeping" would come in 2006). The award-winning design of Ferguson and Pomphrey, two veterans of the "war to end all wars," now formally remembers the fallen of the wars that followed.

———————

In 2003, the provincial government announced a competition for a veterans' memorial to be built at the northwest corner of College Street and Queen's Park Crescent. The jury, headed by retired Major-General Richard Rohmer, favoured the proposal from the architectural team of Kevin Weiss, Larkin Architect Limited and Wayne Swanton. The team's design consisted of three cast bronze monuments, each with a different bas-relief — a cliff face, waves, and clouds — representing the three areas of military service: land, sea, and air. The monuments were configured so that at eleven o'clock each Remembrance Day, they would cast no shadow on the surrounding plaza (Fig. 4-6).

The design team was called back to present the details of their proposal, but, unknown to them at the time, the general election in October 2003 marked the beginning of the end for their scheme. In June 2004, the

Fig. 4-6. The submission of Kevin Weiss, Larkin Architect Limited, and Wayne Swanton that a jury chose as its preferred submission in a 2003 competition for a veterans' memorial. [Kevin Weiss.]

new Liberal government announced it was starting fresh with a second competition. Richard Rohmer continued to head up the jury, but there was a new site: the front lawn of the legislative buildings. The team of Allan Harding MacKay and Phillips Farevaag Smallenberg were announced as the winners of the new competition in June 2005. Their hundred-foot wall of black granite was dedicated in September 2006. Ontario finally had a war memorial, more than eighty-six years after the provincial government had created the Ontario War Memorial Committee.

Chapter 5

GARDINER EXPRESSWAY

1954/BUILT TO DIFFERENT PLANS

FORT YORK ISN'T NORMALLY ASSOCIATED with victory, having been captured and burned by the Americans during the Battle of York in 1813. But in the late 1950s, the fort emerged victorious in a battle of a different kind when three levels of politicians tried (and failed) to push the new Gardiner Expressway through the birthplace of modern Toronto. Foreshadowing future expressway battles, it was local activists, in this case largely forgotten, who rallied to fight the destruction.

Toronto had been planning a "Lakeshore Expressway" since before the end of the Second World War. The master plan prepared by the city's planning board in 1943 proposed a network of depressed or elevated "superhighways" running through the city, connecting to the provincial highway system. A lakeshore component, an extension of the Queen Elizabeth Way, was identified as "Superhighway 'A.'" The Lakeshore Expressway project got into high gear when the newly created Metropolitan Toronto took it over in 1954. By May of that year, Metro's consulting engineers had presented council with detailed plans for the highway.

The board of trade argued that the plan to route the highway south of the exhibition grounds (on twenty-five acres of fill) would ruin the landscaped waterfront there. Metro accepted their suggestion to substitute an alignment along a hydro corridor to the north of the CNE. That solved one problem, but there was another: whether the expressway should be elevated through the city core, between the Don Valley and Bathurst. Metro's forceful new chairman, Frederick "Big Daddy" Gardiner, wasn't about to see work on his pet project delayed by this kind of endless worrying and hand-wringing. Incredibly, he managed to convince council to forget about that issue for the moment and to get on with construction in the east and west ends, on the basis that the middle section of the expressway would be best figured out once cars started using what was already built.

Fig. 5-1. Opponents of the plan to move Fort York attend a public meeting of the fort's operating committee, January 11, 1959. From left are Helen Durie, secretary of the Associated Historical Societies' Committee of Toronto, Harriet Clark, Mrs. John Chase Green, and B. Napier Simpson, Jr. [Clara Thomas Archives and Special Collections, York University, Toronto Telegram Collection, ASC04877.]

It wasn't until 1958, after construction had already started on the western section of the expressway (named after the still-sitting Gardiner the previous year), that Torontonians learned that Metro intended to build the central portion over Fort York. In January of that year, Metro parks commissioner George Bell told the Metro parks committee that an on-ramp from Bathurst would necessitate two piers being constructed in the fort's southwestern wall. One hundred feet of elevated roadway would be constructed as much as fifty feet inside the walls of the fort itself. In other words, part of the fort would be under the Gardiner.

Despite the objections of the Toronto Civic Historical Committee, which had been created earlier in the decade to manage the fort (and had learned of the new expressway plans at the same time as the general public), the parks committee gave its approval to the scheme the following month. Key to its decision was Metro roads commissioner George Grant's opinion that moving the expressway farther south or having it curve was technically impossible. As Grant explained, the six-degree curve in the expressway necessary to avoid the fort would reduce speeds to an unacceptably slow thirty-five miles per hour. Moreover, it didn't appear that more land could be acquired from the railways to allow the entire expressway to be moved south.

Within days of this decision, fifteen historical groups banded together to oppose this cavalier treatment of the fort and its fallen. They organized themselves as the Associated Historical Societies' Committee of Toronto. Gordon Clarry, president of the York Pioneer and Historical Society, was chair, and Helen Durie, second vice-president of the Women's Canadian Historical Society, served as secretary (Fig. 5-1). The AHSC had a couple of factors potentially in its favour. The city still needed permission from the province to convey the necessary Fort York land to Metro. Beyond that, the AHSC knew that when the federal government had transferred the Garrison Common (which included Fort York and the CNE grounds) to the city in 1909, it was subject to two conditions. The first was that the land would revert to the federal government unless the city restored the fort to its original condition (which it had more or less done between 1932 and 1934). The second was that the fort had to be maintained in that condition forever (which, absent any evidence of an expressway over the site in the early nineteenth century, the city was now manifestly not proposing to do).

The AHSC lost no time in publicizing the threat to the fort and the conditions under which the fort had been entrusted to the city. Its submissions to the municipal law committee of the provincial legislature in March resulted in what appeared to be total victory when that committee refused to endorse legislation that would have allowed the transfer of the Fort York lands from the city to Metro. But under pressure from Frederick Gardiner and Premier Leslie Frost, the committee agreed to a compromise suggested by Gardiner himself: Metro could build the expressway on the Garrison Common lands west of Strachan, but could not touch the military cemetery or the Fort.

Gardiner described the compromise as an "honourable retreat" on his part, but it ended up being more of a retrenchment. Less than three months later, he was urging a new approach: if the expressway wasn't to touch the fort or cemetery, then it was the fort and cemetery that should be moved, "piece by piece and brick by brick," to a new location in Coronation Park, just outside the Princes' Gates. The Toronto dailies, which had generally been opposed to building the expressway over the fort, rallied around the much more drastic proposal of moving it entirely. The argument was that years of fill had made the site of the fort ahistoric, since it was no longer on the waterfront. Moving the fort would actually be an act of restoration. And there was an exciting precedent. Just that year, the provincial government had started work on Upper Canada Village, an attraction consisting of pre-Confederation buildings moved out of historic settlements flooded by the St. Lawrence Seaway.

In July, the AHSC organized a memorial service at the military cemetery, which had the effect of highlighting that the fort was not only a collection of buildings, but a battlefield and burial ground, as well. Members of the

Fig. 5-2. A 1961 aerial view shows Fort York keeping Frederick Gardiner's expressway at bay. [City of Toronto Archives, Series 3, File 189, Folio 2.]

AHSC, and anyone else who wondered how you could move a national historic battle site to a more convenient spot, were painted as fussy, elitist members of "hysterical historical societies."

By September, Metro engineers had finalized a new plan, using additional railway and hydro lands, to keep the expressway basically on course while avoiding the fort and cemetery. But if the Gardiner Expressway was for moving, Gardiner the man wasn't. The Metro chair still planned to seek the province's approval to move the fort. Meanwhile, the AHSC, sensing the battle might have to be won at the federal level, had sent out two thousand questionnaires to literary, historical, and archaeological authorities across the continent, to all members of the federal parliament, and to members of all the provincial legislatures. The questionnaires asked respondents if they were in favour of the federal government approving Metro's proposal to demolish Fort York and move the garrison cemetery. Although the federal government wasn't commenting one way or another on whether the fort should be moved, its defenders were encouraged by a warning from the minister of national defense in the House of Commons that any move would require federal approval, since Metro had been taking the position that the feds had no jurisdiction in the matter.

In January 1959, the province and Metro agreed to split the cost of moving the fort. Even though Metro's engineers actually preferred the new route they had come up with to avoid the fort, the idea of moving it had taken on a life of its own. Many politicians, Premier Leslie Frost and Mayor Nathan Phillips among them, had come to the view that moving the fort to the waterfront was just the right thing to do, expressway or no expressway (it was a viewpoint that would resurface as late as 1970, when Metro officials briefly advocated moving the fort

to the newly built Ontario Place). But by now, Fred Gardiner, who had raised the idea of moving the fort in the first place, no longer supported it. He could see that the AHSC would not back down, and had begun to fear that the whole issue of the 1909 agreement would lead to litigation and delay. Even if the federal issue could be resolved, the physical act of moving the fort would hold up construction. At Gardiner's urging, Metro council dropped the matter. Gardiner's biographer, Timothy Colton, writes that it was one of the rare times that the politician backed down from a public position. Fort York would stay where it was; Gardiner's expressway would bend around it (Fig. 5-2).

Chapter 6

SCARBOROUGH EXPRESSWAY
1957/UNBUILT

ISLAND AIRPORT BRIDGE
2002/UNBUILT

I N 1954, WHEN METRO WAS PLANNING what would become the Gardiner Expressway, east-enders questioned how the local roads were going to handle the traffic leaving the expressway's terminus at Coxwell Avenue. There was talk of a link with Kingston Road as a solution, but by 1957 Metro planners had an even better idea: why end the expressway at all? Instead, they recommended pushing it east through Scarborough until it met Highway 401. That same year, Scarborough adopted the concept in its first official plan, and the Ontario Municipal Board gave the green light for Metro to begin expropriating the necessary land.

In the plan, the Gardiner would be extended east of the Don Valley along Lake Shore Boulevard East, heading north through the ravine system east of Coxwell Avenue until it hit the CNR mainline. It would then follow along either side of the tracks as two sections of elevated roadway, continuing east until it met up with the 401 via

Highway 2A, a limited-access roadway that paralleled Kingston Road in east Scarborough.

The extension to Leslie Street opened in 1966, as engineers prepared detailed designs for a further extension. It would continue the expressway to a point just east of Birchmount Road, north of Danforth Avenue. Two years later, the Ontario Municipal Board approved construction of that section. With the highway finally set to become a major presence on the landscape, Metro took the opportunity to formally name it, continuing the Frederick G. Gardiner Expressway designation. But the name "Scarborough Expressway" stuck for the portion east of Leslie (Fig. 6-1).

The continuing construction of the Spadina Expressway had attracted increasing opposition throughout the 1960s (see *Unbuilt Toronto*, Chapter 20). In 1970, opponents asked cabinet to overturn a decision of the OMB approving its completion. In February

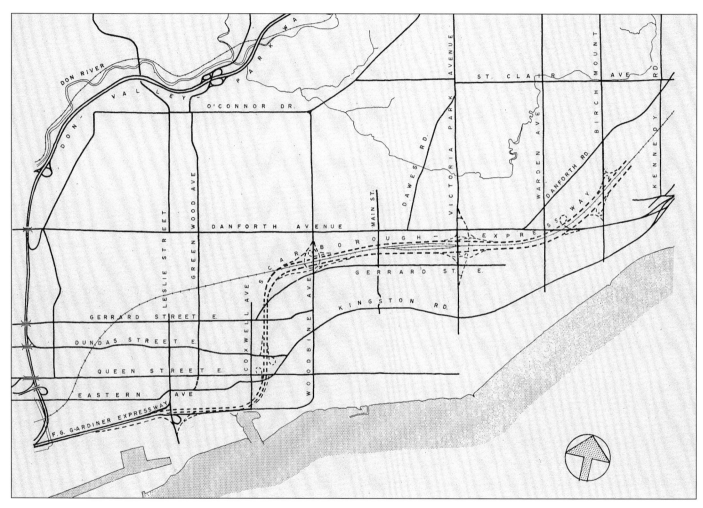

Fig. 6-1. The Scarborough Expressway was an eastern extension of the Gardiner. Heading north through the ravine system east of Coxwell, it would have followed the CNR tracks before connecting with the 401. In 1968, the Ontario Municipal Board approved its construction to a point three thousand feet east of Birchmount Road. [Toronto Public Library.]

1971, with cabinet still deliberating, Spadina was stalled. Metro focused instead on forging ahead with its eastern counterpart, voting to complete the Scarborough Expressway between Leslie and Coxwell. A Beaches-area citizens' group, the ForWard Nine Citizens Association, harnessed the anti-Spadina momentum, asking the OMB to review the Scarborough project. As an interim measure, the board ordered that all work stop until cabinet released its decision on Spadina.

When that decision came down in June 1971, the Spadina Expressway was history. Even so, the province was willing to provide funds for the Leslie to Coxwell segment of the Scarborough Expressway, provided the OMB's review was favourable. Metro asked the board to allow it to go forward immediately on just that extension, but then thought the better of it. It had already acquired a sizeable chunk of land in the expressway corridor, including 216 houses, but it was the tip of the iceberg. It still needed to expropriate about a thousand more properties — a piecemeal solution wasn't going to work. Metro needed some assurance that the rug wouldn't be pulled out from the rest of the enterprise as it had with Spadina. Metro held off on any further construction while it asked the courts to rule that the board had no jurisdiction to review any part of the expressway that it had already approved.

In 1972, the Divisional Court ruled that the OMB did, in fact, have the right to alter any of its decisions on the unbuilt portion of the Scarborough Expressway, right back to the original 1957 approval. It was clear now that if Metro wanted the expressway built, it was going to have to play nice. In 1973, to dampen opposition to the project, it considered an alternate alignment that swung north to the CNR tracks just east of the Don Valley, sparing the ravine system and east-end neighbourhoods that had been such an issue under the approved plan. The revised plan

also replaced the expressway's twin elevated structures with a single, sunken right-of-way that ran south of the tracks. The solution simply shifted the problem farther west, igniting opposition in neighbourhoods that hadn't previously paid much attention.

As the pool of opponents to the expressway broadened, even Metro began to question the expressway's planning rationale. Following the court's decision, Metro instructed the Metropolitan Toronto Transportation Plan Review to consider the new alignment, as well as the case for the expressway generally. The review was a joint provincial-municipal task force that had been set up the previous year to update Metro's transportation plan. After studying the matter for six months, it released its report on the Scarborough Expressway in March 1974. It concluded that the expressway, based on 1960s assumptions, could no longer be justified on environmental or planning grounds, and that a mass-transit solution, such as light rail, was more appropriate. The right-of-way could be retained as a transportation corridor capable of accommodating a mix of transportation uses such as arterial roads and light rail. The nature of that mix was left for future consideration.

Scarborough council responded on May 14, 1974, passing a resolution calling for the immediate construction of the expressway. It gave a nod to the report by saying the design could allow for some form of public transit in the future. It was the expressway's last gasp. Two weeks later, on May 31, 1974, Metro council adopted the report's recommendation that the expressway be scrapped. With Metro no longer pursuing it, the City of Toronto removed any references to the expressway from its official plan in 1980. The portion of the right-of-way through Scarborough lingered on in Metro's official plan as the mixed-use, unspecified "transportation corridor" until 1995 (Fig. 6-2).

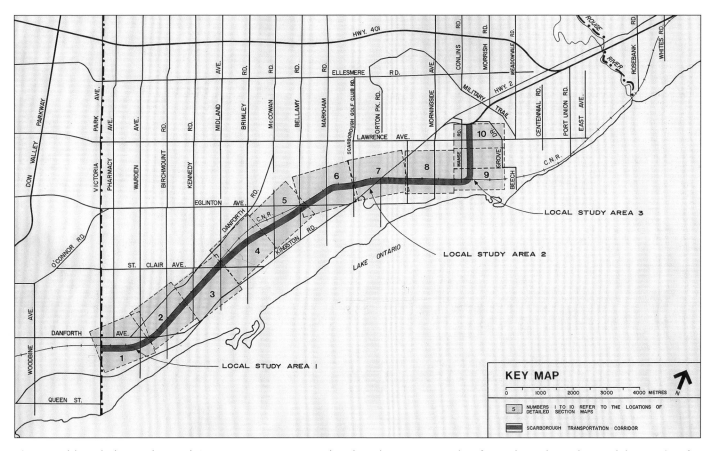

Fig. 6-2. Although the Scarborough Expressway project was abandoned in 1974, its right-of-way through Scarborough lingered on for two decades in Metropolitan Toronto's official plan as an unspecified "transportation corridor." [Toronto Public Library.]

With the Scarborough Expressway dead, the Gardiner east of the Don Valley had become an anomalous bit of elevated overkill. In 1996, Metro's transportation commissioner told council that it made more sense to demolish it than spend the tens of millions of dollars needed to repair it. Local councillor Jack Layton and other grandees officially kicked off the demolition on April 27, 2000, taking ceremonial swings at the orphaned expressway with sledgehammers. A row of its supporting pillars were, however, ultimately retained as landscape features. You can see them, vast and trunkless legs of concrete, near Leslie and Lake Shore.

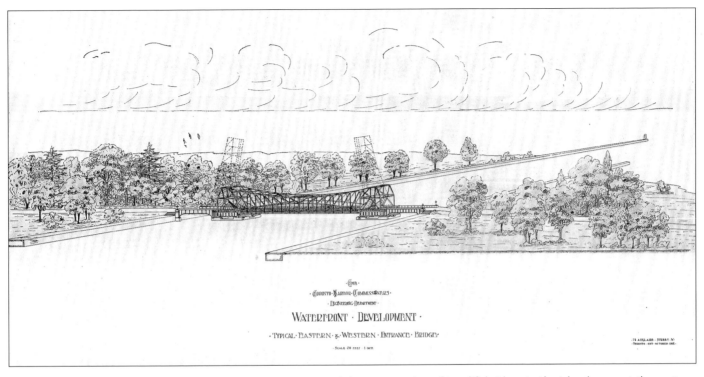

Fig. 6-3. In 1912, the Toronto Harbour Commissioners proposed the construction of two lift bridges to the islands, one at the eastern gap and one at the western. [Toronto Public Library.]

Although the Scarborough Expressway stirred up sustained and vocal opposition, per linear foot of proposed roadway, it's tough to beat the outrage caused by city council's consideration of a "fixed link" to the island airport in 2002.

The Toronto islands used to have at least a tenuous connection to the mainland in the form of an intermittent sandbar at their eastern end. That changed after April 13, 1858, when a storm created the eastern gap, separating them permanently from the mainland. Since its founding in 1911, the Toronto Harbour Commission — now the Toronto Port Authority — has being doing its best to restore a connection. In November 1912, the year after it was created, the commission released its master plan for the Toronto waterfront. The Boston-based Olmsted Brothers firm — whose principals were the sons of Frederick Law Olmsted, designer of Central Park in New York City — were brought on as consulting landscape architects. Though a good deal of it has been ruined by the Gardiner Expressway and other indignities, much of Toronto's parkland on the western lakefront and islands was developed according to the plan. Two elements of the plan that weren't built, however, were the moveable bridges at the islands' eastern and western gaps (Fig. 6-3, see also Fig. 24-1).

In anticipation of the island airport, which opened as Port George VI Airfield in 1939, the city called in the federal funding that had been promised for those bridges (but never delivered) back in 1913. It would now be used to build a tunnel. In 1935, construction actually started, but political changes at both the federal and municipal level saw it cancelled almost as soon as it had begun (see *Unbuilt Toronto*, Chapter 17), forcing the airport to rely on ferry access.

The harbour commission looked at building a tunnel again in 1965, one of several proposals over the following decades for airport bridges, causeways, and tunnels. An intergovernmental staff report from 1993 framed the issue as one of safety, concluding that if a fifty-passenger aircraft crashed at the airport, it could take over two hours to get the necessary emergency vehicles and personnel over. The report recommended the construction of a moveable bridge at the western gap. But there was a problem. The harbour commissioners had an agreement with the city explicitly forbidding the construction of a bridge or any other fixed link. Signed in 1983 as regional air service was ramping up, it was part of a broader deal among the commission, the city, and the federal government over the airport's development. A decade into what was supposed to be a fifty-year agreement, council rejected the notion of amending it to allow a bridge.

Just two years later, however, the city reversed its position. With the downturn in the economy in the early 1990s, travel through the airport had fallen off drastically. The airport was losing passengers as well as money. In 1995, the provincial government stopped subsidizing the airport ferry, leaving the city to shell out more than half a million dollars a year to cover the shortfall. A bridge to replace it suddenly looked attractive. The city approved the construction of one on the blunt condition that "not one penny of City tax dollars will be spent on the bridge or on Airport losses which result from the bridge financing."

As it turned out, there was no financing. The bridge received environmental approvals in 1999, but it was, as the chair of what was now called the Toronto Port Authority would later admit, "non-financeable." The problem was that the airport was continuing to bleed money. From a peak of four hundred thousand passengers in 1987, it was now serving about a hundred thousand passengers a year. In 2001, a report commissioned by the port authority concluded that the status quo wasn't tenable. The airport would have to drastically expand its facilities and operations to become profitable, which would mean serving up to about nine hundred thousand passengers a year with jet or turboprop service.

The next year, the port authority presented the city with the study, as well as a business plan, to increase service at the airport. It included a new terminal facility, expanded turboprop service, and a bridge. The plan was more than academic. A company called Regional Airlines Holdings Inc., otherwise known as REGCO, had now come forward with a proposal to run service to seventeen cities out of the airport on fifteen new turboprop planes. It estimated that it could attract up to nine hundred thousand passengers a year within the first four years of business. The city, which was now subsidizing the port authority's operating expenses to the tune of $2.8 million annually, was faced with the choice of approving the bridge or letting the airport shut down. In November 2002 it voted in favour of the bridge by a wide margin (Fig. 6-4).

Community opposition was strong. Community Airport Impact Review (Community AIR), a coalition of citizens concerned about the impact of a busier airport on air quality and quality of life generally at Toronto's

Fig. 6-4. In 2002, the Toronto Port Authority proposed a bridge to the island airport. Designed by the engineering firm Dillon Consulting and architects Montgomery Sisam, the "twin-leaf bascule bridge" was designed to operate like a double drawbridge. Counterweights would lift its two halves nine storeys into the air in less than a minute, allowing boats to pass through the harbour's western gap. [Montgomery Sisam.]

waterfront, argued that the airport land should be turned into greenspace. The group was headed by Allan Sparrow, a former city councillor and veteran of the fight to stop the Spadina Expressway. He was joined by a legend from that fight, Jane Jacobs. Jacobs, then eighty-six, said that stopping the airport's expansion was as important to Toronto's livability in 2002 as stopping Spadina had been three decades earlier. Council wasn't swayed.

As the port authority worked through 2003 on getting the necessary federal approvals in place for the bridge, Parkdale-High Park councillor David Miller, alone among the major candidates, made opposition to it a major platform in his run for mayor. His victory in the November 2003 election triggered a showdown. In the last week of November, the port authority set up a crane at the water's edge in preparation for construction.

Council responded the following week with another vote on the bridge — this time voting decisively against it. In the face of this sea change, the federal government announced the next day that it was backing council over its own port authority. In May, it agreed to pay $35 million for the authority's expenses arising from the cancellation, covering things such as abandoned steel contracts and a lawsuit brought by REGCO.

The saga was finally over. As the port authority's CEO Lisa Raitt said at the time, "You will never hear about the bridge again." And that's been right, strictly speaking. In 2009, the port authority announced its intention to build a pedestrian tunnel instead.

Chapter 7

UTDC Rapid Transit
1973/Partially Built — Built to Different Plans
Network 2011
1985/Partially built

T HE PROVINCIAL GOVERNMENT'S CANCEL-lation of the Spadina Expressway in 1971 signalled the end of the postwar vision of limited-access highways slicing through established neighbourhoods. What was less apparent at the time was that a new provincial transit vision was emerging, of cities webbed with driverless mini-trains, silently whizzing along elevated guideways. The future had arrived, and it was travelling on a magnetically levitated people mover.

The idea had its origins back in 1969, when the Ontario Department of Transportation and Communications began to investigate intermediate capacity transit systems. Such a system, an "ICTS," could service routes whose ridership was too heavy for buses, but not heavy enough to warrant more expensive subway construction. At the end of 1971, it invited eight companies to submit reports on ICTS technologies that they were developing. The goal was to choose one to design and construct a demonstration project for a driverless ICTS on 3.5 miles of track encircling the CNE grounds.

The government selected three competitors to work up detailed proposals for the test system. When Ford dropped out (rather than adapt its system to the government's specifications), two were left: Hawker Siddeley Canada and the Munich-based KraussMaffei. Hawker Siddeley's proposal seemed to give a glimpse into the world of the future, featuring stations and even vehicle bodies given a futuristic look by Arthur Erickson Architects (Fig. 7-1). *Bus and Truck Transport* magazine — perhaps not an unbiased source — felt it was doomed from the start, however. The magazine editorialized that the province was eager to be dazzled by new technology; even though the Hawker Siddeley vehicle was magnetically propelled by a linear induction motor manufactured by the British Hovercraft Corporation, it still rolled on rubber tires. And rubber tires weren't dazzling.

Fig. 7-1. In Hawker Siddeley's proposal for an elevated transit system at the Canadian National Exhibition, the stations and vehicles were given a space-age look by Arthur Erickson Architects. The system was intended to be up and running for the 1975 fair, serving as a prototype for other lines in Toronto, Hamilton, and Ottawa. [Jim Strasman.]

Magnetic levitation, on the other hand, was. Backed by the West German government, KraussMaffei was working on adapting the magnetic levitation technology it had developed for long-haul trains for local transit systems. In its proposal, driverless, computer-controlled cars would glide above elevated guideways, suspended two-thirds of an inch in the air by magnets on either side of the cars. Accommodating twelve people sitting and eight more standing, those floating cars could travel singly or in a train, at an average speed of forty-five miles

Fig. 7-2. In this photomontage, *circa* 1974, a driverless, magnetically levitated GO-Urban train is shown arriving at Ontario Place Station. The elevated system dipped down at this point to clear Ontario Place's pedestrian bridges. [City of Toronto Archives/TTC Fonds, Series 836, Sub-series 2, File 7.]

per hour. In May 1973, the province awarded KraussMaffei the contract for the CNE test system. It was to be ready for passenger service at the 1975 fair.

While the government was taking a risk backing new technology, the potential payoff was a new transit manufacturing industry in Ontario, since the contract with KraussMaffei gave the province marketing rights for the system in North and South America. To capitalize on them, the province set up the Ontario Transportation Development Corporation (later renamed the Urban Transportation Development Corporation, or UTDC) to develop and market the new ICTS technology, which it was now calling GO-Urban. After the CNE prototype, UTDC planned to build a GO-Urban extension of the Danforth subway line to the Scarborough Town Centre. It would be just the start of a fifty-six-mile network of GO-Urban trains across Metro that would also include radial lines between Union Station and the Toronto International Airport in the west and Malvern in the east, and an Eglinton crosstown line. Systems for Ottawa and Hamilton would follow.

But that was all predicated on the success of the CNE demonstration project, which was running into snags. Within a year, its $16-million construction budget had ballooned to $25 million, even after one of the system's four stations, a connection with the GO Transit station, had been cut. That left stations at the Dufferin and Princes' gates and at Ontario Place, but the minister of transportation, John Rhodes, warned that if costs kept rising, the entire demonstration project might have to be scrapped. At least the government had no qualms about the technology, which Rhodes described as excellent (Fig. 7-2).

He had spoken too soon. In November 1974, reports surfaced that, taking a curve on the test track in Munich, the KraussMaffei vehicle had a tendency to blow a magnet — the equivalent, a government source evocatively explained, of blowing a tire. A trip to the Munich test site designed to show off the system to provincial and municipal politicians was hastily cancelled.

Hard on the heels of that debacle came more bad news: the West German government had decided there was no future for short-haul magnetic levitation systems. It was pulling its funding. With Bonn taking a powder, KraussMaffei informed the province that it couldn't complete the system at the CNE. On November 13, 1974, Rhodes announced its cancellation. Footings for the guideways had been built, and they would be removed the next year. The loss of sixty-six mature trees provided a more subtle, though lingering reminder of the cancelled construction.

After it parted ways with KraussMaffei, UTDC decided to take its ICTS program in a different direction. In the system it ultimately developed, magnets propelled the vehicle, using a linear induction motor. There was no levitation, however, just standard wheels on a track. In 1981, the government convinced the TTC to abandon its plan to connect Kennedy Station to the Scarborough Town Centre using UTDC-designed streetcars, and use its revamped ICTS vehicle instead. The result was the Scarborough RT. Like its CNE forebear, it was designed to be driverless, an idea that safety and union concerns scuttled. What was intended to be the second in a network of innovative rapid transit lines throughout Metro was the first and last.

———————

An even more ambitious proposal for UTDC technology was announced in 1982. It had its origins in a fishing trip that the minister of transportation and communications, James Snow, took to Halifax in the summer of 1981. Flying home, he and his deputy minister, Harold Gilbert, started talking about Toronto's commuter transit problems. Using magic markers and some handy maps, they blocked out a solution, a route for a commuter transit network serving the GTA and beyond.

A little over a year later, in October 1982, Snow formally announced the result of that midair brainstorming session: "GO-ALRT." The "ALRT" stood for Advanced Light Rail Transit. It used a new type of ICTS vehicle designed by UTDC. The linear induction motor was gone, replaced by a conventional rotary motor. Like the Scarborough ICTS vehicle, the ALRT vehicle would be computer-operated, designed for driverless operation. It could run on elevated guideways like the Scarborough RT, but because it didn't use a subway-style hot rail, drawing power instead from overhead lines, it could also run at grade, either method achieving operating speeds of up to 120–130 kilometres per hour.

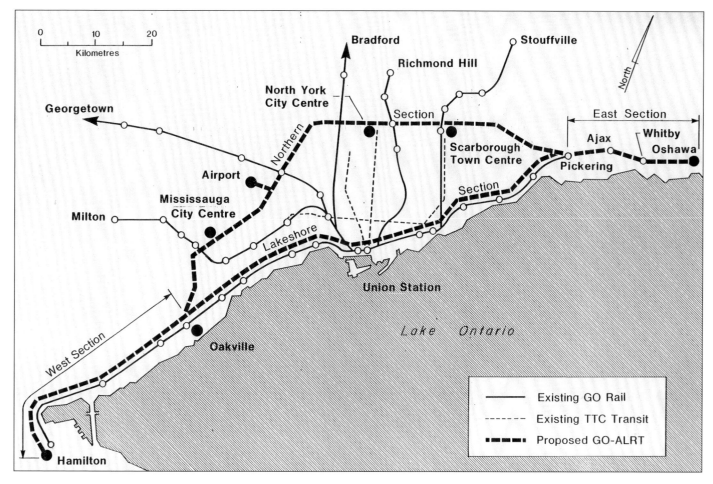

Fig. 7-3. GO-ALRT, proposed in 1982, would have connected communities in the Greater Toronto Area with electrified, light-rail transit service. Its basic system map was sketched out on a fishing trip. [Toronto Public Library.]

The proposed route was basically what Snow and Gilbert had come up with on their fishing trip: a lakeshore line between Hamilton and Oshawa, with a northern line arching from Pickering to Oakville. This northern route would link the emerging city centres of Mississauga, North York, and Scarborough, and include a spur line to the airport. It was as if Sir Adam Beck's dream of publicly owned, intercity radial lines (see Chapter 3), had been revived seventy years on, in a futuristic format that even that great visionary couldn't have imagined (Figs. 7-3, 7-4).

At the time, GO diesel service along the lakeshore ran only between Oakville and Pickering, on track

Mock-up of proposed vehicle for GO-ALRT service

Fig. 7-4. The driverless GO-ALRT vehicle was capable of operating speeds of 120–130 kilometres per hour. [Toronto Public Library.]

largely rented from the CNR. It wasn't an ideal situation. Apart from GO's complaints about the rent, scheduling of its trains always came second to freight transport on the line. The province wasn't willing to extend GO service on the CNR's tracks in those circumstances. Constructed in its own right-of-way, GO-ALRT would mean it didn't have to.

The whole system was projected to cost around $3 billion, but it would be tackled in phases over twenty years. The first phase would bring GO-ALRT rail service to the lakeshore areas between Pickering and Oshawa in the east, and Oakville and Hamilton in the west. The second phase would connect these lines with ALRT service between Pickering and Oakville. The third phase would see the construction of the northern line.

By June 19, 1984, when Snow climbed atop a bulldozer in Whitby to break ground for the twenty-five-kilometre eastern line, things were already starting to unravel. In less than two years, the projected $162-million cost of that line had ballooned to $350 million. In Hamilton, GO-ALRT had become politically contentious, with a group called NO-ALRT protesting the elevated line planned to run down that city's York Boulevard. Even using parts of the old Scarborough Expressway right-of-way (see Fig. 6-2) as was being considered, building the central portion of the ALRT lakeshore line was going to be a difficult and expensive proposition. Now Snow was saying that because of improvements to the existing lakeshore diesel service, it might not happen for twenty years. Transit riders in Hamilton and Oshawa had complained from the start about having to transfer from

GO-ALRT vehicles to diesel trains. They would now have two decades of it to look forward to. As for the northern line, Snow said that the TTC's plans to build rapid transit on Sheppard would delay it for twenty years, as well.

A year after the groundbreaking, the whole plan was history. With Bill Davis no longer premier, and James Snow no longer transportation minister, GO-ALRT had lost its key advocates. In June 1985, George McCague, Snow's successor, announced the cancellation of the ALRT lines to Hamilton and Oshawa. GO would extend conventional diesel rail service to those cities instead. The decision was expected to save $100 million in start-up costs on the Oshawa line and double that on the Hamilton line, provide initial service at least a year earlier than under the ALRT program, and avoid the need to have passengers transfer between two systems. Most significantly, the problem that had made GO-ALRT so attractive in the first place, the scheduling issues on the CNR's lakeshore tracks, was set to disappear. Under federal legislation that had already been drafted, GO's passenger vehicles would be given priority over freight trains, and at significantly reduced fees. GO-ALRT had become a solution to a problem that no longer existed.

———

In May 1985, the month before the cancellation of GO-ALRT, Metro Toronto and the TTC released their own transit strategy, Network 2011. Its name reflected its goal of building the transit system Toronto would need in twenty-five years.

Although Network 2011 was designed to complement the GO-ALRT program, its rejection of innovative technology in favour of subways and busways was in part a repudiation of it. In place of ALRT's nebulous staging, Network 2011 set out five distinct construction phases,

of five to six years each. By the time the last stage was completed in 2014, Torontonians would have a vastly expanded rapid transit network (Fig. 7-5).

A Sheppard subway would be built in two phases, running first from the Yonge line to Victoria Park, it would later be extended to the Scarborough Town Centre. A downtown relief line would start at Pape Station and connect with Union Station via a Pape/Eastern/railway corridor alignment. It would terminate at Front and Spadina, where it could serve the planned domed stadium. As the name implied, it was designed to provide relief to the overcrowded Yonge line, diverting riders travelling downtown from the east. It was anticipated to be a heavy rail subway, although the plan left the final determination of that issue to the future. An Eglinton rapid transit line, expected to be built first as a busway, and also built in two stages, would head west from Eglinton West Station, ultimately terminating at Renforth Drive, west of the 427. Finally, the Spadina subway would be extended north and east, connecting with the Sheppard line. In the middle of each stage, Metro and the TTC were to re-evaluate the next stage in light of current information and travel patterns, making updates as necessary.

The engineers and planners may have agreed on the plan's priorities, but the politicians representing Metro's lower-tier municipalities couldn't. Etobicoke and York argued that the Eglinton line, which passed through their boundaries, should be top priority, and built as a heavy-rail subway from the start. That would not only defer the Sheppard line, which North York and Scarborough wanted, but presumably the downtown relief line, championed by Toronto and East York. As a compromise, in June 1986, Metro council approved the construction of the first phase of the Sheppard line as planned, but made no decision on what would follow it.

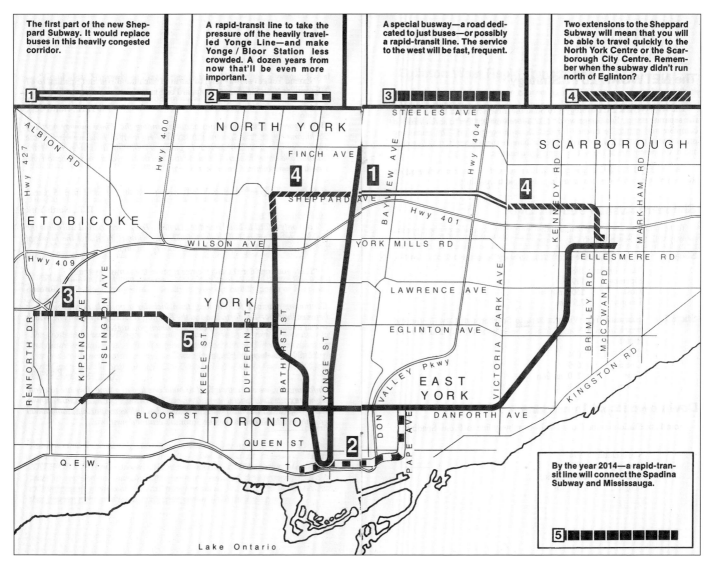

Fig. 7-5. Network 2011 was put forward by Metro Toronto and TTC staff in 1985. A phased program of continuous subway-building, it was intended to take Toronto into the twenty-first century. [City of Toronto Archives/TTC Fonds, Series 836, Sub-series 1, File 19 (Network 2011 map).]

Fig. 7-6. The groundbreaking ceremony for the Eglinton subway line took place on August 25, 1994, at Eglinton and Black Creek Drive, the line's western terminus. Within a year, construction on the line was halted. Premier Bob Rae is shown on the left, accompanied by the provincial minister of transportation, Gilles Pouliot, Metro Chair Alan Tonks, City of York mayor Fergy Brown, and TTC chair Mike Colle. [Archives of Ontario, C 193-9-0-14.]

Staff had estimated that Network 2011's program of continuous construction would cost about $95 to $100 million per year. Since Metro was asking the province to cover 75 percent of it, its inability to get solidly behind its own plan was less than helpful. Apart from that, the Liberal-NDP coalition that had taken power at Queen's Park in 1985 was concerned about Network 2011's price tag. The government also wanted connections with the broader region around Toronto, which neither of the plan's priority lines provided for.

After gaining a majority in 1987, the Liberals agreed to fund a one-stop extension of the Spadina line, up to Sheppard (what would become Downsview Station), as a kind of interim compromise to keep things moving. Metro went along without much enthusiasm. Then, in April 1990, the government announced what it said was the largest rapid-transit expansion program on the continent, a $5-billion scheme that would have looped the Spadina and Yonge Lines in the Finch-Sheppard area, extended the Bloor line to Sherway Gardens, and provided for a Sheppard line between Yonge and the Scarborough Town Centre, and for an Eglinton LRT heading west from the Spadina line.

The plan was short-lived. The Liberals' loss to the NDP that September called the whole thing into question. In 1994, Bob Rae's government came up with still another proposal. It scaled back the Sheppard line to an eastern terminus at Don Mills, turned the Eglinton LRT into a six-station, heavy-rail subway, and extended the Spadina line up to York University. Construction on the Sheppard and Eglinton lines started in 1994 (Fig 7-6), but yet another change of provincial government that year meant yet another change of plans. In July 1995, the month after the Progressive Conservatives swept to power, they announced the "indefinite deferral" of the $750-million Eglinton line as a cost-cutting exercise. Fifty million dollars had already been spent on it, including the excavation of the tail-track, or train-turning area, at Allen Road. But without provincial support, Metro had no choice but to halt construction.

A five-stop Sheppard line finally opened in 2002. With an eastern terminus at Don Mills, it was considerably shorter than even the first phase that Network 2011 anticipated would have been up and running a decade earlier. As the once-distant year of 2011 dawned, apart from the one-stop extension of the Spadina line to Downsview, it remained the only part of Network 2011 built.

Chapter 8

EAST OF BAY DEVELOPMENT

1973/UNBUILT

ATARATIRI

1988/UNBUILT

A MONG THE MAJOR UNBUILT PROJECTS in Toronto's history, the East of Bay proposal had one of the shortest public shelf lives. A mere twenty-three days passed between the government's announcement that it was proceeding with the giant downtown redevelopment scheme, and its announcement that the whole thing was history.

In 1968, as construction continued on the Macdonald Block, the provincial office complex on Bay Street, south of Wellesley (see Fig. 2-9), the Ontario cabinet approved a further consolidation of the province's Toronto-area offices on the east side of Bay. The idea, which had been percolating since 1960 (when the province began to acquire land for it), was to create a government office precinct stretching from Queen's Park Crescent clear over to Yonge Street, between Wellesley and Grosvenor.

In 1970, cabinet decided to hold an invitational architectural competition for the precinct's eastern extension, the 9.8-acre "East of Bay" lands bounded by Yonge, Bay, Grosvenor, and Wellesley. The government wanted 1.35 million square feet of additional office space for civil servants, to be ready in three phases between 1976 and 1987. Under the existing zoning by-law, that would still leave about 2.8 million square feet of unused density on the site. There was a proposal for that, too. In order to avoid what was seen as the single-use sterility of the Macdonald Block, the extra density east of Bay would be taken up by apartments, restaurants, retail, commercial office space — anything to create a lively mix of compatible uses. To achieve it, the land would be leased to a private-sector developer, who would then build on it before leasing the government back its needed office space.

But first a plan was needed. In October 1972, the Ministry of Government Services paid six architectural firms to come up with proposals. While the province still had some of the East of Bay lands left to acquire (largely on Yonge Street), the architects were told to assume that the entire superblock would be in provincial hands, along with Breadalbane Street, which bisected it. As far as design was concerned, the firms were more or less given carte blanche. And, apart from the province's own office space and a mandatory seniors' residence, the same held true for the choice of uses on the site.

To this point, the entire East of Bay project had been progressing behind the scenes, but in November 1972, the *Toronto Citizen*, a midtown community newspaper, broke the story under the headline "Secret Queen's Park Plan Revealed." By the time James Snow, the minister of government services, officially announced the competition on March 6, 1973, there was already alarm over the construction of what the local ratepayers' group was calling a "massive bureaucratic ghetto."

Some comfort might have been taken from the news that the judging panel included urban theorist Jane Jacobs and Eric Arthur, the University of Toronto architecture professor who had orchestrated the competition for Toronto's new city hall. Also, despite the competition, the design process was intended to be collaborative. Taking a page from the Macdonald Block experience (where four firms plus a firm of landscape architects collaborated), the winning firm would be asked to co-ordinate with a representative from each of the other competing firms, jointly producing a new design that would include the best of all their ideas.

What that process might have produced will never be known. On March 29, the day before the models were to be put on public display, Premier Bill Davis announced that the East of Bay project had been shut down. The official reason was that the province didn't like any of the schemes. That might have been true on its face, but there was more to it. In the period between the project's announcement and its cancellation, there had been a by-election in St. George's, the riding in which the development was proposed. The governing Tories had held the seat for thirty years. Although it was considered safe, they lost it to the Liberals. Opposition to the East of Bay project had been a major issue, with the Tories' own candidate, Roy McMurtry, opposing the development. Even outside the riding, government MPPs were taking heat for building offices for civil servants while cutting back on school and hospital construction. East of Bay had become a political liability, in any form.

The timing of the cancellation meant that neither the names of the competing architects nor their proposals were ever made public. The government reportedly destroyed the models and drawings. The Ontario Archives does, however, retain some materials relating to the project that one of the firms, Mathers and Haldenby, later donated (Figs. 8-1, 8-2). Government records show that they were one of six established Toronto firms participating, along with Crang and Boake; Shore, Tilbe, Henschel, Irwin; Clifford and Lawrie; Gordon S. Adamson and Associates; and Dunlop Farrow.

Although the government left open the possibility of resurrecting the East of Bay project in a form the community might find more acceptable, it was a half-hearted suggestion. East of Bay was dead. Perhaps the land had a curse that prevented *grands projets*. In the 1980s, it would be proposed as the site for one of the city's best-known and most contentious unbuilt buildings, Moshe Safdie's Ballet-Opera House (see *Unbuilt Toronto*, Chapter 31).

————

Fig. 8-1. The submission of Mathers and Haldenby in the 1973 Ontario government competition for the area bounded by Yonge, Bay, Wellesley, and Grosvenor. They proposed two forty-storey towers and two thirty-storey towers rising from a two-storey podium that covered the entire site. Overhead pedestrian walkways would lead to the Wellesley subway station across Yonge, and to the Macdonald Block office complex across Bay. [Archives of Ontario, C 315-3, 1673]

Fig. 8-2. In Mathers and Haldenby's conception of the East of Bay development, shoppers enjoy an enclosed retail area overlooking interior open space. [Archives of Ontario, C 315-3, 1673.]

Fifteen years after the East of Bay imbroglio, the province backed an even larger downtown redevelopment scheme: Ataratiri. This time the need wasn't for offices, but for housing. Ataratiri was going to deliver it by transforming a declining industrial area into an entirely new neighbourhood housing up to fourteen thousand people.

As rental vacancy rates in Toronto stayed well below 1 percent in the 1980s, there was a feeling that something had to be done. Toronto needed a major influx of affordable rental housing fast, and neither the private sector nor traditional affordable housing providers were up to providing it. People were calling it a crisis.

On July 13, 1988, the city and the province stepped into the breach, announcing the redevelopment of a massive tract in an aging industrial area just east of the city's core. Excluding the Gooderham and Worts lands, it covered the area between Parliament Street and Bayview Avenue, stretching almost to the Don, bounded to the south by the railway tracks, and to the north by Front, Eastern, and King east of St. Lawrence Street, eighty acres in all.

Whereas the East of Bay project was planned with almost no municipal input, the city would take the lead in this new development, preparing the plans, expropriating the land, and generally getting the area ready for construction. It was a tricky site, requiring environmental remediation to address over a century of industrial contamination, and flood-proofing to address its location in the flood plain of the Don. The predevelopment work alone was going to take hundreds of millions of dollars. The city would have to borrow the money, but the idea was that the sale of development-ready parcels in the new neighbourhood would cover the repayment. If the returns didn't come in as expected, the city would only be on the hook for the first $20 million in losses, with the province guaranteeing the rest to a maximum of $800 million. Since that was almost double what the city expected its costs to be, the prospect of the province ever having to make good on the guarantee seemed unlikely.

The development had been announced with the working name of St. Lawrence Square. With the St. Lawrence neighbourhood already existing on the west side of Parliament, however, a new name was needed to avoid confusion. In January 1989, the city ran a contest to choose one, offering as a prize lunch at the Canary Restaurant, a landmark in the redevelopment area. The submissions ranged from the historical ("First Parliament Town," since Ontario's first parliament had been in the area) to the geographical ("Don's Edge") to the satirical ("Sewerside"). In the end, the advisory council of citizens that the city had appointed to consult on the project chose a name suggested by Humber College professor John Steckley: Ataratiri. It had been the name of a Huron village near Midland that had been destroyed by the Iroquois in 1649. More than 330 years later, a new Ataratiri was set to rise on the banks of the Don.

By the summer of 1990, when the city began widespread public consultation on the proposed site plan, it had acquired all the necessary land to build Ataratiri, either by expropriation, or, in the case of the federally regulated railways (which were immune to the municipal expropriation power), by agreement. Following the example of the successful St. Lawrence neighbourhood, the new development would offer a mix of subsidized and market accommodation in mid-rise buildings. Sixty percent of the six to seven thousand new residential units would be social housing, with the province guaranteeing ongoing subsidies for over half of them for thirty-five years.

In addition, commercial and light industrial uses were contemplated, providing employment for 1,500 people. The site plan prepared by the Kirkland Partnership built on the existing historical grid, extending it and giving it a finer grain. Front Street would serve as the major commercial strip, with terminating vistas over the Don River (Figs. 8-3, 8-4, 8-5).

The first phase of construction was expected to be completed by 1992, but a host of problems was making that unlikely. Flood control, estimated at around $3 million originally, was now expected to cost more than $40 million. Environmental remediation was an even bigger issue. Originally budgeted at $32 million in a worst-case scenario, it was now expected to cost up to $160 million. On top of that, the city was accusing the

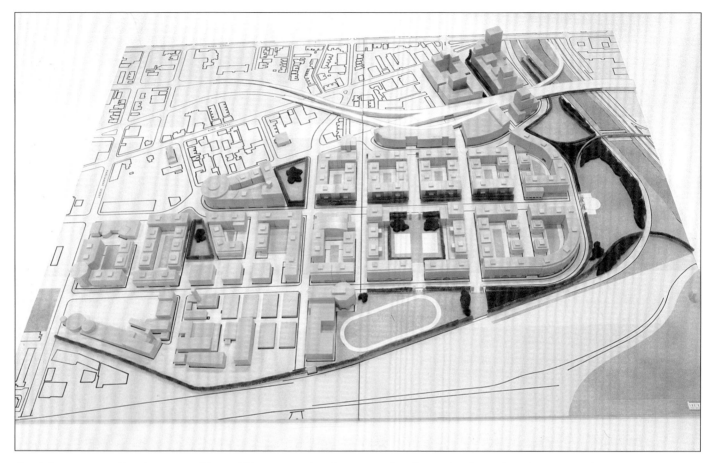

Fig. 8-3. Announced in 1988, Ataratiri would have turned eighty acres of underused industrial land just east of the downtown core into a new, mixed-use community of fourteen thousand residents. In 1990, the city undertook public consultations based on the site plan shown in this model. [City of Toronto Archives, Series 1465, File 635.]

provincial Ministry of the Environment of dragging its feet on the necessary approvals. It was more than an annoyance. The city had already borrowed over $225 million for the project, and each day of delay was costing it $60,000 in interest alone. In fact, interest had become the project's biggest expense.

As the bills racked up, the prospect of covering them with lucrative future property sales became remote. Ataratiri's land had been acquired at the height of the 1980s real-estate boom. In the recessionary 1990s, values had plummeted, turning the cost-recovery assumptions in Ataratiri's business plan into

Fig. 8-4. An August 1990 close-up of the Ataratiri model, looking west down Front Street, the community's planned retail and commercial focus. [City of Toronto Archives, Series 1281, 1990-399, Item 18.]

a pipe dream. The province was now worried that it would have to make good on its entire $800-million guarantee. For its part, the city thought there was a real possibility that it might be on the hook for losses *above* that amount: some forecasts were putting Ataratiri's final bill at $1 billion.

In February 1992, Toronto city council voted to abandon Ataratiri unless the province upped its loan guarantee. The province, headed by a new NDP government, responded the next month by cancelling the project. Even though it would be stuck covering Ataratiri's losses ($413 million by the time they were written off in 1995), the government figured that forging ahead would only make those losses greater. Under the wind-down deal, the province took control of the land, estimated to be worth $15–30 million.

Fig. 8-5. The public inspects plans at an Ataratiri open house, July 17, 1990. [City of Toronto Archives, Series 1281, 1990-328, Item 28.]

In March 2006, federal, provincial, and municipal politicians gathered at the old Ataratiri site to announce the relaunch of a mixed-use neighbourhood there. They were calling it the West Don Lands now, but in built form, it wasn't so different from Ataratiri. The goal was to have more than half of the residential units complete by 2015. A little late to solve the housing crisis of the late 1980s, but just in time to serve as the athletes' village for the Pan-American Games.

Chapter 9

YONGE-DUNDAS SQUARE
1998/BUILT TO DIFFERENT PLANS

TORONTO WASN'T A CITY BLESSED AT birth with public squares. It has wrested what downtown public spaces it has from the no-nonsense military grid provided by its eighteenth-century founders. The best known of these has been Nathan Phillips Square. But a relative newcomer, Yonge-Dundas Square, has arguably become even more central to the city's public life.

Grand schemes to redress Toronto's lack of public squares gained traction in the late-nineteenth and early-twentieth centuries. The construction of Old City Hall was the initial impetus, spurring an 1897 proposal for a square across from it on Queen Street, to be called Victoria Square (see *Unbuilt Toronto*, Chapter 10). There were also various proposals for a square to the west of Old City Hall. It was this concept that came to fruition after the Second World War, with the creation of Nathan Phillips Square. By then, also-rans such as architect F.H.

Marani's 1923 vision of a monumental plaza across from Union Station were long forgotten (Fig. 9-1).

Like Nathan Phillips Square, Yonge-Dundas Square had a conceptual life that stretched back decades. The catalyst that eventually made it a reality was a meeting between two local businessmen, Aaron Barberian, whose father had founded Barberian's steakhouse on Elm Street, and Bob Sniderman, whose father was Sam the Record Man, and who had himself gone on to open the Senator Restaurant on Victoria Street. By the mid-1990s, Yonge Street between Queen and College was becoming associated with crime and a general seediness. They knew that if the area was going to stay economically healthy, something needed to happen.

Soon, other businesses got involved, ranging from the Eaton Centre to street vendors. Separately, they had been voicing their concerns about the area to the city, but in March 1995, they banded together as the Yonge

Fig. 9-1. Architect Frank Marani's 1923 proposal for a monumental square across from the new Union Station. Archways at the eastern and western corners allowed vehicular access to York and Bay Streets. [Toronto Public Library.]

Street Business and Residents Association (YSBRA). With the local councillor, Kyle Rae, championing their cause, council designated the neighbourhood as a "community improvement project area" under the Planning Act. No one objected or complained at the time. Perhaps it seemed to be an innocuous bit of bureaucratic housekeeping, like the city's installation of designer ladybug trash cans in the area. But the ladybugs didn't have broad powers to expropriate land. With the Planning Act designation, the city now did. It was the first legal step in changing the face of downtown Toronto.

Using a grant from the city, the YSBRA hired urban planner Ron Soskolne to devise a revitalization scheme. On December 10, 1996, he revealed it: a complete reworking of the east side of Yonge, focusing on four parcels. "Metropolis," a multistorey, thirty-screen cinema complex featuring retail and themed restaurants would rise on the northeast corner of Yonge and Dundas. The northeast corner of Victoria and Yonge would be redeveloped for a landmark, high-rise hotel and possibly a residential tower, while the southeast corner would be redeveloped for mid-rise commercial uses. The

Fig. 9-2. This exhibit, prepared by architect Terry Brown for a 1976 Ontario Municipal Board hearing, contemplated a square at the southeast corner of Yonge and Dundas, more than twenty-five years before the opening of Yonge-Dundas Square. [Ron Soskolne.]

development would replace the low-end retail the city felt was holding the area back. At the heart of it all would be a new public square, created by clearing the block bounded by Yonge, Dundas, Victoria, and the east-west street known somewhat confusingly as Dundas Square.

The triangular block (or more aptly, rectangular, with one corner cut off) had resulted in the 1920s from the northward rerouting of Dundas Street East, the former Wilton Avenue, to remove a jog at Yonge. In 1923, with the construction of that improvement, controller Albert

Fig. 9-3. The third-place entry, by Bregman and Hamann, in the 1998 Dundas Square competition. It featured lighted glass pavers and a stage floating in a pool. [B+H Architects.]

Hacker called for the creation of a public square in the new block. Although nothing happened at the time, the idea surfaced again more than fifty years later. An exhibit at a 1976 Ontario Municipal Board hearing showed a square on the Yonge-Dundas corner, using it to illustrate the type of public space that was being encouraged under the city's new central area official plan policies. Soskolne had been the city's lead planner for the downtown core when those policies were developed. At the time, the square had merely been an example, a footnote. Now, twenty years later, he was reviving that footnote as the centrepiece of an ambitious plan for the whole Yonge-Dundas area (Fig. 9-2).

But first there were legal hurdles to jump. The city needed to expropriate six privately held parcels to build

Metropolis, and four to build the square itself. After a forty-day hearing in 1998, the OMB approved the plan, confirming as well that the city had the power to expropriate the necessary land. Appeals to the courts by disgruntled landowners were unsuccessful. The city had already chosen PenEquity Management Corporation, a pension-fund manager, to redevelop the Metropolis site according to an agreed-upon design, with the Senator Restaurant redeveloping what would become the Torch building, now the Citytv headquarters. A similar search for someone to build on the hotel site was put on hold after the city chose to focus its expropriation efforts on the square and Metropolis.

For the design of Dundas Square (the "Yonge" would be added before it opened), the city held an international

Figs. 9-4, 9-5. The second-place entry of Oleson Worland featured "Falling Leaves," an overhead, holographic art installation by Michael Hayden. [Oleson Worland Architects.]

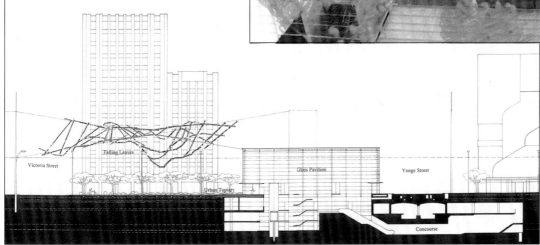

competition. All proposals had to accommodate a 250-space parking garage as well as provide a new subway entrance and theatre-ticket kiosk. Other than that, the city was looking for a flexible, urban space that would fit in well with its surroundings. It had already determined that those surroundings would be typified by Times-Square-style signage (except that, according to the ever-enthusiastic Mayor Mel Lastman, it would be even "bigger and better than Times Square"). A call for interested design teams, sent out in September 1998, brought forty-eight responses from around the world. A committee of design professionals chose six architectural firms to work up submissions: Sterling Finlayson; Oleson Worland; Ian MacDonald Inc.; Bregman and

Hamann; Brown and Storey; and Kohn Shnier. These finalists were given $5,000 each and a little over a month to prepare their designs.

On December 1, 1998, Mayor Lastman announced the results. Third place went to the Bregman and Hamann group. They oriented the square toward the northwest corner. The role of that corner as the main entrance was emphasized by raising the square to the east, and by moving the subway entrance to the south. Glass pavers allowed for light to be projected up into the square, while a stage at the eastern end appeared to float in a lighted pool (Fig. 9-3).

Second prize went to the team led by Oleson Worland Architects. Oleson Worland had won the competition for the Village of Yorkville Park on Cumberland Street, which had opened four years earlier. For their Dundas Square proposal, the integration of art into the public realm played a key role. A glass pavilion housing the ticket kiosk and the garage and subway entrances would define the square's northwest corner. It would face a glass observation tower on the southwest corner. Thanks to holographic film in the glass, both would also serve as giant art installations by artist Michael Hayden, creator of the "Arc en Ciel" neon sculpture at the Yorkdale subway station (which was dismantled in the mid 1990s). The pavilion and tower would help anchor "Falling Leaves," Hayden's overhead light sculpture. Looking up, visitors would see a suspended canopy made of strands of translucent Teflon fabric, its holographic coating refracting the area's natural and artificial light into prismatic colours. Tree-shaped sculptures would rise from the square's south end, providing shade for seating that would incorporate "urban fossils," artifacts uncovered during construction. The history of the site would be further evoked by water jets in the pavement tracing the former path of Taddle Creek. Even something as mundane as the sidewalk air vent for the subway would add to the ethereal sense of place, with reed-like blades in the air shaft creating musical sounds (Figs. 9-4, 9-5).

Given the frenetic backdrop that was planned to surround the square, the jury was looking for less rather than more in the square itself. As a result, they were attracted to the entry by the team led by Toronto architects James Brown and Kim Storey, giving it first prize. In their comments, the jury approved of Brown and Storey's reliance on a few architectural elements to set the square apart from its surroundings without competing with them.

The problem was, when Yonge-Dundas Square opened in May 2003, there wasn't much to compete with. The buildings and signage that were meant as its backdrop were nowhere in sight. For the better part of a decade, the Metropolis land sat empty, surrounded by hoarding, while the developer looked for tenants in a down market. It finally opened as Toronto Life Square in 2007, seven years later than expected. In the absence of the city's assembling a parcel for it, the hotel tower to the east has never materialized. Despite these setbacks, and although not everyone has been convinced by the final result, the square has undeniably become a major site of the city's public life and for many, the image of "downtown."

Chapter 10

JOHN HOWARD PUBLIC BUILDINGS

1834/UNBUILT

ON JULY 1, 1834, THE NEWLY MINTED Society of Artists and Amateurs held an exhibition in the east wing of the parliament buildings on Front Street. John Howard, perhaps best remembered today for donating his estate, High Park, to the city, was one of the society's founders (Fig. 10-1). For the exhibition, he submitted watercolours depicting an astonishing vision of his adopted hometown (he had emigrated two years earlier from England) transformed by fantastic neoclassical public buildings.

On the north side of King Street, west of Church, Howard envisaged a magnificent guildhall. The vast new building was shown between two existing structures that would have been familiar to his 1830s audience, the jail, on the left, and the court house, on the right. In addition to the guildhall, Howard's building would have housed a public library, post office, and merchants' exchange (Fig. 10-2).

Howard also exhibited a design he had come up with the year before for a new residence for the lieutenant governor (Fig. 10-3). The proposed location was Front Street, west of Peter. Unlike the guildhall, the government house design may have been solicited after a fashion, by the lieutenant governor himself, Sir John Colborne. Howard wrote that it had been made for Colborne's "information … and to show the impropriety of expending money in repairing the old government house." Perhaps realizing he had overshot the mark, Howard also designed a slightly pared-down version, shorn of statuary and dome, and with simplified end pavilions. It hardly mattered. Like the guildhall, and a massive, unsolicited proposal for the University of King's College (see *Unbuilt Toronto*, Fig. 27-5), Howard's designs were better-suited to the imperial capital where he had trained than to the colonial outpost where he was now practising.

Fig. 10-1. John George Howard, shown surveying the Toronto harbour, in an 1835 watercolour by George D'Almaine. While D'Almaine painted the portrait of Howard, the background was by Howard himself. He is shown standing in front of the old parliament buildings at Front and Simcoe. In his rendering of them, Howard included a portico that had been planned by the architect, Thomas Rogers, but never realized. [Toronto Public Library, JRR 835.]

Figs. 10-2 (top), 10-3 (bottom). John Howard's 1834 design for a guildhall (top). St. James's Church (now the Cathedral Church of St. James) is shown on the right. Howard prepared a design for a government house in 1833 (bottom). Perhaps realizing it was too extravagant, he later prepared a pared-down version. [Toronto Public Library, JRR 830; Design for Government House, York 1833; John George Howard (1803-1890); watercolour/ink on paper; 25.4 x 52.0 cm; City of Toronto Art Collection, Culture.]

Even so, with his Provincial Lunatic Asylum on Queen Street West (1850), Howard did achieve something of the grandeur depicted in the drawings he had exhibited in 1834. Based on the National Gallery in London, it was a handsome and imposing building even without its planned portico. Sadly, it was demolished in 1975.

That the extravagance of the earlier proposals made them unbuildable in early nineteenth-century Toronto may well have been beside the point. At the time, Howard was the only professionally trained architect in town. As architectural historian Sharon Vattay has pointed out, his beautifully executed watercolours would have served a very practical ulterior purpose, showing potential clients wishing to build more mundane structures just what the man could do. In this light, the over-the-top public buildings displayed in that long-ago exhibition are not a testament to an architect who was out of touch, but to one who knew exactly what he was doing.

COMMERCIAL BUILDINGS

Chapter 11

CONFEDERATION LIFE BUILDING

1889/BUILT TO DIFFERENT PLANS

THE CONFEDERATION LIFE BUILDING IS a survivor. A landmark at the northwest corner of Yonge and Richmond since 1892, it has survived unsympathetic renovations, the lopping off of its towers, the threat of demolition, a fire, even the collapse of the life insurance company that built it. And still it remains one of Toronto's best buildings.

When it announced its decision to build a new head office in 1889, the Confederation Life Association of Canada was just eighteen years old, and would have expected only about twenty of its own employees to be working in the building. But the company's directors wanted a head office that would reflect the firm's importance and potential, if not its current size. In May 1889 they issued an invitation to architects to submit plans in an open competition. The winner was to be decided by a single judge, Montreal architect J.W. Hopkins.

The site was a prime location on Richmond, between Victoria and Yonge. Confederation Life had purchased most of it in freehold in 1888, but had only managed to lease the key parcel at Yonge and Richmond for forty-two years, with perpetual rights of renewal. The company's building program reflected this less-certain tenure by stipulating that the portion of the building on the corner of Yonge and Richmond would be occupied by retail tenants, with the company's own offices to the east, on the land it owned outright.

The asymmetry of the winning design of the Toronto-based Knox, Elliot and Jarvis reflected this distinction (Fig. 11-1). The large, middle tower on Richmond, whose ground-level arch led to an interior court, demarcated the western edge of Confederation Life's non-leased holdings. Seen in this light, the main entrance to the office building, further east on Richmond, is actually centred in the "Confederation Life" portion of the building. This same

Fig. 11-1. The winning entry, by Knox, Elliot and Jarvis, in the 1889 competition for the Confederation Life head office, as depicted in a print from 1890. Its asymmetrical design reflected the underlying land ownership. [Archives of Ontario, C 281-0-0-1.]

Figs. 11-2 (top), 11-3 (bottom). The fourth-place design of Alfred Flockton (top) and the third-place design of James Balfour (bottom). Both exhibited the towers that *The Canadian Architect and Builder* said were necessary for success in the Confederation Life competition. [Thomas Fisher Rare Books Library, University of Toronto.]

Fig. 11-4. The second-place entry of James and James. It is the only symmetrical design of the five prize-winning entries that survive from the Confederation Life head office competition. [Thomas Fisher Rare Books Library, University of Toronto.]

reflection of the underlying land tenure is evident to an even greater degree in the design of Alfred Flockton of Montreal, which tied for fourth place (the other fourth-place entry, submitted under the monicker "Ajax," does not appear to have survived) (Fig. 11-2). Asymmetry and towers also figured in the third-place design of James Balfour of Hamilton (Fig. 11-3). As Edna Hudson writes in *The Romanesque Head Office of Confederation Life Association*, of the six designs known to survive (out of eighteen submitted), only the second-place entry of James and James is symmetrical. Even so, its regular facade concealed two distinct buildings (Fig. 11-4).

Fig. 11-5. The judge in the Confederation Life competition felt that the tower in the entry of Langley and Burke "gave a great deal of character to the edifice," but feared it would put the building over budget. [Archives of Ontario, C 11-613-01, K87.]

James and James were not only in the minority in producing a symmetrical design, they were also in a minority in not being Canadian (the firm's principals, brothers John and Arthur James, had relocated to New York from Britain). Earlier in the year, following another competition, they had been awarded the commission to design the Board of Trade Building at Front and Yonge (now demolished). They found themselves at the centre of a controversy after they were allowed to rework the exterior of their competition design, which the judge hadn't liked. The *Canadian Architect and Builder* found it manifestly unfair that Canadian firms (and specifically Darling and Curry, whose exterior design the judge had raved about) hadn't been given the same opportunity.

For the Confederation Life competition, the choice of another American firm — indeed, the same American firm — would have been a public relations disaster. Knox, Elliot and Jarvis, on the other hand, were acceptably Canadian. The firm had been founded in 1888 by Wilm Knox and John Elliot. The men had met while working in the Chicago office of Burnham and Root. Knox was a Scot, but the fact that Elliot and Jarvis were Torontonians secured their Canadian *bona fides*. Ironically, while the Confederation Life Building was still under construction, Knox and Elliot moved back to Chicago to work for the architect Henry Cobb, who would later design the King Edward Hotel (see Fig. 12-2).

The editors of *The Canadian Architect and Builder* were, naturally, pleased that so many Canadian architects had been finalists, but were otherwise unhappy with the results. They derided Hopkins for disqualifying fully two-thirds of the submitted designs because they failed to include the requisite number of drawings, and for focusing so many of his comments on the quality of the drawings generally — leaving the impression that it was

a drafting competition. They also weren't impressed with what they saw as his blinkered aesthetic judgment: "He certainly seems to think that an elevation without a tower is a rather poor sort of thing. He places designs with towers in first place, and those without nowhere." If so, it didn't help Langley and Burke. Though Hopkins felt that the tower in that firm's design "gave a great deal of character to the edifice," he feared it would put the building over budget. The firm was not given an award (Fig. 11-5). *The Canadian Architect and Builder* even panned Hopkins for choosing a design in which the offices of female typists opened onto public corridors: "What is to prevent them having their friends in to see them all hours of the day?" It all added up to one conclusion: "The result has been that the Association are now preparing to erect a building from a design which would have stood as low down as third, if not lower, provided the expert had been governed by precedent and common sense."

Confederation Life was deaf to the criticism: it was delighted with the building. Even so, in 1898, it modernized the rounded ground-floor arches at Yonge and Richmond; and in 1935, ostensibly for safety reasons, removed the roofs of the building's three towers and the stone tracery of the middle tower, which lost fifty feet in height. In time, a structure that had been far too big for Confederation Life's needs was far too small. The company moved to Bloor Street East in 1955, where it built a stolid, mid-rise, red-brick office building.

It wasn't long before the old building was threatened. In October 1959, a consortium called Queen-Yonge Developments announced that it would be redeveloping the entire block bounded by Yonge, Queen, Victoria and Richmond. Everything on it, including the Confederation Life Building, would be demolished to make way for two office towers designed

Fig. 11-6. In 1981, shortly after this proposal for Confederation Square by Moriyama and Teshima was approved by the city, fire severely damaged the historic 1892 Confederation Life Building. New owners brought on different architects.

[Archives of Ontario, F 2187-1-65.]

by the Toronto firm of Bregman and Hamann. The towers, one twenty storeys and one thirty, would sit on a low-rise podium containing a shopping mall. Thankfully for the Confederation Life Building, this proposal went nowhere. The next major proposal for the block, in 1977, would have saved the facade and roof of the Confederation Life Building, incorporating them into a new Woodward's department store, topped off by a thirty-storey residential building. After Woodward's pulled out, the Thom Partnership, the project architects, were retained as restoration architects for the old building, with Moriyama and Teshima getting the commission to design the new buildings. They proposed two elegant towers, rising up on piers through a nine-storey glass atrium that stretched from Queen Street to the roofline of the Confederation Life Building, which would now be retained in its entirety (Fig. 11-6).

In June 1981, soon after the city granted approvals for the development, a fire ripped through the building, destroying the top floor and severely damaging the roof. Luckily, a heritage easement on the property (which had been required by the Ontario Heritage Foundation as a condition of providing grant money to the project) meant not only that the building had to be restored, but that the owners had adequate insurance to do it. The building was duly repaired and restored the following year, but the second phase of the project, the construction of Moriyama and Teshima's towers, was put on hold. When the developer Bramalea took over in early 1985, it replaced the firm with Page and Steele. They came up with a new design, the single glass tower that was completed on the site in 1990.

Meanwhile, Confederation Life, the company that had started it all back in 1889, was getting its architectural mojo back, having commissioned the Zeidler Roberts Partnership to design for it a fantastical postmodern headquarters at 1 Mount Pleasant, at the top of Jarvis. In its exuberance, it was a worthy successor to the Knox, Elliot and Jarvis building. But this time, the architectural act of bravado was just that: the financially troubled company was wound up in court-ordered liquidation in 1994.

Chapter 12

Toronto Hotels

1895-1926/Unbuilt — Built to different plans

T HE QUEEN'S HOTEL ON FRONT STREET was respectable enough, but like its local competitors, it wasn't a place where you'd be proud to have the actual queen stay. Not in an age of "palace hotels," whose ballrooms and dining rooms — in places like the Château Frontenac in Quebec City and the Waldorf in New York — allowed the upper-middle class to live, fleetingly, like royalty. In January 1895, it looked like Toronto's turn was coming. That month, eighty of the city's leading businessmen signed a circular urging the construction of just such a showpiece for Toronto.

The idea of a palace hotel for Toronto had been floating around for some time, championed by financier Aemilius Jarvis. The circular was intended to kick-start the project by getting the municipal and provincial governments excited. From the city, the promoters were looking for a guarantee of the bonds they planned to issue; from the province, they were looking for two acres

of free land at the northwest corner of King and Simcoe that had become available when Upper Canada College had vacated it four years earlier. They didn't get either, but they pressed on, and by the end of 1898, they were ready to put up their own money for a different King Street parcel, this time just east of Yonge.

The New York firm of Harding and Gooch drew up the plans, which were published in *The Canadian Architect and Builder* in November 1898 (Fig. 12-1). They showed a seven-storey, 325-room hotel in the "free Renaissance style." Two arched entrances, demarcated by towers, provided access from King Street. The principal entrance to the hotel was to the east, with the western entrance opening onto a retail arcade. It allowed pedestrian passage between King Street and Colborne Street, and was aligned with Scott Street to the south (later plans were predicated on Scott Street being punched through the site as an extension of Victoria Street, an improvement the hotel successfully

Fig. 12-1. The design of the American firm Harding and Gooch for the "Palace Hotel" is shown here in an illustration from 1898. New plans and a new name — the King Edward — would follow. [Thomas Fisher Rare Books Library, University of Toronto.]

Fig. 12-2. The King Edward Hotel, depicted in a 1920s rendering. The original 1903 building is on the right. Its top two floors were add-ons, designed by E.J. Lennox after construction had started. The tower addition, on the left, opened in 1921. [Toronto Public Library, 986-2-2]

lobbied for). The palms of a rooftop garden terrace shown in the illustration hinted at the elegance within.

In 1900, Chicago architect Henry Ives Cobb replaced Harding and Gooch, opening up a Toronto office to work on the plans. Construction began in the summer of 1901. Toronto architect E.J. Lennox supervised, leaving his own traces on the design, including the addition of two terra cotta storeys planned after construction had begun (Fig. 12-2). But there was one thing missing — the hotel still had no name. The press had been calling it the Palace Hotel, but that had never been official. The company building it had been incorporated simply as the Toronto Hotel Company (with George Gooderham, its major backer, as president). When the building welcomed its first guests on May 11, 1903, it was as the King Edward Hotel, after Edward VII, who had ascended to the throne two years earlier. Toronto had a hotel not only named for a king, but fit for one, too.

———————

The King Eddy may be the city's original palace hotel, but the closest thing Toronto has to an actual palace is another Lennox building, Casa Loma. The castle's builder, Sir Henry Pellatt, had moved in just prior to the First World War. The interior was still unfinished, and as Sir Henry's finances deteriorated, it stayed that way. In 1923, no longer able to staff or maintain the castle, Pellatt was forced to move out. His dream home had become a millstone. In June 1924, its furnishings, which had cost Pellatt over a million dollars before the Great War, were liquidated in a two-day public auction.

If Pellatt was down, he wasn't out. The next year, he entered into an agreement with the Casa Loma Apartment Hotel Company to convert the castle into a high-class apartment-hotel. The brains behind the operation was local architect William F. Sparling. He planned to take full advantage of the building's quirky grandeur. The principal rooms of the main floor were to serve as common areas, with the upstairs floors converted to seventeen suites. Even the tunnel connecting the castle to the stables would be put to use as a running track. Most significantly, Sparling was designing a new addition for the castle's western end, to house fifty-six additional hotel rooms.

The conversion made sense; certainly there was no market for Casa Loma as a private residence. The problem was, the zoning allowed nothing but. In March 1926, Sparling pleaded his case before city council. Faced with fierce opposition from surrounding homeowners, he returned two months later with revised plans, three storeys lower, and farther back from Walmer Road (Fig. 12-3). It wasn't enough to satisfy the neighbours to the west on Austin Terrace, however. That fall, Sparling submitted an entirely new scheme, with no construction on the western side of the castle. Instead, he proposed two wings for the Davenport side of the building, angled to the southwest and southeast. Access would be from a tunnel off Davenport.

Figs. 12-3 (right, top), 12-4 (right, bottom). Two attempts to operate Casa Loma as an apartment hotel in the 1920s failed. In 1926, William Sparling faced fierce opposition when he proposed an L-shaped addition to the castle's west end. A 1929 proposal, by Cleveland architect A.W. Harris, shifted the new addition to the east side. The inset shows the hotel's manager at the time, E.G. Borden. [Toronto Public Library.]

The Austin Terrace neighbours still weren't satisfied. The most vocal of them was E.J. Lennox, who had built his own mansion, Lenwil, on Austin Terrace a decade earlier. Lennox had once had a warm relationship with Pellatt, but his public comments about his former patron showed those days were over: "Sir Henry has exploited many things before — why should he exploit the neighbourhood?" In November 1926, council granted the request to allow the building to be used as an apartment, on the condition that any additions be in keeping with the castle's original architecture.

In the meantime, Sparling had been busy repairing the damage that had resulted from the building's neglect (Pellatt had stopped heating it), and completing those parts Pellatt had been too broke to finish. The Casa Loma Hotel opened in April 1927, but had to cancel its first major event, a dance. The zoning still wasn't right: it allowed an apartment building, but you didn't hold public dances in apartment buildings. Council passed yet another amending by-law the next month. The Ontario Railway and Municipal Board approved it, noting that when Casa Loma was vacant, it had attracted "undesirable characters" to the area, "some for the purpose of theft and others for purposes most objectionable to the residents of the locality." Whatever those mysterious other purposes were, the residents of Austin Terrace apparently didn't find them as bad as a hotel. Reverend Ben Spence, a temperance advocate, told the board that the hotel would encourage "the evils of drink and all-night dancing," adding "The guests go in there with leaking baggage and come out with much less than they took in."

The neighbours' attempt to get the board's decision overturned by the courts failed. But even though Sparling now had his land-use permissions, financing was still a problem. He tried, apparently unsuccessfully, to get backing in New York, before making a deal in the fall of 1927 with a Detroit businessman, Miles H. Knowles. Knowles planned to take over the property and operate it as a private club. An American firm of architects and engineers were retained in connection with the scheme. Why exactly, is unclear, but it quickly didn't matter. In February 1928, the hotel was forced into bankruptcy, closing its doors on June 18, 1928. Once again, Casa Loma's effects were on the auction block.

A year later, Pellatt, who was still the building's legal owner, let an American group give the hotel idea a second shot. They had Cleveland architect A.W. Harris draw up plans for a $2-million, 350-room addition. It was strategically located on the east side of the building, as far away from the litigious Austin Terrace residents as possible (Fig. 12-4). The Casa Loma Hotel reopened on August 1, 1929, but not for long. As part of the liquidation of the business, on January 20, 1930, the building's contents were auctioned off for the third time in over five years. Pellatt, old, broke, and in ill health, had done all he could to save his castle on the hill. The city took it over for unpaid taxes in 1934.

In December 1926, while William Sparling was busy promoting the Casa Loma Hotel, news came of another ambitious uptown apartment hotel project, the Queen's Park Plaza. It took its name from its location, at the northwest corner of Bloor and Avenue Road, just north of Queen's Park. In a developing commercial district, it didn't have the same problems as Sparling's project, but it had plenty of its own.

The design for the fifteen-storey brick-and-limestone Queen's Park Plaza was the work of architect Hugh G. Holman. In his plan, commercial and office space occupied the first few floors, with hotel suites above. Each hotel suite would have a living room, one or more bedrooms (each with a bathroom), and "en suite refrigeration." In fact, seventy would have "buffet kitchenettes," but residents would presumably prefer to dine in the high-class café or one of the private dining rooms. As for the furnishings, they would be of the highest quality, not, according to a 1927 prospectus, "ornate or gaudy, but rather in keeping with the refinement and atmosphere of the best homes."

The development was being promoted by the Queen's Park Plaza Company Limited, headed by H.W. Burgess, "physician and capitalist." To cover the project's costs, the corporation engaged two companies to sell almost $1.5 million in bonds to the public, secured by first and second mortgages on the property. There were still a lot more bonds to sell when work started in June 1927, but no one seemed worried: the sales would come. After all, the retail space had already been leased out, and it was expected that the rest of the building would be fully tenanted within six months of completion. Even the vendor of the land had sold it to the Queen's Park Plaza Company for only $10 down, on the promise of $150,000 to follow from bond sales, plus some Queen's Park Plaza shares.

Work stopped for a few weeks in 1928, after a decision was made to switch from concrete construction to steel. After it started again, there were obvious cash-flow issues. Contractors began to find that their invoices were being ignored. Under the law, the sums they were owed formed ever-growing liens on the property, even as Queen's Park Plaza bonds continued to be peddled to an unsuspecting public. Another thing the public wouldn't have suspected: the issuer of the first mortgage bonds, the United Bond Company, was commingling the revenue from all the projects it financed (and there were some seventy-five of them in the end) in a single fund, out of which it paid its various obligations as they came

due. In other words, revenue raised for one project could be used to service another.

It worked as long as the money kept coming in from all the different projects, but ultimately, as the Ontario Court of Appeal concluded when considering another United Bond Company project: "This fraudulent course of conduct could only have one result — the speedy exhaustion of the ... fund." In fact, in December 1930, the United Bond Company was in receivership. The Queen's Park Plaza Company, one of its many creditors, claimed it was owed $93,000. Work on the hotel had stopped long before, in the summer of 1929, leaving it unfinished on the inside; an empty shell. It would remain that way for the next seven years (Fig. 12-5).

With both bond companies, the general contractor, and the Queen's Park Plaza Company itself eventually bankrupt, bondholders and construction lien holders were left to compete for any value to be found in the half-completed hulk. Litigation arising from the fiasco in 1932 created a crisis when the Ontario Court of Appeal ruled that, for the most part, even the unregistered liens on the Queen's Park Plaza had priority over the registered mortgages. Lenders on other projects reacted by stopping advances on construction loans, threatening a disastrous domino-effect of bankruptcies across the province.

The legislature fixed the law four months later, but it was too late for the Queen's Park Plaza bondholders, who were trying desperately to find someone to take over the project. In Depression-era Toronto, there weren't a lot of prospects. A proposal in 1931 to convert the building entirely to offices had fallen through, as did a bid the next year by William Sparling — unbowed by his Casa Loma experience — to run it as an apartment hotel. The reality was, there was no money and no market. Even the venerable King Edward was in receivership by year's end.

Fig. 12-5. The Queen's Park Plaza — later simply the Park Plaza — is shown under construction, in a view looking west on Bloor, April 27, 1929. Construction would stop that summer. The building, unfinished on the inside, would remain an empty hulk for the next seven years. [City of Toronto Archives/TTC Fonds 16, Series 71, Item 6776.]

Finally, in October 1934, against the bondholders' objections, the courts permitted the Queen's Park Plaza's receiver to sell the building in order to cover unpaid property taxes. The new owner, the Park Plaza Co., was backed by experienced developer Harry Rotenberg. After the taxes and the liens had been paid out, the bondholders were left with nothing, as they had feared. Chapman and Oxley, whose addition to the Royal Ontario Museum had

opened across the street a couple of years earlier, were brought on to redesign the interiors. On July 11, 1936, the building opened as the Park Plaza Hotel, nine years after construction had begun. A respectable presence on the Toronto scene ever since — currently as the Park Hyatt — her rather sketchy past has been forgiven and (mostly) forgotten.

Chapter 13

BANK OF TORONTO HEAD OFFICE
1910/BUILT TO DIFFERENT PLANS
TORONTO-DOMINION CENTRE
1963/BUILT TO DIFFERENT PLANS

IN JUNE 1910, THE *TORONTO DAILY STAR* reported that the Bank of Toronto was using plans prepared by a New York-based architectural firm, Carrère and Hastings, for its new head office building at the southwest corner of King and Bay. The *Star* gave the impression that there had simply been a competition, and that Carrère and Hastings had won it. But that was only half the story. While it was true that the Carrère and Hastings design had been chosen over those of three Toronto firms, George W. Gouinlock, Sproatt and Rolph, and John Lyle, the bank had actually hired the Americans for the job more than a year earlier, and had asked the Canadian firms to come up with alternate designs only about two months before the *Star* article appeared. Why would the bank hire one firm, work with them for more than a year, and then seek out designs from others — only to go with what they already had? (Figs. 13-1, 13-2, 13-3, 13-4.)

The initial choice of Carrère and Hastings was not surprising. One of the premiere American firms of the era (best known today for their New York Public Library), they had come to Canada four years earlier to design the head offices of the Traders Bank at Yonge and Colborne (see Fig. 16-2). Barrie-born Eustace Bird, who was working for the firm in New York, was dispatched to Toronto to supervise the project, and to head up the firm's new Toronto office. From that point, Carrère and Hastings took on a number of high-profile commissions in Canada. They were even asked to design the new Union Station (the commission would ultimately go to Ross and MacFarlane working with Carrère and Hastings alumnus John Lyle) (Fig. 13-5). The firm had also designed a number of branches for the Bank of Toronto. So it was natural that the bank would approach them when it was looking to move out of its 1862 head office at Church and Wellington streets and follow the commercial movement over to the west side of Yonge.

Fig. 13-1. When the Carrère and Hastings–designed Bank of Toronto head office opened in 1913, it was hailed as one of the most beautiful buildings in Canada. Comments by one of its designers, however, caused an uproar among Canadian architects. It is shown here in 1939. In the foreground, demolition has taken place for the new Bank of Montreal headquarters (see Chapter 18). [TD Bank Financial Group Archives (photograph by Pringle and Booth).]

Fig. 13-2. George W. Gouinlock's 1910 design for the Bank of Toronto's head office was one of three commissioned more than a year after Carrère and Hastings had been hired for the job. [Thomas Fisher Rare Books Library, University of Toronto.]

Figs. 13-3, 13-4. The Bank of Toronto head office proposals submitted by Sproatt and Rolph (top) and John Lyle (bottom) in a limited competition in 1910. [Thomas Fisher Rare Books Library, University of Toronto.]

The hiring of American architects had been a longstanding source of resentment among the profession in Canada, going back at least to 1886 and the Ontario government's awarding the commission for the provincial legislative buildings to the American Richard Waite (see *Unbuilt Toronto*, Chapter 8). By 1910, however, Canadian architects were fighting back in an organized way. The Ontario Association of Architects and the Toronto Society of Architects formed a joint committee to lobby government on the issue and to rally public opinion against the hiring of foreign talent. It was more than a matter of national honour: the architects were compiling statistics to show the economic loss to the country over the past four years had been in the millions, since the hiring of an American architect often led to the hiring of American contractors. In an open letter dated April 26, 1910, and published in the May edition of *Construction*, the joint committee criticized banks in particular for failing to support Canadian architects. An editorial accompanying the letter specifically criticized the Bank of Toronto for hiring Carrère and Hastings to design its new head office.

It seems almost certain that the Bank of Toronto's eleventh-hour decision to invite the three local firms to come up with competing plans was an attempt to address the criticism that Canadians hadn't been given a chance. *Construction* questioned the fairness (and implicitly, the good faith) of the exercise altogether in noting that the Toronto firms were given about two months to come up with their plans while those of Carrère and Hastings, by the firm's own admission, had been the result of more than a year of "great care and deliberation." The issue might have died with that lingering criticism had it not been for the comments of Eustace Bird in a *Star* article, in which he suggested that the choice of the American firm was a foregone conclusion for a very different reason, namely, that Canadian firms just weren't up to the job:

Fig. 13-5. Carrère and Hastings' unrealized 1907 plan for Union Station. [Toronto Public Library.]

In any new country architecture is necessarily undeveloped. As in any other branch of art it is necessary for us in Canada to rely on established principles which have been perfected in New York or Europe. In doing this there is no intention of boycotting Canadian industry but only an attempt to secure a satisfactory design. Carrère and Hastings are conceded to be the leading architects of North America, and surely Toronto wants the best buildings that can be secured.

The response to Bird's comments from an already-sensitive profession was immediate. The *Star* published a letter from Alfred Chapman in which, using the Traders Bank Building as an example (see Fig. 16-2), the architect dismissed the notion that Carrère and Hastings should have any claim to competency, much less pre-eminence. The debate continued in an even more vitriolic way in the pages of *Construction*, whose editors railed against Bird's comments as "a gross breach of professional ethics" and "an insidious attack upon Canadian architects." The *Star* had reported that Bird had actually designed the new building in Toronto, and that the plans had simply been reviewed and approved by Carrère and Hastings in New York. *Construction* seized on this tidbit to attack Bird personally:

> We know of no work he has done in Canada or elsewhere that would justify his assuming that his architectural training or practice has been such as to place him in a position where he might consistently deprecate the inferiority of

Canadian architects, when discussing in the public press a competition with which are connected the names of such men as Sproatt and Rolph, G.W. Gouinlock and J.M. Lyle.

Carrère and Hastings responded with an outraged letter to *Construction*, calling its editorial a "gratuitous, unfair and unseemly attack," adding that, "We cannot believe that any architect of standing and good repute can possibly sympathize with your motives, or with your manner of presenting your case." *Construction* gave no ground in its response:

> So remember! Canadian architects, that if you resent the inference that you are untrained because you live in a country where architecture is undeveloped — if you do not agree that it is only reasonable that large Canadian corporations should go to New York for architects to design their buildings — if you agree with the resentful spirit of an article that undertakes to protect the profession against the insidious attacks of a representative of a foreign architectural firm, then, mark you! Because of these things you are not an architect of "standing and good repute."

By the time the Bank of Toronto head office opened in July 1913, all was clearly forgiven. *Construction* dedicated a good chunk of its September edition that year to a profile of the building, with its marble banking hall topped by a ceiling of glass and cast bronze. It could not have been more approving of the result, concluding that "as a work of art it is destined to take its place as one of the notable structures of the present time" (Fig. 13-6).

Eustace Bird and Carrère and Hastings must have felt vindicated. They moved their offices to the new building, but by 1916, with Canada in a war economy, Carrère and Hastings had closed their Canadian operations. Bird, who had created such an uproar in defending the firm, was left to fly solo.

———————

In 1955, the Bank of Toronto merged with the Dominion Bank to form the Toronto-Dominion Bank. In 1962, New York developer Webb and Knapp tried to convince the TD Bank to add its lands to "Finance Plaza," a redevelopment scheme it was preparing for the Canadian Imperial Bank of Commerce (Fig. 13-7). TD had no interest in redeveloping with its larger competitor across the street, but, spurred by Webb and Knapp's proposal, TD chair Allen Lambert began to explore the redevelopment opportunities of its site. At his recommendation, the bank partnered with another developer, the Fairview Corporation, which was controlled by the Bronfman family. Initially, the plan was to replace the Carrère and Hastings building with a tower on the same site, but as the partnership acquired more land in the area, its

Fig. 13-6. The banking hall in the Bank of Toronto's head office in a view that emphasizes the room's glass-and-cast-bronze ceiling, looking toward the main entrance on King. This photograph was taken in 1913, immediately after the building's completion. [TD Bank Financial Archives Archives (photograph by Pringle and Booth).]

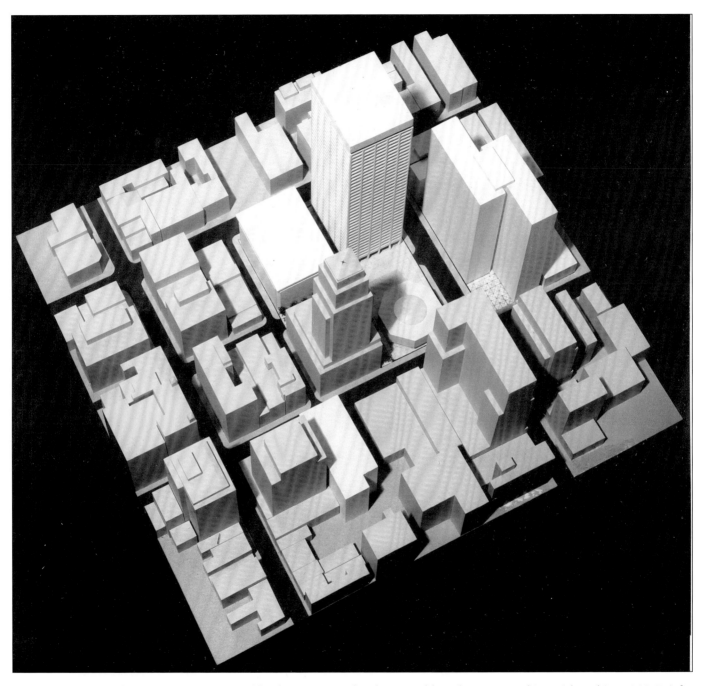

Fig. 13-7. Finance Plaza was a 1962 proposal by the American developer Webb and Knapp, working with architect I.M. Pei, for a redevelopment of the King and Bay holdings of both the Canadian Imperial Bank of Commerce and the Toronto-Dominion Bank. [CIBC Archives.]

development ambitions grew. It hired two Toronto firms, John B. Parkin Associates and Bregman and Hamann to prepare preliminary plans. But history seemed to repeat itself when the bank and the developer concluded that what they really needed was the heft and experience of an internationally known architect.

The bank, which had the final say on the design of the complex that would bear its name, wanted Gordon Bunshaft of Skidmore, Owings and Merrill. Fairview advocated for Ludwig Mies van der Rohe, who had designed the Seagram Building in New York for the Bronfman-controlled distillery, on the recommendation of Samuel Bronfman's daughter, architect Phyllis Lambert. Daniel Stoffman writes in *The Cadillac Fairview Story* that the bank felt Bunshaft could come up with something more original. As it happened, Bunshaft's design was so original, it lost him the commission.

Though no drawings of the proposal appear to have survived, Phyllis Lambert and others who were involved remember it well, if not fondly. Bunshaft proposed a single, sixty-storey tower, whose concrete columns would taper upwards from the building's broad base in great, sweeping lines. These exposed, concrete columns would support the weight of the building. They would inevitably expand and contract in the blazing Toronto summers and freezing Toronto winters, but Bunshaft had a way to deal with that. Phyllis Lambert would later describe it in an essay on the Toronto-Dominion Centre: "All expansion of the continuous eight-hundred-foot-high concrete structure was to be resolved by hefty stainless steel piston-like slip joints placed at the top of the building — a daring and unproved solution."

As Stoffman relates, Fairview and the bank retained the head of structural engineering at the Massachusetts Institute of Technology to review the proposal; he agreed

it was problematic. In an exchange of telegrams while Bunshaft was on vacation, the developers asked the architect to come up with a more conventional design. Bunshaft, who was designing smaller buildings at the time with metal slip joints (including the Beinecke Rare Book and Manuscript Library at Yale University), refused. He was fired. Two later designs by Bunshaft in New York City would give form to his conception of an office tower with a monolithic curving silhouette, the W.R. Grace Building (1973) and Nine West 57th Street (1974), though neither employed the stainless-steel slip joints that had lost the architect the Toronto job (Fig. 13-8).

TD and Fairview next turned to John B. Parkin Associates, who prepared designs for a single tower, with conventional curtain-wall construction. The banking pavilion was located below ground, with access through a freestanding pavilion. Concerned about the Parkin firm's lack of track record in high-rise design, Fairview proposed to bring in a New York architect to supervise. At this point, Phyllis Lambert, a silent part owner of Fairview, intervened. She felt that the arrangement would lead to conflict. On what she would later describe as her "insistent recommendation," Mies was interviewed. After the Bunshaft ordeal, Mies's reputation for designing conventional curtain-wall skyscrapers certainly helped him get the commission, but, as Ms. Lambert recounts, his rhetorical question to the bank chair on viewing the Parkin proposal also had its effect: "Do you want to have your bank in a *basement?*"

Mies unveiled the model of the TD Centre to a team from the bank and Fairview who had assembled in Carrère and Hastings' now-doomed head office building. The elements that would go on to create a Toronto landmark were all there: the two towers, the banking pavilion, and the plaza. Everyone seemed to agree it was pretty

Fig. 13-8. The W.R. Grace Building, one of two New York skyscrapers in which architect Gordon Bunshaft realized the sweeping silhouette he had wanted for the TD Centre.

[Loren Kolar.]

smashing, except for one thing. Both Allen Lambert and Samuel Bronfman felt the major tower should be pushed up to King Street to solidify the building's association with the King and Bay intersection. Mies told them that his buildings would go just where he had planned them to go. The development team was again being told they could take or leave the design of the architectural star they had retained. This time, wisely, they took it.

Chapter 14

CANADIAN BANK OF COMMERCE BUILDING

1912/BUILT TO DIFFERENT PLANS

COMMERCE COURT

1968/BUILT TO DIFFERENT PLANS

WHEN IT OPENED IN 1890, THE Canadian Bank of Commerce head office building at King and Jordan Streets was one of the tallest commercial buildings in the city. The sandstone and brick structure, by Buffalo architect Richard Waite (whose Ontario legislative buildings were then under construction), was also one of the city's most luxurious (Fig. 14-1). But by 1912, the bank had outgrown it. Seeking to expand, it acquired the adjacent parcels west along King and south to Melinda. The local firm of Darling and Pearson, who had designed buildings for the bank across the country, were hired for the big hometown job, a new head office building on the expanded King Street site. Their seven-storey, beaux-arts design — described by one bank officer as "a most beautiful Grecian temple, adapted to banking" — was similar to the magnificent branches that the firm had recently produced for the bank in Montreal (1909) and Winnipeg (1911).

Construction was expected to start in 1914, but the First World War ensured that that didn't happen. After the war, the bank waited for building costs to stabilize through the 1920s, as Darling and Pearson continued to refine their scheme. In July 1925, however, bank officials announced that they were taking an entirely different approach: now the idea was simply to add on to the existing building. A westward extension would make Waite's asymmetrical composition symmetrical. The building would be similarly extended to Melinda Street in the south. Although Waite's self-described "modern example of the Italian Renaissance" was far from the height of 1920s fashion (it was described in a history of the bank at the time as "more elaborate than the best architectural talent would now employ"), it was only thirty-five years old, and its (at least partial) steel-frame construction made extension with modern additions a feasible and economical option (Fig. 14-2).

Fig. 14-1. When it opened in 1890, Richard Waite's Canadian Bank of Commerce head office was one of the tallest and most luxurious commercial buildings in the city. [City of Toronto Archives, Series 387, Item 21.]

Even as the bank announced that construction on the extensions would start by year's end, Darling and Pearson were back producing plans that required the demolition of the building, continuing to update and rework their seven-storey pre-war design through 1926 (Figs. 14-3, 14-4). The next year, however, in order to ensure adequate space for future growth (and no doubt to take advantage of a booming 1920s real-estate market), the program shifted dramatically again, when the bank decided to build a skyscraper. And not just any skyscraper: at thirty-four storeys, it would be the tallest in the British Empire.

Having decided it wanted a skyscraper, the bank brought in the New York architectural firm of York and Sawyer, keeping Darling and Pearson on as supervising architects. York and Sawyer had made a name for themselves as experts in bank design, and had designed the twenty-two-storey Royal Bank Building in Montreal, then nearing completion.

Fig. 14-2. Abandoning plans to build a neoclassical new head office building, the Canadian Bank of Commerce announced in 1925 that it would enlarge its existing headquarters, copying its Victorian Romanesque exactly in the extensions. [CIBC Archives.]

Fig. 14-3. This rendering, *circa* 1925–26, shows the architects Darling and Pearson continuing to work with the basic concept for the bank's head office that they had planned prior to the First World War. [CIBC Archives (illustration by S.H. Maw).]

Fig. 14-4. An alternative scheme for the Canadian Bank of Commerce head office from 1925 to 1926 reflected a stylistic departure from Darling and Pearson's pre-war plans. [CIBC Archives (illustration by S.H. Maw).]

Fig. 14-5. In this perspective, from November 1927, Darling and Pearson's proposed seven-storey Canadian Bank of Commerce Building becomes the base for a tower, designed with the New York architects York and Sawyer, who had now joined the project. [CIBC Archives.]

Fig. 14-6. An illustration by S.H. Maw from December 1927 shows what may have been intended to be the final design for the Canadian Bank of Commerce head office building. [CIBC Archives.]

Fig. 14-7. The plans that were released when the head office tower of the Canadian Bank of Commerce was formally announced in January 1928. [Toronto Public Library.]

For the Toronto tower, the bank's limited frontage on King Street drove the design. The decision was made early on not to construct a building that rose straight up on all sides, which would have resulted in the most imposing facade being on Jordan Street. Instead, the tower would rise straight up from King Street only, emphasizing that facade as the principal front, while being set back on its other three sides. Interestingly, despite the radical shift from planning a seven-storey building to planning Canada's tallest skyscraper, the project's long history remained — and remains — discernable in its massing. The banking hall and all of the bank's offices were contained in the tower's seven-storey base, with the tower itself used for rental office space. In effect, the skyscraper's base was the seven-storey banking building that Darling and Pearson had been planning since 1912, freshened up stylistically and topped off with a tower. In one version, from November 1927, the beaux-arts styling was retained, making this connection all the more apparent (Fig. 14-5).

In a perspective produced the following month, the colonnaded base gave way to a massive entrance arch, while still retaining Corinthian details. The rendering was done by Samuel Herbert Maw. Trained as an architect in his native England, Maw had worked with Darling and Pearson after immigrating to Canada in 1912, developing a reputation as one of the best architectural renderers in the country. One suspects that the building depicted in his December 1927 illustration — a month before the project was formally announced — was initially considered the final design. How else to explain the time and attention lavished on it, compared to the more hurried rendering ultimately provided to the press? (Figs. 14-6, 14-7.) Clearly, the plan had continued to evolve, with the decision ultimately made to dispense with classical detailing entirely. Its replacement was a neo-Romanesque/art deco combination that allowed for greater whimsy than a Grecian temple of banking ever could. In addition to the sixteen massive heads that survey the city from high atop the tower (in a last-minute adjustment, they replaced more typical-looking gargoyles), the Melinda Street entrance — now the courtyard entrance — is flanked with stylized carvings of bulls and bears, apparently with ticker tapes in their mouths.

Massive as the Canadian Bank of Commerce head office building was for its time, within twenty-five years of its completion, it too had become too small. In 1956, the bank announced what was being called the single largest development proposal in Canadian history: a $50-million expansion to its head office, on adjacent land that it had acquired on King Street. As with the extension of the bank's 1890 building, nothing came of this announcement. It was for the best. When the bank merged with the Imperial Bank of Canada in 1961, becoming the Canadian Imperial Bank of Commerce, there was the possibility of an even more ambitious project. That was because the Imperial Bank's assets included its valuable landholdings at the southeast corner of King and Bay, the site of *its* head office.

The CIBC continued to assemble land in the King/Bay/Wellington/Jordan superblock throughout the 1960s. In 1962, the bank worked with the American developer Webb and Knapp and its architect, I.M. Pei, on a proposal for Finance Plaza, a scheme that included a tower for the CIBC at Bay and Wellington, a low-rise, octagonal pavilion to house the CIBC's banking hall, as well as a new Toronto stock exchange. Although the TD Bank declined an offer to participate in Finance Plaza,

Webb and Knapp showed various versions of a new TD tower at the southwest corner of King and Bay integrated with the complex (see Fig. 13-7).

After the bankruptcy of Webb and Knapp in 1965, the CIBC continued to work with I.M. Pei and Associates, who partnered with Page and Steele, all the while publicly denying any specific development plans. The bank's silence didn't stop Mayor Phil Givens from making his own announcement. In a 1966 election speech, he "revealed" that the CIBC was planning an eighty- to ninety-storey tower. When the bank finally went public with its Commerce Court project in August of 1968, Givens's information was shown to be more civic boosterism than reality. Even so, the proposal was impressive: a soaring tower (ultimately fifty-seven-storeys) as the centrepiece of a complex which, with the addition of five- and fourteen-storey buildings to the south and east, covered the superblock surrounding the 1931 head office. The new tower at King and Bay would recapture, at least for the three years before First Canadian Place topped out, the tallest-building crown recently lost by the CIBC's 1931 tower, now renamed Commerce Court North (Figs. 14-8, 14-9).

Before construction could start, there was a glitch that had to be dealt with: the bank's investigations had revealed that a grave-sized parcel south of the Canadian Bank of Commerce Building had not been sold in 1815 with the rest of its surrounding plot, apparently because the vendor's daughter, Stella Vanzant, was buried there. In 1969, in an effort to find the gravesite, the bank undertook an archaeological dig, supervised by Mount Pleasant Cemetery, the provincial government, and the Anglican Church. After hand-digging to a depth of twelve feet without any sign of Stella's remains, all parties agreed that further searching would be futile. Construction could begin in earnest on Commerce Court.

Figs. 14-8, 14-9. A model and rendering, *circa* 1968, show I.M. Pei's Commerce Court West in its near-ultimate form. The tower's flared base and the dramatic tree columns of the banking hall would be jettisoned. [CIBC Archives (illustration by Helmut Jacoby).]

The *Globe and Mail* had earlier announced that the CIBC's plans meant that its 1931 head office building was doomed, but this never seemed to have been the case. On the contrary, at great expense, the landmark was given a painstaking, eighteen-month renovation and restoration from top to bottom, including facing the brick-clad western portion of the building's base (now exposed because of the demolition of its neighbour) in Indiana limestone to match the rest of the building. Moreover, in setting the new tower back from King Street, the old head office would actually be given increased prominence from the west. "Commerce Court North" may not have been Toronto's tallest building any longer, but it was still one of its best.

Chapter 15

Canadian National Building
1925/Unbuilt

When Canadian National Railways took over the Grand Trunk Railway in 1923, it acquired, among other assets, what was left of the Grand Trunk's lease on its Toronto head office at the northwest corner of King and Yonge. The lease had five years left, but the CNR was not willing to risk losing the prime location when it expired. Whether the CNR out-and-out expropriated the building (as the newspapers reported) or "virtually" expropriated it (as a judge would later write), the Imperial Bank, which was its owner, would not have complained: it got $1.2 million for the building, the highest amount ever paid to that point for real estate in Canada (Fig. 15-1).

For the CNR, the location justified the price. In the period immediately before the First World War, King and Yonge had transformed into "canyon corners." The CNR's largest competitor, Canadian Pacific, had built the tallest building in the British Empire at the southeast corner

in 1913. The record was surpassed two years later by the twenty-storey Royal Bank Building on the northeast corner. In the year between, the Dominion Bank erected its own twelve-storey skyscraper at the southwest corner (see Fig. 16-2). There were reports that the CNR intended to build something that would surpass any of these, a building that would "look scornfully upon the roof of the Royal Bank Building." The failure of the Home Bank in August 1923 provided an opportunity for the CNR to acquire its adjacent head office building, creating an even larger development parcel.

It was all very attractive, but by the end of 1924, the railway had decided that it didn't want to play the development game. That's when James Forgie, a lawyer who had acted for the CNR when it acquired the Yonge Street property, suggested a way that it could leave that to others, while still occupying a landmark tower. In his proposal, Forgie would buy the CNR's land for $1.25

Fig. 15-1. The Grand Trunk Building at the northwest corner of King and Yonge (shown here in 1912), which the Canadian National Railway "virtually" expropriated in 1923. Two years later, the CNR entered into an agreement that would have seen it and the head office of the Home Bank (immediately to the west) demolished. [Toronto Public Library, E2-16b.]

million, $50,000 more than the railway had paid. He would also spend $500,000 to buy the Home Bank land, building a twenty-six-storey skyscraper on the combined parcel. The CNR would agree to lease the ground floor and the next three floors in the building for thirty years. In recognition of its lead-tenant status, the building would be called the Canadian National Building.

It seemed like a win-win situation, and the CNR was eager to proceed, but the deal still needed the federal government's ratification. That came by way of an order-in-council on July 29, 1925. By that time, the city's property committee had approved what would be the Empire's tallest building, the third at King and Yonge to carry that title. The architect was Eustace Bird.

In a two-page feature, the *Star* enthused that Bird's CN tower would not only be Toronto's tallest, but its most distinctive. The newspaper reported that Bird had prepared sketch plans for the Canadian National Building in both "Florentine" and Gothic styles. Either way, the building would be constructed of buff Manitoba limestone, making it a stand-out among Toronto skyscrapers. Its shape would also be distinctive, the *Star* likening it to a mountain peak. A perspective published later in the newspaper showed Bird's building rising straight up for its reported height of twenty-six storeys, before stepping back for five more storeys and finally terminating in a two-part château-style roof complete with dormers (Fig. 15-2).

The Gothic style and the château roof had become hallmarks both of Canadian federal buildings and of

Fig. 15-2. Eustace Bird's 1925 design for the Canadian National Building. At twenty-six full storeys, and crowned with ten additional tapered storeys, it would have been the third building at King and Yonge to take the title of tallest in the British Empire. [Toronto Public Library.]

Canadian railway architecture. Bird's use of them on the Canadian National Building would have suggested the presence of the federally owned railway company. It was not something people needed to be reminded of. In September 1925, the governor general, Lord Byng, dissolved parliament at the request of Prime Minister William Lyon Mackenzie King. Opposition leader Arthur Meighen made an election issue of the CNR's involvement in such extravagant non-essentials as hotels, golf courses, and, not least of all, the proposed Canadian National Building. The minister of canals and railways, George P. Graham, defended the deal: "Remember that Canadian National Railways is not spending one dollar in what Mr. Meighen terms a skyscraper. The public is being misled…. There is not a business man in Canada, if he wants to be fair, will say that this was not an ideal transaction."

The transaction may have been ideal, but it was getting more and more complicated. Forgie had got financial backing for his scheme from J.R. Anglin, president of Anglin-Norcross, the construction firm that would later build the Royal York Hotel and the Canadian Bank of Commerce Building. Anglin agreed to provide the down payments for the CNR and Home Bank properties. In return, he would get a 25 percent interest in Dominion Building Corp., a company that Forgie had incorporated to hold the land. Anglin-Norcross would also get a $1.75-million contract to construct the building. Dominion Building Corp. would raise the rest of the capital it needed by issuing bonds to the general public, who could feel comforted by the solid revenue stream assured by the long-term government leases.

The CNR, which had been operating out of the site for over two years, moved out on September 19, 1925. On September 25, three days before the land deal was set to close, Dominion agreed to flip the property to the William Wrigley Jr. Co. Ltd. for just over $2 million. Anglin-Norcross would still build Bird's skyscraper, but now it would be for the chewing-gum manufacturer. The Wrigley's deal brought needed capital, but it caused other problems. Not surprisingly, Wrigley's (whose American arm had a brand-new, self-named skyscraper in Chicago) insisted that the CNR give up its naming rights, something that the railway refused to do. Further, Wrigley's wouldn't close unless an agreement that Forgie had reached to lease five floors to the Department of Customs and Excise was ratified by cabinet. Although an order-in-council approving the lease had been prepared at the beginning of September, once parliament had been dissolved, its fate was in limbo.

The federal election of October 29, 1925, resulted in a hung parliament, with no party having a majority. Mackenzie King stayed on as prime minister, even though his Liberals had fewer seats than Meighen's Conservatives. A rumour spread that, given the precarious political situation in Ottawa, the Canadian National Building had been cancelled. Eustace Bird told the *Star* at the end of November that it wasn't true: "There is absolutely no truth to the rumour…. I think that it is an assured fact that the recent election has in no way altered the plans of those responsible for the erection of the new structure. The whole thing is a storm in a teacup." Bird's assurance seemed more than credible when, a few days later, tenders were requested for the demolition of the old Home Bank and CNR buildings.

Demolition was to have started in December, but with the order-in-council for the customs and excise floors still outstanding, that month came and went with no activity. On January 26, 1926, A. Graham Bell, deputy minister of railways and also a director of the CNR, announced that Dominion Building Corp. had failed to perform under its contract with the government, and had forfeited its $25,000 deposit. The government had continued to negotiate with Dominion, but it was also in talks with another developer by this point, presumably the same group whose proposal for a building by architect Charles Dolphin was published in the *Star* the following year (Fig. 15-3).

Even if the government ultimately went with Dominion, it wanted new terms. The CNR now wanted only two floors in total, not four. On the bright side, on February 1, 1926, cabinet finally approved the order-in-council permitting the rental of five floors by the Department of Customs and Excise. It was what Dominion was waiting to hear. The next day, it gave notice that it was ready to close. But it was too late. The minister of railways and canals informed Dominion that the contract was terminated.

In December 1927, the CNR reopened its offices at King and Yonge. The building had sat empty for more than two years, pending the ill-fated redevelopment. As for Dominion Building Corp., in September 1926, a month before it originally expected to hand the federal government the keys to its new offices in the Canadian National Building, it instead served notice that it was seeking damages of almost a million dollars. Before it was all sorted out, there were three separate appeals to the Supreme Court of Canada, and, at a time before that court was truly supreme, two to the Judicial Committee of the Privy Council in England. In 1935, Dominion was finally awarded $75,000 for breach of contract. It also got its $25,000 deposit back — the one it had paid a decade earlier.

Fig. 15-3. The competing twenty-six-storey design of architect Charles Dolphin for the Canadian National Building. [Toronto Public Library.]

Chapter 16

TORONTO'S NEW SKYLINE
1928/UNBUILT — BUILT TO DIFFERENT PLANS

T O READ THE TORONTO DAILIES OF THE late 1920s is to enter a world of secret land assemblies, competing real-estate syndicates, and breathless reports of the new hotels, office buildings, apartments, and subdivisions that were changing the face of the city. The development activity was nowhere more exciting than in the downtown core, where a sea of skyscrapers was rising in the King and Bay area. The party would come to a crashing end with the collapse of the economy in 1929, but on January 16, 1928 — when the *Evening Telegram* published an illustration titled "Toronto's down-town area as it will be when projected developments are completed" — the future was an exciting place to be (Fig. 16-1).

1. **Royal York Hotel** (Front and York). **Built to different plans.**
   The hotel as shown in the illustration is familiar, yet not. It's blockier and more severe than the completed structure, with lower eastern and western wings. There are no obvious elements of the château style that had typified Canadian Pacific's hotels across the country, and that would ultimately distinguish the Royal York among Toronto buildings. But this rendering is in keeping with the perspectives that had been released to the press at the time. Ross and Macdonald, the Montreal firm that was partnering with Sproatt and Rolph to design the building, had announced that for this urban, downtown hotel, they didn't intend to follow the CPR's château precedents. Instead, they would design a "modern" hotel. Presumably, the client had other ideas.

2. **The Commerce and Transportation Building** (northeast corner, Front and Bay). **Built (now demolished).**

Fig. 16-1. Published in January 1928 in the *Telegram*, this aerial perspective projected what Toronto would look like when all the proposed developments of the day were completed as planned. Many never would be. [Toronto Public Library.]

As the name suggests, this ten-storey building by N.A. Armstrong was designed to house facilities for commerce (office and retail) and transportation (a bus terminal and six-storey parking garage). Opened in 1928, it was demolished in the 1980s to make way for what is now Brookfield Place.

3. **The Mail and Empire Building** (northeast corner of King and York). **Built to different plans.**

At the end of November 1927, there was buzz that a prime parcel on the northeast corner of King and York had been bought by a "powerful local syndicate." Architects Herbert G. Duerr and Earle Sheppard released plans showing a thirty-storey skyscraper in the tiered style that had developed in New York as a result of that city's 1916 zoning by-law. Within days, rumours that the building would be the new head office for the *Mail and Empire* were confirmed. A decade passed before any construction took place, however. In 1936, William Wright bought both the *Mail and Empire* and the *Globe*, merging them into the *Globe and Mail*. The William H. Wright Building, the newspaper's new headquarters, opened the following year. Mathers and Haldenby's beautiful seven-storey, art deco creation was demolished in 1974. The newspaper salvaged its ornate bronze doors, installing them at its modernist Front Street location (the old Telegram Building).

4. **The Toronto Daily Star Building** (King, between Bay and York). **Built (now demolished).**

A little east along King Street, another newspaper was planning new headquarters. Excavation had already begun for Chapman and Oxley's twenty-three-storey Toronto Daily Star Building when the *Telegram* ran its illustration (see Fig 17-8). The building would open the following year. Like the North American Life Building (see Fig. 17-8), the Bank of Montreal Building (see Fig. 18-7), the William H. Wright Building, and others, the Toronto Daily Star Building was a casualty of the First Canadian Place complex.

5. **The Holt Gundy Building** (southeast corner, King and Bay). **Unbuilt.**

Holt Gundy and Company was a privately held investment firm started by financier and Royal Bank president Sir Herbert Holt and Wood Gundy co-founder James Gundy. In October 1927, it was reported that the firm had purchased Darling and Pearson's 1911 Union Bank Building at King and Bay, as well as its neighbour to the east on King. Both were to be demolished to make way for a twenty-eight-storey skyscraper designed by Chapman and Oxley. It was supposed to be the tallest in the Empire, and the tallest concrete skyscraper in the world, but less than two weeks after its depiction in the *Telegram*, the Holt Gundy Building was history. The firm had flipped the land at a tidy profit to the Imperial Bank. The Depression delayed the bank's plans for the site, but in 1935 it finally had a spiffy new King and Bay head office, thanks to Darling and Pearson's thrifty expansion and modern re-cladding of the 1911 structure.

Fig. 16-2 In an operation that took a year and a half, the terra cotta of the 1913 Canadian Pacific Building at the southeast corner of King and Yonge was replaced with Indiana limestone. In this photograph, taken on June 30, 1929, the re-cladding is shown nearing the top of the building. Immediately to the south (right) is the Bank of Hamilton Building, built as the Traders Bank Building in 1905. To the north is the 1915 Royal Bank Building. Barely visible in the foreground, at the southwest corner of Yonge and King, is the Dominion Bank Building, from 1914. [City of Toronto Archives, Fonds 1639A, Item 3N.]

6. **Canada Life Assurance Building** (northeast corner, King and Bay). **Unbuilt**.

Canada Life had been planning a new headquarters on this site going back to 1920, when W.F. Sparling designed a forty-storey tower as the company's new headquarters (see Fig. 21-2, *Unbuilt Toronto*). The company was still planning to build at King and Bay in 1928, but the following year decided on a new site at Queen and University, where they remain today.

7. **Northern Ontario Building** (northwest corner, Bay and Adelaide).

This sixteen-storey office building by Chapman and Oxley was completed in 1925.

8. **Atlas Building** (southwest corner, Bay and Temperance).

Announced in early 1927 as a speculative project by the Commercial Lands and Building Company, the thirteen-storey Atlas Building made the most of its location. Its Bay Street frontage was narrow, but terminated the vista looking west down Temperance. Architects S.B. Coon and Son took advantage of this street presence with liberal use of decorative embellishment. The architects provided a recess on the north side of the building so that after the other side of narrow Temperance Street inevitably redeveloped, the Atlas Building would continue to get as much light as possible.

9. **Sterling Tower** (southwest corner, Richmond and Bay).

Toronto's first skyscraper with ziggurat-like setbacks was realized in 1929 with the opening of this twenty-storey skyscraper by Chapman and Oxley. Other examples, such as the Canada Permanent Building, the Toronto Daily Star Building, and the Bank of Commerce Building, would quickly follow.

10. **Canadian Bank of Commerce Building** (southwest corner, King and Jordan). **Built to different plans**.

The bank had been planning a new headquarters on this site for fifteen years, but had decided to build a tower only in 1927 (see Chapter 14).

11, 12, 12a. **Toronto Towers** (King and "Toronto Towers Street" [unbuilt street]). **Unbuilt**.

The newspapers were full of the Toronto Towers project when it was announced in November 1927. Truly massive in scope, it would have resulted in a forty-storey office tower (building 11 in the *Telegram* illustration) rising from a fourteen-storey podium. The tower would front the west side of a new street, "Toronto Towers Street," running between King and Adelaide, west of Yonge. On the east side of that street would be a nine-hundred-room, twenty-nine-storey hotel fronting on Adelaide (building 12A), and a bank tower, shown at the same height, fronting King Street (building 12). The buildings as shown here are true to the designs prepared by architect Charles Dolphin. The Toronto Towers proposal, which is discussed at greater length in *Unbuilt Toronto*, was cancelled for lack of funding by April 1928.

13. **Dominion Bank Building** (southwest corner, King and Yonge).

Now incorporated into the 1 King Street West complex, this 1914 building by Darling and Pearson was headquarters for the Dominion Bank, which would later merge with the Bank of Toronto (see Fig. 16-2).

14. **Bank of Hamilton Building** (northeast corner, Yonge and Colborne).
This fifteen-storey skyscraper had opened as the Traders Bank Building in 1905. Designed by the New York architects Carrère and Hastings, it was Toronto's tallest (see Fig. 16-2). The commission led them to open an office in Toronto in 1906, and to other Toronto jobs, such as the 1913 Bank of Toronto head office (see Chapter 13).

15. **Canadian Pacific Building** (southeast corner King and Yonge).
At eighteen storeys, this was the tallest building in the Empire when it opened in 1913. By 1929, its ornate terra cotta exterior cladding had been damaged by sixteen Canadian winters. In an operation that took a year and a half, the terra cotta was replaced with Indiana limestone, under the supervision of the building's original architects, Darling and Pearson. The bottom three storeys, which were granite, were left untouched (Fig. 16-2).

16. **Royal Bank Building** (northeast corner of King and Yonge).
Another "tallest" when it opened in 1915. The bank brought in the Montreal firm of Ross and Macdonald to design this twenty-storey office building. The firm would have a big impact on Toronto's skyline over the next fifteen years, working on such landmark buildings as Union Station, the Royal York Hotel, and Maple Leaf Gardens. On this job, they partnered with Carrère and Hastings, who handled the interior public spaces (see Fig. 16-2).

17. **Metropolitan Building** (southwest corner, Adelaide and Victoria).
This building, designed by W.F. Sparling, was touted as "twenty-one storeys of office perfection," as well as the tallest commercial building in the Empire when it opened in 1925. It was still shy of the Royal Bank Building if you measured from street level to cornice, but the Metropolitan Building's seventy-eight-foot penthouse sent it over the top. It became the Victoria Tower later in life, the name it retains today.

18. **Excelsior Life Building** (southwest corner Adelaide and Toronto).
This twelve-storey office building, begun in 1914, was E.J. Lennox's last major work.

19. **King Edward Hotel** (King Street East, east of Victoria).
In 1912, E.J. Lennox was asked to draw up plans for a fourteen-storey, three-hundred-room annex for the hotel he had co-designed in 1903 (see Chapter 12). It would have been on the south side of Colborne Street, at Scott, linked to the main building by a bridge seven storeys in the air. Although a tower addition did open in 1921, it was on King Street, at Leader Lane. And it was by Buffalo architects Esenwein and Johnson, not Lennox. True, Lennox had effectively

Fig. 16-3. Toronto's Ford Hotel, shown here nearing completion, opened in 1928. Demolished in 1974, it was identical to owner Richard T. Ford's hotels in Buffalo and Montreal. [City of Toronto Archives, Series 387, Item 319.]

shut down his practice in 1917, but it seems possible that the Americans would have got the job, anyway: in 1918, controlling interest in the King Eddy had been acquired by the United States–based United Hotels Company of America (see Fig. 12-2).

20. **Ford Hotel** (northeast corner, Bay and Dundas). **Built (now demolished).**

Richard T. Ford opened his first hotel in Rochester in 1915, and by the end of the 1920s had expanded into five cities. The 750-room Toronto location, which cost $2 million to build, opened in 1928. It was a replica of the twelve-storey building that Rochester architect J. Foster Walker had designed for Ford in Buffalo (1923), and that he would duplicate again in Montreal (1930). Of these three sister structures, only the Montreal building survives, although it hasn't operated as a hotel in over sixty years, serving now as an office building. As for Toronto's Ford Hotel, its reputation as a destination for respectable, budget-minded tourists disappeared long before the building itself. It was demolished in 1974 (Fig. 16-3).

21. **Dominion Building** (northeast corner Bay and Albert). **Built (now demolished).**

This twelve-storey office building by Chapman and Oxley was announced in February 1927 as the "Commerce Building." The name was changed to the "Dominion Building" before it opened in 1928, continuing the nationalist nomenclature of the developers' earlier downtown towers, the Federal Building (1923) and the National Building (1926).

In 1946, after the city expropriated it for municipal office space, it had another name change, becoming the City Hall Annex. A fire seriously damaged the building in 1977 and it was demolished the following year.

Chapter 17

SIMPSON TOWER

1928/PARTIALLY BUILT — BUILT TO DIFFERENT PLANS

NORTH AMERICAN LIFE BUILDING

1931/PARTIALLY BUILT

B Y THE TIME SCOTTISH IMMIGRANT Robert Simpson died in 1897, the little dry goods business he had started near the southwest corner of Queen and Yonge twenty-five years earlier had grown to make his name a household word. The progression hadn't been without drama: in 1895, after it had been open for only a few months, fire ripped through the imposing, six-storey building that arcitect Edmund Burke had designed for him, destroying it. Undaunted, Simpson operated from temporary premises while the store was rebuilt, even taking the opportunity to expand it.

Simpson's death came a year after the Queen Street building had reopened. The store's new owners continued its expansion, both south to Richmond and west along Queen. In 1923, Simpson's constructed an eight-storey addition on what had been a privately owned extension of James Street, between Queen and Richmond. The department store now occupied more than a full city block. This might have seemed the crowning achievement of thirty years of almost constant building, but Simpson's was nervous. Eaton's had been secretly planning a massive new flagship store at Yonge and Carlton well before the First World War. Architect Daniel Burnham drew up plans in 1912 that surpassed even the opulent department stores that he had recently designed for Marshall Field's in his hometown of Chicago and for John Wanamaker in Philadelphia (Figs. 17-1, 17-2). The war had scuttled those plans, but by the 1920s, there were rumours that Eaton's was again planning something spectacular to replace its Queen Street store, this time at Yonge and College (see *Unbuilt Toronto*, Chapter 22).

If Eaton's was leaving Queen Street, Simpson's would have to up its game to continue to attract shoppers to the area. It quietly began buying surrounding properties, and by April 1928, it was ready for its big announcement: a $4-million expansion that would take it all the way over to Bay Street. Along Richmond, starting at Yonge, the new

Figs. 17-1, 17-2. In 1912, Eaton's hired Chicago architect Daniel Burnham to design its magnificent new flagship store at Yonge and Carlton. Though the First World War scuttled Eaton's plans, rumours that they were back on in the 1920s spurred rival Simpson's to come up with a grand scheme of its own. [Collection Centre Canadien d'Architecture/Canadian Centre for Architecture, Montreal.]

Simpson's would rise in three westward progressions; beginning at six storeys, it would increase to twelve, before finishing in a twenty-storey Bay Street tower. Chapman and Oxley, who had designed several of the newer skyscrapers in the King-Bay area, were hired as architects. They proposed to continue the heavy street-level piers that characterized the 1896 building. The first three storeys of the addition would be faced in polished Ontario black-grained granite, and decorated with applied bronze-work. Two cornices would flank a band of heavily carved stone on the third floor. The tower's buff brick would match that of the existing buildings (Fig. 17-3).

Fig. 17-3. Simpson's expansion plans at Bay and Richmond, as announced in 1928. The planned twenty-storey tower on Bay was to be constructed in two stages, but only the first nine storeys were ever built. [Toronto Public Library.]

Fig. 17-4. Simpson's as built. Looking east down Richmond across Bay, *circa* 1930. [City of Toronto Archives, Fonds 1244, Item 2465.]

Fig. 17-5. Chapman and Oxley's design for the new entrance to Simpson's at Bay and Richmond, part of its major expansion of 1928. [Archives of Ontario, C-18-11.]

The project was intended to be built in stages. Construction on the first stage would start right away, so that the sales floors could open in time for Christmas shopping. It would consist of a nine-storey extension over to Bay Street. As demand warranted, the middle section of the store (including the addition over James Street) would be extended to twelve storeys. Finally, eleven storeys would be added onto the Bay Street frontage, increasing it to its ultimate height. The building's footings and structural steel were engineered to take the additions.

By the time construction started, the exterior design had changed. The aesthetic of the building was lighter, with the proposed dark granite of the base replaced with smooth limestone. Decorative metal grillwork partially covered the first- and second-floor windows. The ground-floor piers continued from the 1896 building were jettisoned, but large arched entrances seemed to be a reference to the earlier building (Fig. 17-4).

As announced, the first phase of the expansion was ready for Christmas shopping. The extension to Bay Street gave Simpson's the world's longest store aisle, at 583 feet, as well as the world's largest department store restaurant, the Arcadian Court, occupying the eighth and ninth floors. The year after the Bay Street extension opened, Chapman and Oxley reworked Simpson's Yonge Street frontage, creating an enclosed arcade that ran between Queen and Richmond Streets. The arcade was described as a "Peacock Alley," where Torontonians could stroll on marble floors and under a vaulted ceiling while looking at the display windows on either side. It developed, in a more elaborate way, the treatment of the Bay-Richmond entrance (Fig. 17-5).

Simpson's stated intention was that the skyscraper addition would be built "as the future demands." The Depression and the Second World War meant that the demand for any major construction would be long delayed, however. Even so, starting in the 1930s, Simpson's continued to acquire adjacent properties around Queen and Bay. By 1964, it owned the entire superblock bounded by Queen, Richmond, Bay, and Yonge. A proposal simply to expand the store onto the newly acquired land, perhaps with a few floors on top, developed into the announcement, in October 1964, of a new skyscraper at Bay and Queen, to be designed by John B. Parkin and Associates with Bregman and Hamann. Simpson's planned an aesthetic modernization of its older buildings as part of the project, happily abandoned, in which they would be re-clad to match the new tower (Fig. 17-6).

It may have been in a different spot, and completed decades later, but when the thirty-three-storey Simpson Tower opened in 1968, Simpson's finally realized its long-ago dream of a Bay Street skyscraper.

———

Simpson's wasn't the only building in the financial district whose foundations anticipated a future tower. In an effort to demonstrate its financial solidity during the Depression, in August 1931 the North American Life Assurance Company announced that it would be building a new head office building on the location of its existing headquarters at 112 King Street West. Any commercial building project was rare in those dire times, but architects Marani, Lawson and Morris had designed a building that actually looked forward to better times. In its ultimate build-out, the seven-storey structure would increase in height to fifteen storeys, and its depth would be doubled. In anticipation of these extensions, the foundation for the tower was completed to the full depth of the lot, with both the foundation and the steel frame of the completed building engineered for the additional storeys to come (Fig. 17-7).

Fig. 17-6. Simpson's redevelopment plans in October 1964 not only included a skyscraper at Bay and Queen, but a complete re-cladding of all its historical buildings to match. [Courtesy Ivanhoe Cambridge.]

BUILDING NOW UNDER CONSTRUCTION

COMPLETED BUILDING

Fig. 17-7. North American Life's head office on King Street West was announced in 1931, in the depths of the Depression. The first phase, of seven storeys, was to be increased to fifteen when circumstances permitted. [Toronto Public Library.]

Fig. 17-8. Looking east on King, 1936. The North American Life Building is in the foreground to the left. The Toronto Daily Star Building rises in the background. [City of Toronto Archives, Fonds 1231, Item 81.]

There was a nearby precedent. Two years earlier, the owners of the Trusts and Guarantee Building had doubled the height of their own building at 302 Bay Street by adding six storeys, something that had been planned way back in 1916 when it was built (it is shown completed on the right of the perspective drawing at Fig. 18-2). But the North American Life Building would be even grander. The *Contract Record and Engineering Review* said that, on its ultimate build-out, it would "rank in size and appearance among the most imposing office buildings in the city." Even half-finished, it still looked pretty good (Fig. 17-8).

Alas, it would never achieve its planned-for heights. It was razed in the 1970s — an obstacle to the First Canadian Place complex, and the skyscraper dreams of a less patient generation.

Chapter 18

BANK OF MONTREAL BUILDING
1938/BUILT TO DIFFERENT PLANS

WHEN THE BANK OF MONTREAL announced in 1938 that it would be moving its Ontario head office from Yonge and Front (in the building that is now the Hockey Hall of Fame) to the site of the former Mail and Empire Building at the northwest corner of King and Bay, it was a homecoming. The bank's main Toronto branch had been on that corner almost a century earlier, from 1842 until 1845. But in July 1938, the real news was that the bank was building anything at all. It was seen as a symbol that the Depression was lifting. No one could have known that the building's partially completed steel frame would soon serve as a symbol that an even more perilous era had arrived.

In considering the move, the bank had originally looked at a larger parcel at Bay and Adelaide, but at that location it would have continued as the only bank in Toronto with a local or national head office that wasn't on "bankers' row," the stretch of King between Bay and Yonge. The King Street site had become available when the *Mail and Empire* moved out in 1937, after merging with the *Globe*. It may have been more prestigious than Bay and Adelaide, but it was also more expensive. The bank justified it by deciding to build an income-producing office tower as part of the project.

Chapman and Oxley— who had designed the twenty-two-storey Toronto Daily Star Building just west on King (see Fig. 17-8) — were chosen as architects. They would be assisted by K.R. Blatherwick and H.S. Maxwell of the bank's premises department. For inspiration on this new project, Alfred Chapman looked to the bank's head office building in Montreal. Between 1901 and 1905, the original 1847 structure had been rebuilt to plans by McKim, Mead and White. Chapman considered the banking hall they produced to be the finest in the world, and he consciously paid homage to it in his plans. The Toronto banking hall would take up almost the entire ground floor, and within

Fig. 18-1. The model of Chapman and Oxley's 1938 proposal for the Bank of Montreal's Ontario headquarters gives a glimpse of the neoclassical styling and twin colonnades that paid tribute to the bank's national headquarters in Montreal. [Archives of Ontario, C 18-1.]

Figs. 18-2 (top), 18-3 (right). A perspective drawing and model of the 1938 proposal for the Bank of Montreal Building show the building's two functions delineated in its architectural styling. The base, with its neoclassical cues, housed the banking hall, while the rental office tower on top showed art deco influences. [Archives of Ontario, C-18-1; Corporate Archives, BMO Financial Group.]

the site, its proportions were intended to replicate those of the Montreal banking room. The twin colonnades down the length of the room, with their dark green marble columns (grouped in pairs) echoed the green granite columns of the Montreal building. Chapman described the style as "modernized classical" (Fig. 18-1).

The only obvious exterior classical embellishment, modernized or otherwise, was restricted to the building's

two-storey base, and specifically, to the entrance to the banking hall off King. It served to give that entrance prominence over the entrance to the office tower, which was off Bay. The tower itself, rising to sixteen floors, was contemporary, both in its terminating setback and in its art deco treatment on top. The result was a tower and base that looked as if they could have been from two different buildings. It may have been that the bank

Fig. 18-4. The steel frame of the uncompleted Bank of Montreal Building at King and Bay was a fixture in wartime Toronto. It is shown here in a photograph taken on September 6, 1941. [City of Toronto Archives/TTC Fonds, Series 71, Item 13896.]

insisted on the more traditional architecture for its banking hall, but by 1938, this would have seemed dated in an office tower. Chapman seemed to acknowledge the tension: "Our problem was to design a building in the simpler classic form, as modern as we dared to make it …" (Figs. 18-2, 18-3).

The site was cleared by April 1939 (see Fig. 13-1), and excavation for the new tower started in July. With the threat of war looming in Europe, the bank's directors considered shelving the project, but decided to push ahead. By August, the building's steel frame was starting to rise. Then, on September 10, 1939, Canada declared war on Germany, and the brighter future that the building's construction had heralded vanished instantly. Seventeen days later, with the basement and three storeys of steel structure completed, the bank stopped all construction so that materials and labour could be redirected to the war effort. The building would sit in this unfinished state for almost seven years, serving for the duration of the war as a daily reminder at the city's financial crossroads of the fighting overseas (Fig. 18-4).

In September 1943, the bank began to plan for the resumption of construction after the war. But by then, Alfred Chapman had taken ill. The bank considered several local firms to assist Chapman's firm (now Chapman, Oxley and Facey), and at James Oxley's recommendation, they chose Marani and Morris. The two firms joined as Chapman, Oxley and Facey, Marani and Morris for their rework of the pre-war scheme. K.R. Blatherwick continued to assist. The steel structure that had been built was retained, but the orientation of the tower that would top it changed significantly. Instead of being set back on the north and south sides, the building would now be set back on the east and west. Chapman had given prominence to the main bank entrance off King Street using neoclassical cues, but this precise solution was no longer possible, as the reworked building was shorn of historicist ornamentation. In the new plan, the lobby for the office tower was given its own entrance, at half-height, and shunted to the side of the King Street frontage, with the banking hall given more prominent entrances centred on the King and Bay facades.

The building's sculptural program was concentrated on the banking hall entrances. Six Toronto sculptors (including Emanuel Hahn: see Fig. 1-4) produced two reliefs each of human figures representing Canada's provinces and territories. They were placed in the six entrance alcoves to the banking hall. Reliefs of Canadian animals by Jacobine Jones were on the curved lintels over these entrances. Inside, Chapman's basic arrangement for the banking hall was retained, including his paired columns. But as with the exterior, there was no classical ornamentation. F.H. Marani still described the building as "contemporary classical," but admitted that "this subject is good for an evening's argument at almost any time." If bank officials had wanted an ornate banking hall before the war, that was not the case now; they asked the architects to simplify their proposed ceiling treatment, finding it "too rich for the simplicity of treatment indicated elsewhere…." (Figs. 18-5, 18-6).

Construction planning resumed in earnest in February 1946, but it was slow going. It would be half a year more before steel work continued. Finding willing and skilled workers was a constant problem in the postwar economy, a situation unfathomable in 1938. And even then, strikes caused delays. Material shortages were also an issue, although steel was not a problem: most of the building's steel beams had been received before the war and had remained in storage (the bank had offered them to the

Figs. 18-5, 18-6. The reworked banking hall of the Bank of Montreal Building as proposed in 1946 (top) and as constructed (bottom, shown in 1949). The ornate ceiling was simplified at the bank's request. The two rows of paired columns were a link to the original pre-war design. [Archives of Ontario, C 18-1; Corporate Archives, BMO Financial Group.]

federal government for the war effort, but no suitable use was found). The building had originally been estimated to cost just under $3 million, but ended up costing $6 million as a result of inflation and delays. It had been scheduled to open in April 1940, but had its official opening instead on September 6, 1949 (Fig. 18-7). It was demolished in 1975, during the construction of First Canadian Place, in this case more than usual, the building coming down much more quickly than it had gone up.

Fig. 18-7. The Bank of Montreal Building as completed, September 1949. [Corporate Archives, BMO Financial Group.]

Chapter 19

Wittington Place

1989/Unbuilt

Sapphire Tower

2004/Unbuilt

WHAT'S AT THE NORTHEAST CORNER of Yonge Street and Highway 401? Chances are you can't say. Or maybe the question brings to mind some vague field of suburban condo towers. In Toronto's alternate history, you'd probably know. "Wittington Place," you'd say — picturing clearly the winning proposal from an architectural competition that had put that intersection on the map.

In April 1987, the *Toronto Star* reported on a development proposal that, according to the newspaper, was being discussed on a "hush-hush" basis in the corridors of North York City Hall. Westnor Ltd., controlled by Loblaws magnate Galen Weston through his family firm, Wittington Investments, had an option on the twenty-four-acre Maclean Hunter lands at Yonge and the 401. Maclean Hunter had run its printing operations there since 1947, but was ready to cash in. A lot had changed in the past four decades: the 401 had

arrived in the 1950s, the Yonge subway had tunnelled through in the 1970s, and North York had transformed itself from a sleepy, semi-rural township to the second-largest city in Ontario. All of which left the industrially zoned Maclean Hunter parcel woefully underdeveloped. But with Yonge Street already congested, there was a problem: how to accommodate all the traffic that a redevelopment would produce?

It was an issue that Westnor had seriously considered. In its view, a new interchange with Highway 401, and a connection to the Sheppard subway station to the north, perhaps via a moving-sidewalk "people mover," could unlock one of the prime development parcels in Metro, allowing for a master-planned extension of North York's city centre. There had been interest in redeveloping the site before, but this time North York mayor Mel Lastman was impressed, not only by the transportation solution that would allow hotels, offices, and condos

Fig. 19-1. In the 1989 Wittington Place competition, distinguished architectural firms were invited to submit proposals for a twenty-four-acre parcel of land at the northwest corner of Yonge Street and Highway 401. Moshe Safdie and Associates saw the site as a gateway, reflecting that theme in a series of buildings with monumental arched openings. [Safdie Fonds, John Bland Canadian Architecture Collection, McGill University Library.]

to rise on the site, but by Galen Weston's vision of a landmark skyscraper that would dominate it all. "I get the impression he wants to create one of the greatest buildings in the world," Lastman said. It would, he felt, be a "world-class architectural achievement."

In February 1989, Westnor wrote to a select group of architects in Canada and the United States, gauging interest in designing what was now being called Wittington Place. The program included 3 million square feet of high-rise office space, 1 million square feet of medium- and high-rise condominiums, a four- to six-hundred-room hotel, and three hundred thousand square feet of retail. In addition, Wittington Place would be home to the Canada Coliseum, a twenty-thousand-seat venue for hockey, basketball, and concerts. Maple Leafs majority-owner Harold Ballard was already interested in moving the Leafs there, and Westnor was actively looking to land a resident NBA team to join them. The Canada Coliseum also officially made it into Toronto's proposal for the 2000 summer Olympics as the venue for basketball (see Chapter 27).

From the responding firms, three finalists were chosen: Moshe Safdie and Associates, Arthur Erickson, and Ehrenkrantz Eckstut and Whitelaw. Each was paid to prepare a plan for the site, including building elevations and a scale model. On June 4, 1989, they presented their proposals at the Westnor offices at St. Clair and Yonge.

Moshe Safdie saw Wittington Place as a gateway: to North York from the south, east, and west, and to Toronto from the north. His firm's proposal gave literal form to this concept, through buildings that were themselves gateways, forming two-hundred-foot-high arched openings (Fig. 19-1). In the architects' preferred plan, three buildings of twenty-five storeys each — two office towers and a hotel — ran on an east–west axis, linked by a retail galleria that would draw travellers from a new subway stop that was now being planned to service the development. A fifty-storey corporate headquarters, also with a monumental gateway cut through it, would rise at the corner of Yonge and the 401. It would form the southern base of a second, north–south axis of parks and gardens that terminated in a crescent-shaped residential building to the north.

Arthur Erickson also placed a tower, fifty-seven storeys high, at the southwest corner of the site. In his plan, two more towers, one thirty storeys and one thirty-seven, faced Yonge Street to the north. On the east side were the condominium buildings, hotel, and coliseum. Erickson's entire scheme was designed around Fountain Place, a monumental circular commons bordered by a traffic circle (Fig. 19-2).

In keeping with Westnor's requirement from the outset that all teams include Canadian designers, New-York-based Ehrenkrantz, Eckstut and Whitelaw partnered with Baird/Sampson, A.J. Diamond and Partners, J. Michael Kirkland Architect, and Kuwabara Payne McKenna Blumberg (KPMB). Their plan showed a fifty-storey tower in the northwestern quadrant of the site, behind three lower towers on Yonge Street that housed offices and a hotel. Most of the retail was placed on the second level, in a weather-protected pedestrian skywalk system that connected all the buildings and converged on a cloistered colonnade called "Wittington Court." The octagonal court was perched over the development's major intersection. Mid-rise residential towers bordered on a traffic circle in the northeast, with the Canada Coliseum to the south (Figs. 19-3, 19-4).

A grand unveiling had been anticipated once the winning entry was picked, but still facing a complex approvals process, Westnor chose to keep the competition

Fig. 19-2. Arthur Erickson's proposal for Wittington Place, shown here in an illustration by Michael McCann, was dominated by a fifty-seven-storey landmark skyscraper. [Michael McCann.]

Fig. 19-3 (left). New-York-based Ehrenkrantz Eckstut and Whitelaw envisaged Wittington Place dominated by a fifty-storey tower rising behind three lower towers fronting Yonge Street. [Ehrenkrantz Eckstut and Kuhn Architects.]

Fig. 19-4 (top). In the Ehrenkrantz Eckstut and Whitelaw plan for Wittington Place, a second-storey, octagonal court spanned the development's central intersection. The Canada Coliseum is shown on the bottom right. The twenty-thousand-seat arena, a required feature of all proposals, was being promoted as the basketball venue in Toronto's bid for the 1996 Olympics, as well as a future home for the Leafs. [Ehrenkrantz Eckstut and Kuhn Architects.]

submissions confidential. Westnor needed to get the buy-in of three levels of government, two school boards, and neighbouring residents before anything could happen on the site. Presenting one of the monumental entries as if it was a *fait accompli* didn't seem like the best way to make that happen.

In the end, no winner was chosen. When Westnor finally made its formal application to the municipality in January 1992, it was based on a site plan by KPMB. There were more changes to come. The scope of the transportation improvements necessary for Wittington Place was staggering, including a new lane on the 401 with a widening of the Don Valley Bridge, an underground interchange between the 401 and a new service road, a widening of Yonge Street, and a new subway stop. When you threw in the cost to acquire the necessary land, the package was estimated at $110 million. Westnor had looked for funding from a federal-provincial infrastructure program, without luck. Things seemed to have reached an impasse. North York's transportation commissioner didn't see that situation changing, suggesting that, "Maybe the ultimate vision is no longer realistic." Westnor agreed. By that point, traffic wasn't the only problem; the recession of the early 1990s had blown the bottom out of the office market.

In July 1995, Westnor revised its plan to something the municipality could get behind: 2.3 million square feet of residential space, and no more than five hundred thousand square feet of the more traffic-intensive commercial space. The Ontario Municipal Board gave its approval in 1997, clearing the path for the condo towers and stacked townhouses that occupy the site today. Not a bad development, but not exactly Wittington Place.

———

The rise and fall of another of Toronto's might-have-been landmarks, the Sapphire Tower, played out much more publicly.

The Sapphire Tower was the brainchild of developer Harry Stinson. In 2003, as his 1 King West high-rise was climbing ever closer to its full fifty-one storeys, he began marketing another: the Downtown Plaza. Planned for a surface parking lot at the northeast corner of Temperance and Richmond Streets, south of City Hall, the location of the proposed fifty-five-storey hotel-condominium was first-rate. But its staid styling wasn't going to be grabbing any headlines. The problem was, the financial district's other planned residential tower *was* grabbing headlines. In March 2004, Donald Trump relaunched plans for a condominium and hotel building at Bay and Adelaide bearing the Trump name. It had originally been proposed back in 2001. As revamped by developer Talon International Development, it was now sixty-eight storeys with a new, punchier design by the Zeidler Partnership. It spurred Stinson to rethink the Downtown Plaza. As Stinson told the *Toronto Star* at the time, "We've decided to up the ante to see if we can trump Mr. Trump."

Gone was the Downtown Plaza's century-old look. In its place were two connected cylinders by Turner Fleischer Architects. Rising sixty-two and eighty-one storeys respectively, they would house over a thousand hotel-condominium units. Subsequent refinements to the design saw the higher tower crowned by a giant sphere that was itself surmounted by a spire. The sphere would not only allow the building to cut an instant figure on Toronto's skyline, it would serve a practical purpose, acting as a mechanical damper to counteract the tower's sway in high winds. Even with fewer floors, Trump's building, with its higher ceilings, was still winning on height. But Stinson had won on pizzazz. He

said that he had been advised to name the skyscraper after himself, *à la* Trump, but in the end, he gave it a name that evoked the deep-blue glass of its curtain walls: Sapphire Tower (Fig. 19-5).

At the end of 2004, Trump announced the addition of two floors to his tower, taking it to seventy (it would later be reduced to sixty-one). In turn, after acquiring an adjacent lot, Stinson reconfigured his building again. The lower tower became broader and rectangular, while the eighty-one-storey cylindrical tower was pushed up to ninety storeys. At 1,122 feet, including the spire, not only would it top Trump's building, but it was set to become Canada's tallest residential tower.

Critical reaction was good. Bureaucratic reaction was not. At a time when the city was planning an international competition to revamp Nathan Phillips Square, city staff concluded that the Sapphire would cast unacceptable shadows on it. Council agreed, killing the proposal in December 2005. Turner Fleischer prepared new plans to address the concern. With its terraced roof treatment, two-storey family units, and reduced height of sixty-two storeys, there was little to link the new Sapphire Tower stylistically to its rejected forebear, save the blue curtain wall that ensured the relevancy of its name.

As the city's planners considered the revised scheme in early 2007, a new storm was gathering, stirred up by the $27.6 million in debt that the long-delayed project had racked up. The holders of a $10.5-million mortgage

Fig. 19-5. This eighty-one-storey version of the Sapphire Tower was proposed by developer Harry Stinson in 2004. Not only would the crowning sphere have cut an instant figure on Toronto's skyline, it would have acted as a mechanical damper, counteracting the tower's sway in high winds. [Turner Fleischer Architects.]

Fig. 19-6. In March 2011, more than three years after the Sapphire Tower was cancelled, a banner on its proposed site attests to what might have been. The tower, which went through several redesigns, is shown here in the ninety-storey version that was rejected by city council in December 2005.

on the Temperance Street site called in their loan after the Sapphire Tower Development Corp. defaulted. In July, the company sought protection from creditors.

In August 2007, the Ontario Superior Court ordered the sale of the Sapphire property. A new development has since been proposed for it, but as of this writing, seven years after Stinson began his friendly rivalry with Trump, it remains a parking lot. As the Trump tower nears completion, a five-storey banner on the Temperance Street site that once heralded the Sapphire Tower's coming now serves as its transitory memorial (Fig. 19-6).

Chapter 20

JOHN MARYON TOWER

1971/UNBUILT

ON OCTOBER 16, 1971, BOTH THE *Toronto Daily Star* and the *Globe and Mail* reported that Toronto engineer John Maryon, a recognized expert in skyscraper design, was proposing the world's tallest building for Toronto. The 140-storey tower would be built on the site of Eaton's College Street store, between Yonge and Bay. The plan was that the 1,650-foot-tall, 2.85-million-square-foot structure would be built in the customer parking lot behind the store, north of Hayter. Once Eaton's had decamped to its planned new Eaton Centre farther south, the 1931 building could be demolished, allowing for a suitable approach for the new building. It would, after all, be the world's tallest, with Maryon aiming to surpass the World Trade Centre, then partially completed (Fig. 20-1).

It was exciting stuff, but three days later, the *Star* ran a tiny article under the banner "Eaton's has not approved 140-storey tower." In the article, an Eaton's spokesman clarified that it had not been in discussions with Maryon or anyone else for the sale of its College Street holdings.

Although the *Star* had reported that Maryon was in negotiation with developers to build the structure, and that "Australian or European capital could be involved in its financing," it seems that the model was not so much a definite projection of tomorrow's Yonge and College as an example of what was possible in 1971 in tall building design. Maryon's tower, for example, used a concrete, central core to provide support for the building's triangular skeleton. The triangular shape itself was intended to reduce wind resistance.

Maryon formally unveiled his model and plans at the International Building Exhibition at the CNE on October 20, in conjunction with a speech he gave on tall building construction. The next day, the *Telegram* published a photograph of the engineer with his model, but talk of

Fig. 20-1. In 1971, engineer John Maryon proposed a 140-storey tower — the world's tallest — for College Street, between Yonge and Bay. This illustration by artist Mathew Borret depicts how it would look in the context of modern-day Toronto. [Mathew Borret.]

its construction on the Eaton's site was now much more equivocal. The newspaper reported that the tower had been designed for the Eaton's College Street site, "but could be erected elsewhere in the city."

The *Telegram* ran its story two weeks before it ended publication for good, after nearly a century in business. Even so, the moribund newspaper had more actual life in it at that point than the prospect of the world's tallest skyscraper at Yonge and College. Its story completed the news cycle surrounding that intriguing notion.

ARTS, LETTERS, AND LEISURE

Chapter 21

TORONTO REFERENCE LIBRARY
1903 AND 1968/BUILT TO DIFFERENT PLANS

WORD CAME IN JANUARY 1903 THAT the Scottish-American philanthropist and former steel magnate Andrew Carnegie was giving the city $350,000. It meant that for the first time in its history, the Toronto Public Library would have buildings that were actually built as libraries. Since it had opened as the Toronto Free Library in 1884, the central reference library had been housed in the old Mechanics' Institute at Adelaide and Church. On freezing days it couldn't be heated above fifty-five degrees Fahrenheit, on rainy days it leaked, and they were stacking books on the floor for lack of shelf space. The Carnegie Foundation's gift, and its other gifts that would follow, allowed the construction of eleven new libraries within the boundaries of modern-day Toronto between 1907 and 1916, including the jewel in the crown, the central library at College and St. George.

As always with Carnegie's library donations, it was a condition that the city provide operating funding,

and also that it supply the land. This latter requirement turned out to be contentious in the case of the central library. Not because it was in any way unreasonable, but because the library board and city council couldn't agree on where to build. The board unanimously wanted something "uptown," in the area bounded by Yonge, Spadina, College, and what is now Dundas. In the board's view, a central library should be central, which, based on population, meant moving north and west, a move that would also take it away from the smoke, crime, congestion, and fire-hazard of the downtown core.

City council was not convinced. Early on, it had decided that the central library should be downtown, leaving it to its property committee to figure out where exactly. While the committee made suggestions that were, literally, all over the map, council continued to avoid making any decision. On the evening of April 19, 1904, a great swath of that map was destroyed, as fire raged

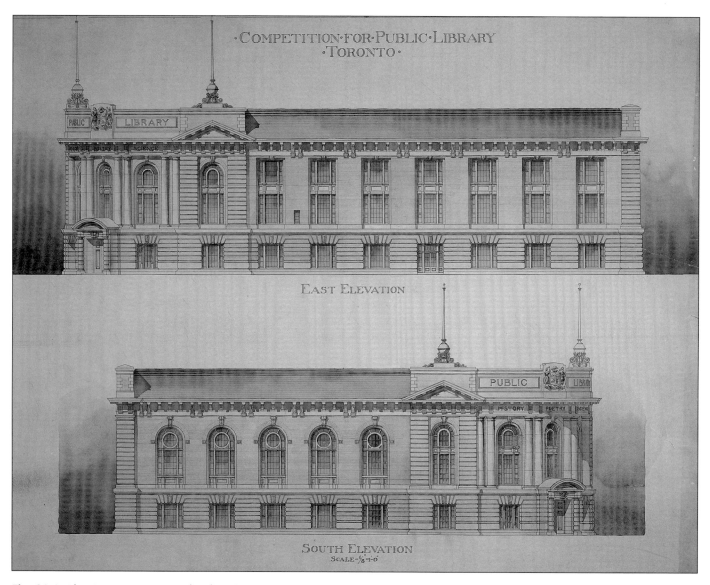

·COMPETITION·FOR·PUBLIC·LIBRARY·
·TORONTO·

PUBLIC LIBRARY

EAST ELEVATION

PUBLIC LIBRARY

SOUTH ELEVATION
SCALE ⅛"=1'-0"

Fig. 21-1. The St. George Street (top) and College Street elevations of the unsuccessful entry of W. Ford Howland in the 1905 competition for the central library. The Toronto library board had wanted the building's main entrance to be on College, near to St. George. Howland responded by placing it right on the corner. [Toronto Public Library Archives.]

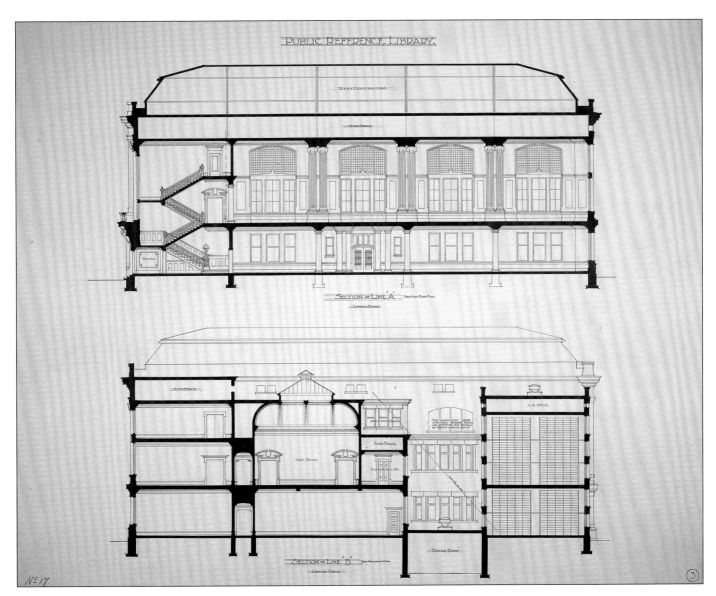

Fig. 21-2. A cross-section of Langley and Langley's proposed central library, showing the reading room with its large windows facing College Street. [Toronto Public Library Archives.]

through twenty acres of the downtown core, destroying over a hundred buildings. Among them was the printing plant where the library's brand new, multi-volume catalogue was being bound. Luckily, the plates were offsite and out of the fire zone. Even luckier, of course, so were the library's actual books. The library board had consistently warned against the fire hazard of a downtown location. Perhaps this close call swayed a recalcitrant council. In any event, in December, it agreed to buy a site at the northwest corner of College and St. George.

An architectural competition would determine the design. The call for plans went out at the end of October 1905. As reflected in the competition brief's detailed specifications, the library board had a clear idea of what it was looking for. And as ever in sensible Toronto, a clear idea of what it wasn't looking for. The brief scolded interested architects that: "The building is for a library and is to be planned for library work. It is to be essentially a work place and not a show place." Nineteen plans were submitted by the deadline of January 31, 1906, including those of W. Ford Howland and Langley and Langley, the only competitors whose work now survives in the library's archives (Figs. 21-1, 21-2). The selection committee didn't find any of the submitted plans to be suitable, asking four firms to re-submit: Alfred Chapman, working in association with Wickson and Gregg; Gordon and Helliwell; J.A. McKenzie (all from Toronto) and William Newlands, from Kingston.

On April 27, 1906, still with no winner announced, Andrew Carnegie arrived in town. Chief Justice William Glenholme Falconbridge, the library board's chairman, thanked Carnegie for his $350,000 gift, to which, according to the board's minutes, Carnegie "made a felicitous reply." One thing he reportedly declined to do, however, was examine any of the plans from the competition. Visiting City Hall later in the day, he explained himself: "I do not wish to interfere in the selection of sites or in the class of building you desire to put up.… I am not going to put my hand in a hornet's nest by interfering with the architects.…"

Soon after Carnegie's visit, on May 12, 1906, the scheme of Chapman and Wickson and Gregg was announced as the winner (Fig. 21-3). Construction started that fall, and the new building opened in October 1909. In an era when rigid planning and formal composition made many libraries difficult to add on to, the library board had insisted that the new building allow for future additions, while still exhibiting "architectural unity and completeness" from the outset. This foresight paid off when Alfred Chapman seamlessly extended the building northward in 1929. In 1985, his son, Howard Chapman, worked with Howard Walker to modify the building for continued service as the University of Toronto's Koffler Student Services Centre, the role it still fulfills.

———————

When the Municipality of Metropolitan Toronto was created in 1954, libraries were left as a local matter, with each of Metro's thirteen original municipalities running its own. Legislative amendments in 1966 created a new metropolitan library board, responsible for central reference services for all of Metro starting in 1967. The feeling at the new board was that the sixty-year-old central reference library on College wasn't up to the demands that were coming. A new building was in order, one that could consolidate the collection from the old building and several other locations. In 1968, the board began to plan for one.

Ironically, in light of its history, the new Metro library board felt that the 1909 building was too far west. They wanted something within walking distance of Yonge Street and the subway, between Queen and St. Clair. In 1971, architect Raymond Moriyama prepared a report evaluating several available locations that fit those criteria, settling on three: the northwest corner of Yonge and Asquith; the northwest corner of Yonge and Church; and the block immediately south of Eaton's College Street, north of Gerrard. With its easy access to two subway lines, the Yonge/Asquith site was the hands-down winner. Metro began to assemble the necessary land, while Moriyama set about designing the building that would go on it.

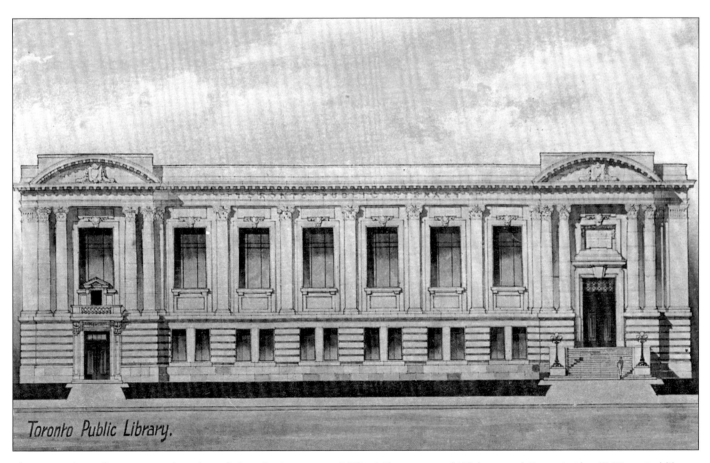

Fig. 21-3. The College Street elevation of the winning entry of Alfred Chapman and Wickson and Gregg in the 1905 central library competition. The end pavilions demarcated separate entrances to the branch library and the central reference library. With slight modifications (e.g. converting the double columns on either side of the pavilions to pilasters, dispensing with proposed crests) the completed building reflected this drawing.

Fig. 21-4. Raymond Moriyama's original, 1973 proposal for the Metro Central Reference Library is shown in an illustration by Michael McCann. [Archives of Ontario, F 2187-1-20.]

He unveiled his plans for the first time at City Hall on November 19, 1973. They revealed a 327,000-square-foot building, rising up five storeys from Yonge and Asquith in sheer walls of mirrored glass (Fig. 21-4). The timing couldn't have been worse. In September, even as the world's tallest freestanding structure was being built in the railway lands, council had voted to prohibit any new projects over forty-five feet high or forty thousand square feet in the downtown core. It would go on to pass what would be known as the "forty-five-foot by-law" in December, but was treating the policy as effective immediately. It was an initiative of the so-called reform faction that had gained a majority on council the year before. Until the city's official plan policies could be reviewed, the forty-five-foot by-law was intended to provide a respite from what the reformers saw as untrammelled development in the downtown core, requiring large new development applications to be considered on a case-by-case basis.

Figs. 21-5, 21-6. Two watercolours by Michael McCann show the radical exterior redesign of Raymond Moriyama's proposed Metro Central Reference Library between late 1973 (top) and early 1974 (bottom). The building's setbacks, massing, and materials were changed in the face of political and neighbourhood opposition. [Archives of Ontario, F 2187-1-20; Toronto Public Library Archives.]

The new library blew the by-law's numbers out of the water. And there were other criticisms. Reform alderman Colin Vaughan, an architect, thought the interior of the building was well thought out, but considered the exterior monolithic and out of scale with the surrounding neighbourhood. Another reformer, Karl Jaffray, likened it to the Bastille. To the outrage of local architects, he later summed up his assessment even more pithily: "simply awful." Reformers were joined in their opposition to the design by suburban councillors such as Mel Lastman, who were balking at the project's cost, which was estimated at $30 million, including land.

Lawyer Walter Cassels, Metro's appointee to the library board and also its vice-chair, was dismayed to see years of work dismissed so quickly: "I have no idea what they want us to do. Each individual who voted to defer this seems to have a different idea of what he wants." Frustrated, he resigned. The full Metro council, meeting the next week, not only refused to accept his resignation, they reversed the executive committee's decision, giving Moriyama's plans the green light with a 21–5 majority. The library still needed approval at Toronto city council, however, and that wasn't going to come so easily. The next week, city council gave a historical designation to a 1840s building on the site that had served as the Victoria College medical school. Legally, at the time, council couldn't prevent its demolition, but it requested that the library not demolish it until approvals were in place for the new building. On that front, they resolved that they did not intend to exempt the new building from the forty-five-foot height by-law "until the Council has been satisfied that the height and bulk of the proposed building is necessary for library purposes."

In January and February of 1974, the library board worked with city planning staff and the North Midtown Planning Group, a residents' association, to hammer out a compromise. By April they had one. The total floor area was only slightly reduced, but Moriyama radically altered the exterior of the building to diminish its presence. The sheer walls on Yonge and Asquith were replaced by successively recessed tiers. The first, at street level, reflected the height of the surrounding historic buildings. The building was moved closer to the lot line, but full arcades were provided along Yonge and Asquith. Street-related uses such as an art gallery and cafeteria with direct access to Yonge would continue that street's retail continuity. Except at the corner of the building, which was now raked back, the mirrored glass was jettisoned, ultimately in favour of orange-brown brick. The interior continued Moriyama's original conception of a tiered central atrium with plants and water features (Figs. 21-5, 21-6).

Council approved the revised plans in April 1974, and the building opened three years later, on October 19, 1977. In 2010, the library began a phased revitalization program for the building, now called the Toronto Reference Library. The first and most striking component planned was a new entrance pavilion, designed by Raymond Moriyama's son, Ajon. Jutting out into the small open area at Yonge and Asquith, his addition took a highly symbolic form given the building's history — a glass cube.

Chapter 22

ROYAL ONTARIO MUSEUM

1909/BUILT TO DIFFERENT PLANS

ART GALLERY OF ONTARIO

1912/BUILT TO DIFFERENT PLANS

I N THE 2001 COMPETITION FOR THE ROYAL Ontario Museum's Bloor Street addition, Berlin-based architect Daniel Libeskind submitted his conceptual sketches on napkins from the museum's restaurant. It struck some people as cheekily amusing. Others as cheekily arrogant. Either way, it was a bit of history repeating, since almost a century earlier, the museum's original layout had been dashed off on a moving train by another high-profile architect from Europe, in one account, on an envelope.

In the spring of 1908, Charles Currelly, who would become the ROM's first director of archaeology, was heading back to London after a visit to Windsor Castle. As it turned out, he was sitting beside Sir Aston Webb. The British architect, who is perhaps best known today for the main facade of Buckingham Palace, was then finishing a major addition to the Victoria and Albert Museum. At the time, the ROM was in the planning stages, and Currelly took the opportunity to ask the celebrated architect's advice on its buildings. He was in luck. Although he had been constricted by the Victoria and Albert's existing buildings, Webb knew what he would build if he could start from scratch, saying he had evolved the "perfect" museum plan. It would be made up of long ranges of sixty-foot-wide buildings, separated down the middle into thirty-foot-wide galleries, and arranged around one or more quadrangles. He quickly sketched out some drawings and measurements.

Currelly sent the drawings to Edmund (soon to be Sir Edmund) Walker, who was the president of the Canadian Bank of Commerce and one of the Toronto museum's great proponents and benefactors. When Darling and Pearson were retained as the museum's architects, Walker gave them Webb's sketches. In *Bold Visions*, his architectural history of the ROM, Kelvin Browne writes that, at the time of their chance meeting, the quadrangle-based

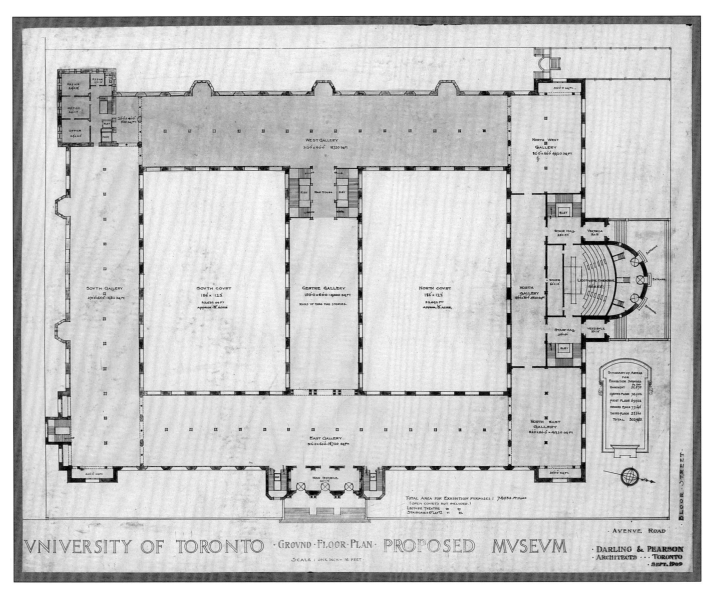

Fig. 22-1. Darling and Pearson's 1909 plan for what would become the Royal Ontario Museum followed designs hastily sketched out by the English architect Sir Aston Webb on a train heading into London. The western galleries (shown shaded) opened in 1914, followed in 1933 by the Queen's Park galleries to the east and a central connecting gallery. [University of Toronto Archives, A65-001(044).]

NORTH ELEVATION

SCALE. ⅛IN.=1FT. JAN. 1910..   VNIVERSITY OF TORONTO   PROPOSED MVSEVM   DARLING AND PEARSON ARCHITECTS, TORONTO

Fig. 22-2. Darling and Pearson's unrealized Bloor Street wing for the Royal Ontario Museum. It would have stood where Daniel Libeskind's Crystal addition is now. [University of Toronto Archives, A65-001(042).]

arrangement that Webb was recommending to Currelly had been influential in European museum design for over a century, and would presumably have been well-known to a firm such as Darling and Pearson — and likely used regardless of Webb's sketch. Whether Webb's "perfect" museum scheme was news to Darling and Pearson or not, the plans that they drew up in 1909 show that they duly followed it, with ranges of sixty-foot-wide buildings,

divided lengthwise into parallel galleries, and arranged around two courtyards (Fig. 22-1).

The site chosen to build their design was at Bloor Street and Queen's Park Crescent. Although legislation in 1912 would style it the Royal Ontario Museum, the museum was originally conceived as a collegiate institution, drawing from existing collections in the various University of Toronto departments (Darling and

Fig 22-3. The Royal Ontario Museum as completed by 1914, showing the temporary Bloor Street entrance.

Pearson refer to it as the "University of Toronto Proposed Museum" in their plans). Given this association, it was logical that a 1906 commission on the university had recommended that it be built on campus, and adjacent to a major thoroughfare. College Street was the first choice, but with no suitable site being found, two lots at Avenue and Bloor were acquired. There was some grumbling about the out-of- the-way location, but Sir

Edmund Walker argued, correctly, as it turned out, that the growing city would catch up to it.

As ultimately planned, the museum's main entrance would be off Queen's Park Crescent (a rendering of Darling and Pearson's Queen's Park elevation does not appear to have survived), with an impressive facade featuring twin towers on Bloor (Fig. 22-2). Budgetary constraints meant that the museum would have to be built in phases. Construction began in the fall of 1910 on the first phase, the west wing along Philosopher's Walk (shown shaded in Fig. 22-1). An entrance off Bloor would provide access to the building until it was ultimately covered by the Bloor Street wing. The governor general, the Duke of Connaught, officially opened the building on March 14, 1914, a little less than five months before Canada entered the First World War (Fig. 22-3).

After the war ended, the museum's directors were eager to continue construction, but the province didn't commit the funds until 1929, turning the expansion into a make-work-project once the Depression hit. The new buildings opened in 1933. As with the Whitney Block (see Chapter 2), only Ontario materials were used, and the foundation was dug by hand. Chapman and Oxley had taken over as architects, using an art deco updating of the Romanesque style long associated with the university. Much greater changes were coming, however.

When the museum finally undertook a major expansion of its gallery space, between 1978 and 1984, the Darling and Pearson scheme was abandoned entirely. A curatorial building filled the south quadrangle, and the Queen Elizabeth II Terrace Galleries filled the north. Both were by Moffat, Moffat and Kinoshita. The latter building was obliterated within twenty years of its formal opening, to make way for Daniel Libeskind's Crystal. Although it confirmed that any idea of completing Darling and Pearson's scheme was well and truly dead, Libeskind's plan did much to rehabilitate what had been realized of it. The 1914 building was restored to its former glory. The windows that had been such an important feature were unblocked after years, and the central axis between the 1914 and the 1933 buildings, also long since blocked up, was reopened. It was a little-noted feature of the renovation program, which many saw as purely iconoclastic.

The physical evolution of Toronto's other great museum, the Art Gallery of Ontario, followed a similar trajectory to the ROM's: a pre–First World War, courtyard-based plan by Darling and Pearson was pursued over two stages of construction in the first half of the twentieth century, thoroughly abandoned in the second half, and quietly highlighted in the twenty-first century through the intervention of a "starchitect."

The incorporation of the Art Museum of Toronto in March 1900 was a milestone in the Ontario Society of Artists' dream of procuring a permanent public art gallery. The incorporation was confirmed three years later in special provincial legislation. Significantly for a non-governmental body, it gave the museum expropriation powers. Although they were set out in general terms, Edmund Walker, who was the museum's president, privately had a specific use in mind for them: the houses to the north of the Grange, fronting St. Patrick Street (now Dundas Street West). Shortly before, Walker had been approached by Harriet Boulton Smith and her husband, Professor Goldwin Smith, who were looking for estate-planning advice. Since they were both in their late seventies, there was nothing particularly remarkable about that. But unlike most people, Mrs. Smith owned an actual "estate" — the Grange — at the top of John Street, which she had acquired in a previous marriage. Walker successfully made the pitch for the fledgling Art Museum of Toronto.

The public knew nothing of the bequest until Mrs. Smith's death in 1909. She had left her husband a life interest in the Grange, but with his death the following year, the Art Museum of Toronto finally had a home. A deal with the city in 1911 (and more provincial

Fig. 22-4. This 1914 rendering by S.H. Maw shows Darling and Pearson's original scheme for the Art Museum of Toronto, what is now the Art Gallery of Ontario. The Grange, the Georgian residence that had been bequeathed to the gallery, is visible behind the proposed new buildings. [Art Museum of Toronto, 1914; Darling and Pearson Architects, Toronto; S.H. Maw — watercolour; Edward P. Taylor Research Library and Archives; ©2010 Art Gallery of Ontario.]

Fig. 22-5. The sculpture court from Darling and Pearson's art museum plan is shown in another 1914 perspective. Half of it opened as the Walker Court in 1926. A planned expansion to the north was not pursued. [Art Museum of Toronto, 1914; central gallery with glass roof removed; S.H. Maw — watercolour; Edward P. Taylor Research Library and Archives, ©2010 Art Gallery of Ontario.]

Fig. 22-6. The Art Gallery of Toronto as it looked between 1926 and 1935. Unlike the original 1918 stone building to the rear, the 1926 additions shown here were faced in brick and stucco — an acknowledgement that they were ultimately intended to be engulfed by further expansions. [City of Toronto Archives, Series 372, Subseries 41, Item 314.]

legislation to back it up) saw the city taking possession of the grounds as a public park, in return for ongoing funding for the gallery. The Grange mansion served as initial gallery space, but expansion was a problem. Any additions to the south would ruin its Georgian architecture, not to mention the city's new park. Under the plan that Edmund Walker had conceived a decade earlier, the museum would have used its statutory powers of expropriation to acquire frontage on St. Patrick Street. Under the new partnership, however, the city ended up doing that dirty work.

In 1912, Darling and Pearson prepared plans for the complex that would go on the museum's inherited and expropriated lands, updating them two years later. As with their ROM design, ranges of galleries, some thirty in all, would surround open courtyards. Whereas the ROM had two courtyards, the art gallery would have three, an eastern court with an English garden, a western court with an Italian garden, and a central sculpture court (Figs. 22-4, 22-5). Again, as with the ROM, the work was intended to proceed in phases over a number of years. The first wing, three rooms adjacent to the Grange, opened on April 4, 1918. The next year, in order to avoid confusion with the ROM, the museum became the Art *Gallery* of Toronto.

The second phase of Darling and Pearson's master plan opened in 1926. It consisted of half of the central sculpture court, now covered, and was named after Sir Edmund Walker, who had died two years earlier. It was built immediately to the north of the 1918 building, along with two more galleries flanking it on each side, with an entrance off what was now Dundas Street. Unlike the 1918 building, the new additions had a modest brick and stucco exterior. As *Construction* magazine pointed out, there was a reason: "Eventually, when further extensions are carried out, the entire building will be enclosed with stone, the

only portion in which stone is now employed is the south end. The present walls will then form the necessary division between the various courts. This likewise to the present front and entrance, which are only temporary and will ultimately be replaced with a permanent front more interesting in architectural character."

The gallery was extended to the east and west in 1935, but its "temporary" Dundas Street front would be its face to the world for the next forty-eight years (Fig. 22-6). In 1968, architect John C. Parkin set out to change that, with an ambitious three-phase expansion plan. The idea had been hatched in 1966, when the gallery got yet another new name, the Art Gallery of *Ontario*, matching its new status as the art gallery not just of the province's capital, but of the province as a whole. The first stage of Parkin's plan, including his Henry Moore Sculpture Centre and a restoration of the Grange, opened in 1974. The second stage, a series of new galleries spreading west to Beverly Street, opened three years later.

For over a decade, funding issues delayed the third phase, planned as additions to the southwest and a final northern extension of the Dundas Street facade. But in August 1986, the AGO got the ball rolling again by seeking expressions of interest from Ontario architects. From twenty-eight responses, four firms were ultimately invited to submit anonymous design proposals: A.J. Diamond and Partners; Moriyama and Teshima Architects; the Zeidler Roberts Partnership; and Barton Myers Associates. In January 1987, a seven-member jury, which included architect Moshe Safdie and Canadian Centre for Architecture founder Phyllis Lambert, chose the Barton Myers entry. A firm founded by Myers's former associates, Kuwabara Payne McKenna Blumberg, worked on its completion after Myers moved to Los Angeles (Figs. 22-7, 22-8, 22-9, 22-10).

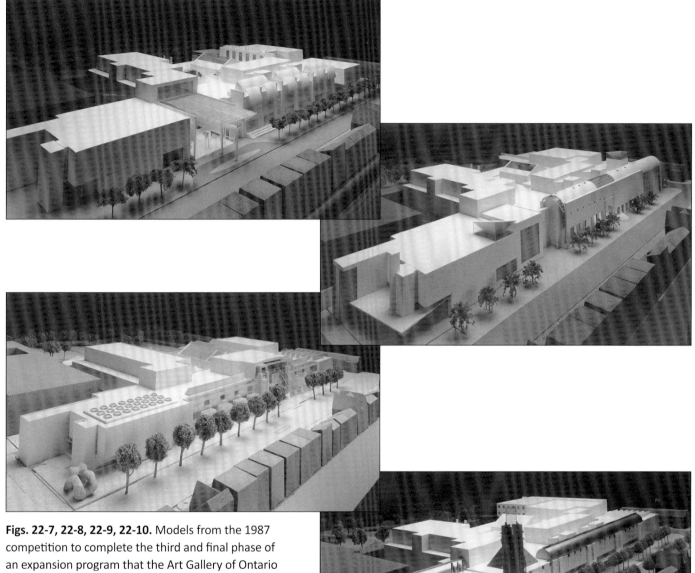

Figs. 22-7, 22-8, 22-9, 22-10. Models from the 1987 competition to complete the third and final phase of an expansion program that the Art Gallery of Ontario had planned in the 1960s. A.J. Diamond's Dundas Street elevation (top left) was marked by a glass-roofed entry court, while Moriyama and Teshima's (top right) had a vaulted entrance. The Zeidler Roberts entry had a crystalline porte-cochère (bottom left). The winning entry of Barton Myers Associates (bottom right) featured an entrance tower. [Ryerson University Archives and Special Collections.]

A tower gave the museum's new entrance, and the gallery generally, increased prominence, serving as a beacon at the terminus of a planned pedestrian mall between the gallery and University Avenue, on the south side of Dundas. A major portion of that mall had already been achieved in the plaza in front of the 52 Division police station, a building whose height and pre-cast concrete exterior were meant to complement Parkin's Moore gallery. The city's failure to prevent the erection of a condominium tower up to the street line in the block between St. Patrick and McCaul spelled the end of the promenade plan, however. Remarkably, by then, the AGO's new tower was also doomed, along with the rest of the additions along Dundas. Intended as the final piece of an expansion plan spanning three decades, they were obliterated within a decade and a half by Frank Gehry's 2008 reconstruction.

Chapter 23

TRINITY COLLEGE

1913/BUILT TO DIFFERENT PLANS

INNIS COLLEGE

1966/BUILT TO DIFFERENT PLANS

T HE IMPRESSIVE ENTRANCE GATES TO Trinity Bellwoods Park on Queen Street West — built in 1904 as the gates to Trinity College — are the most obvious indication that the college was once there. It's ironic then, that even before they were completed, Trinity's days on Queen Street were numbered: the year before, the college had agreed to federate with the University of Toronto on a trial basis.

When he founded Trinity in 1851, Bishop John Strachan had chosen the Queen Street location in order to literally set the college apart. With federation, this distance became a problem, and the college began to acquire land for a right-of-way for a private streetcar or bus service connecting its campus to U of T's. That plan didn't get very far before the provincial government, following on the recommendations of a royal commission into the University of Toronto, enacted the University Act. Among other things, it made provision

for a site for Trinity on the U of T campus, and a loan to help it make the move.

In 1909, after two-and-a-half years of negotiations, the University of Toronto's board of governors offered Trinity two rent-free sites, one on Hoskin Avenue for the college itself, and an additional site on Devonshire Place for St. Hilda's College, the women's residence. The college formally agreed to the university's terms the following year, and Trinity's period of trial federation became permanent in 1911. The university's offer was contingent on Trinity's moving within five years. In August 1912, Trinity sold its Queen Street lands to the City of Toronto, on the condition that it be allowed to remain there without charge for five years.

The next year, the college retained Darling and Pearson to design the buildings for its new campus on Hoskin. Frank Darling was an alumnus of the college, and had designed several additions to the Queen Street campus, including the entrance gates. Over the next two years, the firm worked through various proposals, all neo-Gothic, and based generally on grouping the college's buildings around two quadrangles. They had another common feature: the firm had been specifically instructed that in whatever it came up with, the Hoskin Avenue facade must "preserve … as close a resemblance as possible" to Kivas Tully's 1852 Queen Street building. In this sense, the new building would be twice removed from its source: as architectural historian Graham Owen has written, on Strachan's instructions, Tully himself had adapted the plans from St Aidan's Theological College in Birkenhead, England.

By 1915, plans for the Hoskin Avenue campus had been finalized. They showed the college's functions grouped around two great quadrangles, which the college planned

Fig. 23-1. A 1920s fundraising brochure described this as an "aeroplane view" of Darling and Pearson's 1915 plan for Trinity College. It shows the Henderson Tower dominating the campus, linking the Chancellors' Quadrangle and the Founder's Quadrangle. [Trinity College Archives (illustration by S.H. Maw).]

to call the Founder's Quadrangle (after John Strachan) and the Chancellors' Quadrangle (after the college's various chancellors). The quadrangles were joined by a large central tower, the Henderson Tower, named after a leading benefactor. Classroom space for 350 students was provided, as well as laboratories, a library for twenty thousand books, a chapel, convocation hall, gymnasium, and squash court. Residence accommodation was provided for staff and faculty, as well as for male students. Female students would be housed in the yet-to-be-designed St. Hilda's College. As instructed, Darling and Pearson very nearly recreated the old Queen Street facade as the college's public face on Hoskin, now in stone instead of brick (Figs. 23-1, 23-2).

The outbreak of the First World War in 1914 put any start on construction out of the question. In the circumstances, the city extended Trinity's rent-free

Fig. 23-2. The Chancellors' Quadrangle, looking southeast towards the chapel, in Darling and Pearson's 1915 plan for Trinity College.
[Trinity College Archives (illustration by S.H. Maw).]

occupancy on its old buildings into 1919. But inflation and decreased revenue from low war-time enrollment meant that the college was in no position to proceed even after hostilities ended. The city granted it a further five-year extension on the Queen Street campus. The extra time was fully needed. In 1923, the year of Frank Darling's death, construction finally started at the new campus, with the first building, consisting of the Hoskin Avenue range, ready for the 1925–26 academic year.

Converted houses and an apartment building served as student residences until the construction, by other architects, of St. Hilda's College in 1938, and the men's residences three years later. The college got a purpose-built chapel in 1955, and further additions in 1961 completed the campus in a modern, though sympathetic, style. None of the construction followed Darling and Pearson's master plan. In the end, the only portion of it that was built was the one that had been required to mimic someone else's work.

———————————

By the 1950s, it was clear that the postwar baby boom was going to result in a massive increase in university students. In 1956, the University of Toronto's "Plateau Committee" (so called because the increase in students would not be a temporary "bulge," but a new "plateau") recommended that U of T roughly double its enrollment of twelve thousand, accommodating the additional students in suburban satellite campuses and in two new downtown colleges.

In the 1960s, the increase that the Plateau Committee had predicted became a reality. The first of the new downtown colleges recommended by the committee was founded in 1963 and, appropriately enough, called New College. The second followed quickly. In January 1964, University of Toronto president Claude Bissell announced the creation of Innis College, which admitted its first students the following September. It was named after Harold Innis, a political economist and communications theorist who had taught at U of T for over thirty years, until his death in 1952.

Architect Macy Dubois designed a two-building complex to house both institutions. New College would occupy the northern building, at Classic Avenue and Huron Street, and Innis would occupy the southern building, at Spadina and Wilcocks. The colleges would not only occupy sister buildings, they would be sister institutions, each with nine hundred students, and each with residence space for three hundred men.

Work began on New College's building in the fall of 1964. The university intended that construction on Innis would follow immediately, with parts of its building ready for use by the 1965–66 school year, but 1965 came and went with no start on Innis. The university had decided that Innis' planned building should instead be used to accommodate the expansion of New College (the southern building did, in fact, open as part of New in 1969). In the meantime, Innis operated out of what had been intended as a temporary wartime building beside the old University of Toronto observatory, south of Hart House. It later acquired a Victorian house at 63 St. George Street, as well.

The idea now was to construct Innis on a two-hundred-by-four-hundred-foot lot at the corner of St. George Street and Sussex Avenue, stretching back to Huron Street. In the summer of 1966, Innis retained architect Hart Massey to prepare a feasibility study for accommodating its needs on the new site. Massey had served as a juror on the architectural competition that his father, the former governor general, Vincent Massey,

Fig. 23-3. Looking toward Sussex Street from St. George, this perspective shows the twin towers that would have marked the eastern and western ends of the Innis College quadrangle in Massey and Flanders's plan from 1967. [University of Toronto Archives, A1970-0016 (illustration by Barry Padolski).]

had organized in 1960 for Massey College. The resulting building, by architect Ron Thom, had opened at Hoskin Avenue and Devonshire Place in 1963. Innis wanted to replicate its approach of an inward-looking campus, centred on a courtyard.

It was going to be tough on such a small lot. Innis was planning now for 1,400 students, with residence space for five hundred men and women. Massey knew that distributing the mass of such a large complex equally around the perimeter of the site, as had been done at Massey College, would put the courtyard in perpetual shade. Instead, he recommended four residence towers, each approximately 150 feet high, at the east and west ends of the site, joined by low-rise buildings to the north and

Fig. 23-4. In this 1966 photograph by Gilbert Milne, William Davis inspects a model of the four eighteen-storey towers announced for the campus of the Ryerson Polytechnical Institute, two on the west side of Victoria Street, and two on the east side of Church Street. Only the western towers were built, in altered form. As minister of education and minister of university affairs, Davis oversaw a massive expansion of the province's post-secondary system. [Ryerson University Archives and Special Collections.]

south. Massey admitted that the high-rise scale would be different from the traditional university residence, but in his view, that wasn't necessarily a bad thing: "… the environment created would be a vital, urban one, similar to that experienced often in large city dwelling."

In 1967, Massey and his associate, John Flanders, partnered to create Massey and Flanders. The plans drawn up by the new firm continued the approach set out in Massey's feasibility study. The four towers became two nine-storey towers, but they were anything but conventional high-rise slabs. Instead of arranging residence rooms off long corridors, the architects grouped them around two common rooms on each floor, encouraging interaction and a feeling of community despite the high-rise setting. The plan also aimed to increase interaction between residence students and those living off campus. Apart from the actual residence floors, the college's facilities were designed for the use of all Innis' students. These common areas were arranged so that they were a flight up or down from the courtyard level. The courtyard itself was surrounded by an arcade, and featured a large open area and staircase to the concourse below. A theatre, dining room, and other common facilities were located on the concourse. Like Massey College and New College, Innis would be characterized by highly articulated building walls facing the courtyard, in this case in pre-cast concrete (Fig. 23-3).

By now, however, the prospects of the college being built as planned were in serious doubt. Under the leadership of William Davis, the provincial minister of education and minister of universities, the province had been making massive investments in post-secondary education (Fig. 23-4). Unfortunately, Innis was late to the party, seeking $10 million for construction at a time when the province was trying to keep a lid on university expenditures. In February 1968, the Department of University Affairs had advised that it would not fund Innis' plans unless it could trim $3 million in costs. The problem seemed largely to be the residence towers. Innis had wanted to avoid building just another high-rise slab, but the government was now basically telling Innis that it would only fund another high-rise slab. As a government spokesman advised, it was what the students wanted: "They're the chief advocates of low-cost living facilities."

The college managed to reduce its construction budget by 20 percent, but even so, it was clear by 1969 that there would be no federal or provincial money to build anytime soon. With the full support of University of Toronto president Claude Bissell, a demoralized college faculty and student body resolved that Innis should be closed down if the province didn't provide building funds. In a cruel twist, with Massey and Flanders's design in serious jeopardy, *Canadian Architect* magazine gave it an Award of Excellence for 1969.

The University of Toronto asked Massey and Flanders to come up with cheaper plans. But Innis' principal, Robin Harris (Fig. 23-5), was now questioning the validity of the program they were based on. Times had changed since the mid-1960s, and Innis itself had evolved. It had grown to about seven hundred students, and had managed to secure residence accommodation in existing buildings for about a hundred of them. To Harris, that felt just about right:

> Does it make sense in the 1970s to have 576 students in one building? Does it make sense in the 1970s to develop a college community of 1500? Does it make sense for Innis College,

Fig. 23-5. Robin Harris, principal of Innis College, is shown in July 1969, in front of the building that served as the college's temporary home. He is holding plans for the new Innis campus. [University of Toronto Archives, A1978-0050/005(04) (photograph by Robert Lansdale Photography).]

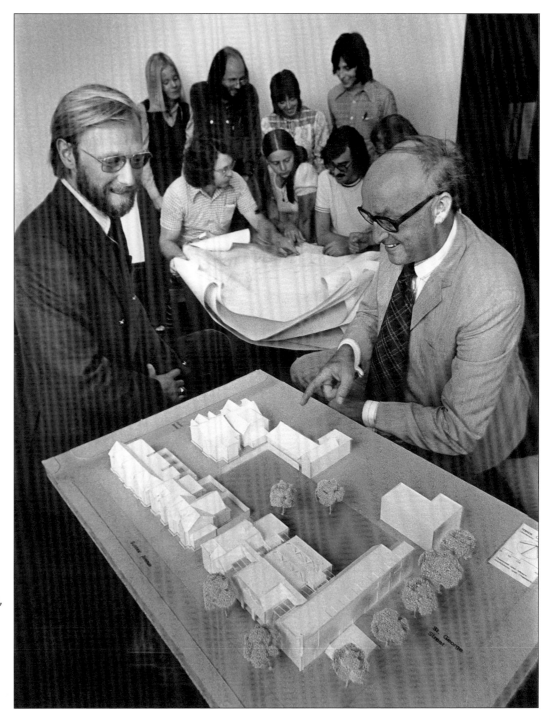

Fig. 23-6. Innis principal Peter Russell points to the new design for Innis College, as college administrator Art Wood looks on, October 1973. [University of Toronto Archives, A1978-0050/005(18) (photography by Robert Lansdale Photography).]

in light of the style and tradition it has developed during the six curious years of its existence to encase itself for half a century in a building, the plans for which were based on the knowledge and experience possessed by its students and staff in the period 1964–1968?

To Harris, the answer was clearly no. U of T's board of governors agreed. In June 1972, it approved construction of a 27,000-square-foot building on the St. George Street site. A.J. Diamond designed a low-rise scheme in orange brick that incorporated the site's Victorian houses (Fig. 23-6). The provincial government provided no direct funding. Appropriately, when the new buildings opened in January 1976 — more than a decade later than planned — it wasn't a ribbon that the new principal, Peter Russell, cut to mark the occasion, but a shoestring.

Chapter 24

PALACE PIER

1927/PARTIALLY BUILT

METRONOME

1993/UNBUILT

DUKE ELLINGTON, COUNT BASIE, BENNY Goodman, Rosemary Clooney, Peggy Lee … the list could go on and on. In the heyday of the big bands, these were only a few of the big names that played Toronto's Palace Pier, a venue whose history, a mix of trouble and triumph, would end in the most spectacular show of its existence.

By the 1920s, "pleasure piers" in seaside resorts, such as the Steel Pier in Atlantic City and the Palace Pier in Brighton, England, had a proven track record as money-making tourist draws. It was an association that the directors of the Provincial Improvement Corporation consciously drew on when they announced plans for Toronto's own Sunnyside Palace Pier in the summer of 1927. The Harbour Commission had approved a spot in Sunnyside Park for the attraction, which was being advertised as the largest pleasure pier in the world. For the commission, the approval was a natural, the

realization, in amended form, of the "recreation pier" that its own Toronto Harbour Plan of 1912 had called for in front of the CNE (Fig. 24-1). The parties couldn't reach a deal on the lease, however. It was a possibility that the promoters had planned for, with Montreal considered as a fallback location. Ultimately, they found a much closer alternative, a site on the west side of the Humber Bay, in Etobicoke — just outside the commission's jurisdiction.

John Westacott, the staff engineer at the Brighton Palace Pier, was brought from England to design the Toronto attraction. His plans centred on four principal buildings: a ballroom for three thousand couples; a "palace of fun" with roller skating in summer, ice skating in winter, and bowling year-round; a bandstand that could seat 1,500 covered and another 1,500 in the open; and a 1,400-seat theatre. The pier would jut 1,762 feet into Lake Ontario, its buildings connected by covered walkways with shops, refreshment stands, and rest areas,

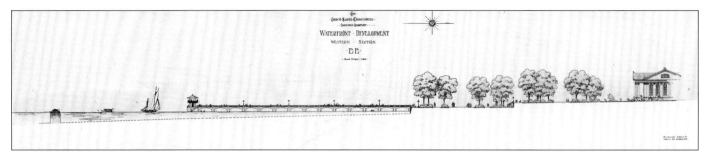

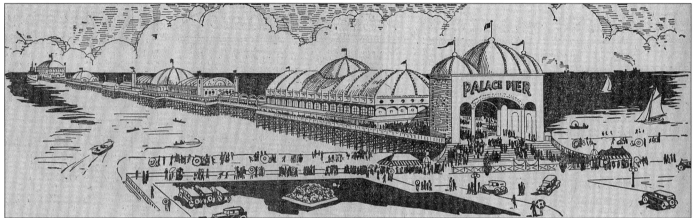

Figs. 24-1 (top), 24-2 (centre), 24-3 (bottom). In 1912, the Toronto Harbour Commissioners proposed a three-hundred-foot recreation pier in front of the CNE (top). In 1927, the idea of a waterfront pleasure pier was revived. John Westacott, the engineer for the Palace Pier in Brighton, England, drew up the plans, shown here in a drawing from 1929 (centre). The Toronto architectural firm of Craig and Madill updated the pier's design in 1931. Lit from below with coloured lights, it would have looked like a Technicolor, art deco dream (bottom). [Toronto Public Library.]

Fig. 24-4. What was intended to be only the first phase of the Palace Pier sat empty for almost a decade, before finally opening in 1941. In the years that followed, the biggest names of the big band era played the venue. It is shown here in a photograph taken for the Toronto Harbour Commissioners on June 1, 1960, to document dredging activity at Humber Bay. [Toronto Port Authority Archives, PC 14/5354.]

all of it surrounded by a nineteen-foot-wide boardwalk. Patrons could arrive by land, or by ship at one of the pier's three docks (Fig. 24-2).

But first, the Provincial Improvement Corporation needed $1.25 million to get it all built. For that, they were selling $10 shares in the venture to the public. Stocks sold slowly. It was January 10, 1931, before the cornerstone was laid, by Prime Minister Arthur Meighen. Even then, there was only funding for the first phase, consisting of the ballroom. By that time, the Toronto-based architectural firm of Craig and Madill had been brought on board. Where Westacott's pier had looked back to its Victorian antecedents, Craig and Madill, who later designed the CNE Bandshell, brought the concept stylistically up to date. Lit from below with floodlights that would change colour every fifteen minutes, the Palace Pier ("Sunnyside" had now been dropped from the name) would be like something out of a Technicolor, art deco dream (Fig. 24-3).

The press reported that construction on the rest of the pier would resume "at the earliest possible moment," but that moment never came. As it turned out, the Depression wasn't a great time to open a massive amusement venue. The building would sit empty for the next decade. By 1937, the owners were three years behind in their property taxes and had defaulted on their mortgage. A foreclosure action followed. By the time the litigation was all sorted out and the Palace Pier was ready to open its doors, it was 1941.

The pier operated initially as a roller-skating rink, but things really took off when it started to offer dancing to live orchestras. After the big band era ended, the Palace Pier continued to perform yeoman service into the 1960s, sometimes booked seven nights a week for private parties, wrestling matches, even spiritual revivals (Fig. 24-4).

And then it was all over. At about 3:00 a.m. on the morning of January 7, 1963, the night sky lit up. Flames, visible from as far away as Buffalo, shot two hundred feet into the air. The Palace Pier was providing its final spectacle, the work of an arsonist. The building, which had been touted as fireproof during its construction, was gone. Today, condominiums on the site continue the Palace Pier name, if not the music.

———————

Thirty-five years after the loss of the Palace Pier, another musical landmark was proposed on Toronto's lakeshore: Metronome Canada. But where the Palace Pier had been identified with American musical legends, Metronome's purpose was to promote Canada's homegrown talent, in a venue that would also pay tribute to the waterfront's industrial heritage.

Opened originally in 1928, and expanded in 1944, the Canada Malting silos at the foot of Bathurst Street were built for the centuries (see Fig. 5-2, top, centre right). The massive concrete silos were also built for a single purpose: storing barley before its conversion to malt for brewing and distilling. When Canada Malting discontinued operations at the site in 1987, there was an obvious question: what to do with them? By that time, the silos had come under the ownership of the federally controlled Harbourfront Corporation. It answered that question to its own satisfaction by conveying them to the city in 1993, on the condition that they be used for "public purposes." The city attempted to answer the question itself by putting out a call to developers the same year for expressions of interest, following it up with a formal request for redevelopment proposals in 1996.

Figs. 24-5, 24-6. Metronome, a 1993 proposal to transform the abandoned Canada Malting silos at the foot of Bathurst Street into "Canada's Music City," featuring museums, performance and education venues, offices, restaurants, and pubs. [24-5: illustration by Bruce K. Darrel; 24-6: photograph by Steven Evans, model by Richard Sinclair.]

A creative response to the request for proposals was the conversion of the silos into a gigantic waterfront mausoleum, housing 6,500 crypts for coffins and five thousand niches for urns. Since the windowless silos had been designed for storage, perhaps a new type of storage use made some sense (one of the better ideas to come out of a 1992 brainstorming session had been the relocation of the Ontario Archives to the site). Even so, the city took a pass. A proposal to build three hundred units of seniors' housing might have been somewhat livelier, but it would also have necessitated demolishing the larger, smooth-walled 1944 complex on the northern portion of the site. "Metronome Canada," on the other hand, reused the silos, almost in their entirety, for a mix of commercial and cultural uses. It was the brainchild of John Harris, a long-time veteran of the business side of the music business. In 1989, he had founded the Harris Institute for the Arts, offering post-secondary courses in the production and commercial aspects of the music industry. Its success got him to thinking: what if there was a single complex that could serve as the central focus of the music business in Canada, allowing for synergies among its various branches? It could house not only educational facilities and performance and recording venues, but offices for agents, promoters, and record companies.

Metronome had been in talks with the city since the request for expressions of interest in 1993, when it was Music City Canada. By the time of the 1996 proposal call, the project had its new name, broad industry support, and a design for the silos by architects Kuwabara Payne McKenna Blumberg that had already won an Award of Excellence from *Canadian Architect* magazine (it would go on to win one later in 1996 from the Ontario Association of Architects, as well) (Fig. 24-5, 24-6).

In the award-winning design, Bruce Kuwabara inserted a dramatic, multi-storey opening into the north complex. An opening would also be cut between the northern and southern complexes, allowing for the insertion of a glass-clad elevator shaft. Three-storey additions on top of the silos would house music industry offices, as well as a restaurant with panoramic views of the harbour. The southern silos would house a music museum. Visitors would travel to the top of it by escalator and then descend through seven floors of exhibits. The northern silos would contain a music-themed, boutique hotel in the upper portion, and the Canada Malting Museum below. Its working scale model of the malting complex would actually turn grain into malt, which could then be used to make beer at an on-site brew pub. New construction to the west would house an eight-hundred-seat theatre and a music education centre. Finally, the Riverboat, a ship moored at the complex, would contain coffee houses recalling the music scene in 1960s Yorkville.

In March 1999, after five-and-a-half years of discussions, the city finally granted Metronome a ninety-nine-year lease on the silos. Metronome's directors had a report from a major accounting firm saying that once the complex was up and running it would be economically self-sustaining. The catch was that it would cost $70 million to get it up and running, and on Metronome's business plan, only $12 million of that would be borrowed against future revenues. That left a lot of construction capital to be raised. There was no time to lose: under the agreement with the city, if Metronome didn't raise the first $10 million within a year, the deal was off.

The city later extended that deadline by a year, and then, in February 2001, extended it again to the end of 2001. By then, Metronome had a ten-year, $5-million commitment from Panasonic, part of $14.2 million in cash and in-kind donations it had attracted. But the city wasn't satisfied that $10 million of it related to the first phase of construction, as its lease required. More time might have solved that problem, but there was worse news to come. In March 2002, the provincial government's announcement of $92 million in capital funding for Toronto arts venues didn't include a $15 million grant that Metronome had been counting on. It was a double blow, since that also meant the loss of $15 million in federal matching funds. The spiral continued, as the lack of government support seemed to spook potential private donors. Metronome chose not to ask the city to revive the lease agreement. Ten years of effort and planning had come to an end.

In 2005 the city approved the silos as the site for another cultural attraction, "Humanitas," (later known more descriptively as the Toronto Museum Project). The municipal museum was supposed to open in 2015, but the plan was scrapped in 2009 after a private-sector partner failed to materialize. The city's chief corporate officer recommended that council demolish the silos, but it opted instead to stabilize them, demolishing only some attached ancillary structures. The silos themselves were designated under the Ontario Heritage Act in 2010. By that time, they had sat empty for almost twenty-five years.

Chapter 25

Spadina Gardens

1931/Unbuilt

Union Station Arena

1997/Unbuilt

T HE PRESS RELEASE WAS DATED JANUARY 9, 1931, and signed by Conn Smythe, part owner and general manager of the Toronto Maple Leafs. It was a reaction to the lead story in that morning's *Mail and Empire* about Spadina Gardens, a $1.5-million, sixteen-thousand-seat arena being proposed by a syndicate of "Montreal interests" for the old Knox College site on Spadina Crescent, north of College (Fig. 25-1). *The Mail and Empire* fawned over the preliminary plans prepared by local architects A.J. Everett and J.D. Wilson, noting that it was "thought practically certain" that, among other sports, professional hockey would find a home in the building. Smythe didn't know how that could be. In Toronto, professional hockey meant the Leafs, and the Leafs had no intention of becoming tenants at Spadina Gardens. Why would they? As Smythe affirmed in his press release, the Leafs were actively working on plans for their own arena.

Smythe didn't mention where the Leafs' new arena

would be, or what it would be called. By February 12, 1931, when he was before the city's property committee seeking zoning approval for it, the answers to both questions were known. The location was the northwest corner of Carlton and Church streets (a site at the foot of Yonge Street had been an earlier contender). As for the name, a number of possibilities had been privately mooted, including Central Gardens, Midtown Arena, and the Metropolitan, before what now seems the only choice possible was settled on: Maple Leaf Gardens.

Maple Leaf Gardens wasn't the only major arena seeking quick approval before the property committee that day. Spadina Gardens was still in the game, and its promoters were making the same request. For Maple Leaf Gardens, the plea worked. The committee voted in favour of it at a special meeting the following week, with council giving its approval on February 23. For Spadina Gardens, on the other hand, things didn't go so well.

Fig. 25-1. In 1931, a syndicate of "Montreal interests" proposed to build Spadina Gardens on the old Knox College site at Spadina Crescent, in direct competition to Maple Leaf Gardens. [Toronto Public Library.]

The required neighbourhood poll to gauge opinion on its rezoning hadn't been taken, and nothing could happen until it was. Already, however, the neighbours were up in arms. They feared that the facility, which included parking for a thousand cars and a ring of retail shops facing the street at grade level, would ruin the residential character of the area. Speaking to the committee, Salem Bland, a United Church minister who lived nearby, colourfully summed up the sentiment: "If this arena goes up, the district will be forever doomed — forever damned — you might say." Council provided the *coup de grâce*, killing Spadina Gardens on March 10, 1931.

By then, Montreal-based architects Ross and Macdonald were busy completing the working plans for Maple Leaf Gardens. Twenty years earlier they had designed the space where the Leafs were currently playing: Arena Gardens on Mutual Street. They had also been the architects for the new Eaton's College Street store (now College Park), which had just opened up at Yonge and College. It wasn't the only Eaton's connection, since the Maple Leaf Gardens site was on part of the so-called "mystery block" bounded by Yonge, Church, Carlton, and Alexander. Eaton's had clandestinely assembled it prior to the First World War (hence the name), before deciding to build west of Yonge instead (see Figs. 17-1, 17-2).

In March 1930, even before Eaton's ownership of the mystery block was common knowledge, the Leafs had approached Eaton's agent about building on part of it. Eaton's, however, wasn't at all sure that an arena fit in with its high-end vision for the area. It offered the Leafs a parcel to the north, between Wood and Alexander streets. But the Leafs wanted the profile of Carlton Street. Eaton's capitulated. The lure of bringing 2 million people a year to the area, coupled with Ross and Macdonald's assurances that the arena could be designed sympathetically, proved persuasive. It was written into the deal, however, that Eaton's had design approval of the arena, and that retail uses, which Eaton's felt would help integrate the building into the district, would front on Church and Carlton.

The Gardens was constructed at breakneck speed in a little less than six months and opened on November 12, 1931. With seats for 12,473 hockey fans, the building could seat a third more people than the old Arena Gardens, but it still couldn't fit all the people who wanted to see the Leafs play. The Gardens' management squeezed in more seats in 1947 and still more in 1962, bringing the capacity to 13,718, but there was still a waiting list for season's tickets that was nine-thousand names long. In May 1963, Leafs vice-president Harold Ballard arrived at the city's works committee with an audacious plan to fix that by adding an additional 4,020 seats.

The building was already at the lot line on all sides, but Ballard didn't see that as a problem. He filed drawings, prepared by architect Peter Allward, showing extensions that cantilevered fifteen feet in the air over Carlton Street to the south and Wood Street to the north, supported by a series of piers on the edges of the sidewalks. The assistant city solicitor said that council couldn't approve such a scheme even if it wanted to, and special legislation would be needed to permit the encroachment. That wasn't going to happen anytime soon, if at all, and Ballard was eager to have at least one of the extensions ready for the next hockey season. Replacing existing seats with narrower models, and using every last cranny, he managed to add another 1,743 seats within the arena's existing four walls in 1965.

Fig. 25-2. In April 1997, the Maple Leafs released plans, by architects HOK Sport and Roger du Toit, to build a nineteen-thousand-seat arena on a platform four storeys above the tracks at Union Station. [Roger du Toit.]

Fig. 25-3. The Leafs' Union Station arena development as viewed from the southeast. At the time, the Air Canada Centre was under construction. In the Leafs' plan, the site of the ACC (seen to the left) was to be turned into a bus terminal. [Roger du Toit.]

Even more seats were squeezed in during the 1970s, but it still wasn't enough. It had become clear that a new venue on a larger site was the only way to increase ticket sales, as well as provide for the corporate boxes that had become a lucrative feature of more recent professional sports facilities. Ballard, who was now majority shareholder in Maple Leaf Gardens, actively considered the possibilities through the 1980s (see, for example, Fig. 19-4). After his death in 1990, a new ownership consortium led by Steve Stavro took up the cause in earnest.

The NBA's awarding of the Raptors pro-basketball franchise to Toronto in September 1993 was a game-changer. A joint hockey/basketball facility made a lot of economic sense. Realizing that, the Raptors abandoned the location at the southeast corner of Dundas and Bay that they had originally intended to build on when it became clear it was too small to accommodate hockey. In November 1996, the Raptors closed on a new site, the old Postal Delivery Building on Bay Street, between the Gardiner and Union Station. With the new site came a new name, the Air Canada Centre. There were discussions about the Leafs joining them there, but they still found it too cramped, and an unworthy location to build a replacement for the venerable Maple Leaf Gardens. Stavro stated firmly that the site was of "no interest" to the hockey team.

Although the Leafs were adamant that they wouldn't move to the ACC, they were still hopeful they could lure the Raptors away from it. Since the Raptors had now started construction, that was going to take something extraordinary. At a press conference on April 17, 1997, the Leafs unveiled something they thought would do the trick: a nineteen-thousand-seat arena built behind Union Station, on a platform raised four storeys over the railway tracks. The great hall of the station would actually serve as a grand entrance to the arena, which would open to a new plaza to the south. Designed by HOK Sport with Roger du Toit Architect Ltd., the scheme complemented Union Station, but also tied in aesthetically to the Raptors' development. Two twenty-storey towers flanking the arena took their cue from the ACC's proposed tower, and the front elevation of the new arena itself was strongly reminiscent of the Postal Delivery Building which, under the plan, would be converted to a bus terminal (Figs. 25-2, 25-3).

Now it was the Raptors' turn to be unimpressed. Majority owner Allan Slaight said the Raptors couldn't possibly leave the ACC. For one thing, they had already put $80 million into it. For another, they were obligated to the NBA to have it up and running by February 1999. The Leafs' new arena wouldn't be ready until almost a year after that, at the earliest. Slaight said the concrete was going to start pouring at the ACC within days, and there was no hope of changing that: "We cannot conceive of anything in the world that can have us move off the Air Canada site."

It wasn't quite as straightforward as all that, however. Slaight was looking to sell his 79 percent interest in the club. Raptors general manager and minority shareholder Isiah Thomas signed a letter of intent to buy it on April 21. Unlike Slaight, Thomas made it clear that he was interested in joining the Leafs at Union Station. Toronto city council voted unanimously to fast-track the Union Station arena's land use approvals, and by mid-May, discussions between the Leafs and Thomas were going so well that a fall construction start was being predicted.

There was still another huge obstacle, though: the Leafs didn't own the land, and acquiring it wouldn't be easy. The city owned most of the land on which Union Station was built, but had leased it out in perpetuity in

1906 to the Toronto Terminals Railway, which owned the building. The TTR, which was wholly owned by the CNR and CPR, had been paying only $55,000 a year in rent since 1947, even though there were supposed to have been market-value adjustments in 1968 and 1989. An arbitrator had recently awarded the city $21 million in back rent, but the city was challenging the decision, arguing it was owed more than three times that amount.

The Leafs had offered to pay the TTR $50 million to walk away from its lease, including $21 million to cover the back rent to the city. Under the proposal, the Leafs would then take ownership and management of the station, leasing the land underneath for a fifty-year term. They would pay the city $13 million upfront for a thirty-five-year term, or $1 million per year, whichever the city preferred. The city would share in the rents of the office towers once they were built, and from year thirty-six to forty-nine, the Leafs' rent would be based entirely on profit-sharing from development on the site. In year fifty, the Leafs would have the right to another fifty-year lease of the station (based on market value), and could lease the arena in perpetuity, with fifty-year rent adjustments.

On June 19, 1997 the city rejected the offer, later saying it would accept a payment of $46 million to satisfy the TTR's back rent and $6 million in rent for thirty-five years or $100 million up front. That was too rich for the Leafs, who tried to take their case directly to the public, in full-page ads in the daily newspapers titled "An open letter to the citizens of Toronto." It was no use. On July 19, the newspapers reported that both sides considered the deal truly dead.

In November 1997, the Leafs had a new proposal for an arena on the site of Exhibition Stadium. In December, at its last-ever meeting before the creation of the megacity in January 1998, Metro council approved a fifty-year lease of a site at the Ex that would include room not only for an arena and parking, but also complementary development that the Leafs might wish to undertake. The Leafs had eighty days to perform their due diligence prior to the deal's going firm. During that eighty days, the landscape shifted completely.

In a bombshell announcement on February 12, 1998, the Leafs revealed that they were buying the Raptors, including their Bay Street arena. Clinging to at least one aspect of their previous proposal, the Leafs initially envisaged the station's great hall serving as the main entrance to the ACC, before finally abandoning the idea. The Air Canada Centre, the venue that the Leafs had said was of no interest to them, hosted its inaugural game on February 20, 1999. The Leafs beat the Habs, 3–2 in overtime.

Chapter 26

CANADIAN BROADCASTING CENTRE

1939/BUILT TO DIFFERENT PLANS

THE TECHNOLOGIES MAY HAVE DIFFERED, but like the construction of the transcontinental railway in the nineteenth century, the founding of the Canadian Broadcasting Corporation in the twentieth was an attempt to unite a nation that spanned a continent. By comparison, building some studio and office space so the CBC could get on with the job should have been a snap. But it would take over five decades and several false starts before a central Toronto facility was built, the controversial Canadian Broadcasting Centre on Front Street.

In January 1939, the CBC announced that it was planning to build studios for its major English and French production centres in Toronto and Montreal. It made sense. The broadcaster had been up and running for a little over two years — having been founded in November 1936 — and new facilities would allow it to consolidate its operations in each city (in Toronto, it was working out of three different buildings). Montreal firm Ross and Mac-donald created a preliminary perspective of the Toronto proposal, which survives to this day. Dated June 1938, it shows a handsome, modern building, interestingly identified as combined CBC headquarters and medical arts building (Fig. 26-1). No location was identified, but two months later the CBC bought a block-long parcel on the east side of Yonge Street, at Jackes Avenue, just north of Summerhill. The locally based Marani, Lawson and Morris took over as architects. In November 1939, however, construction plans were cancelled. Canada was at war now; the CBC buildings would have to wait.

The CBC managed to get its Toronto operations under a single roof for the first time after it took over the former Havergal College property on Jarvis Street at the end of 1944 (then being used as a training facility for the Women's Division of the Royal Canadian Air Force). It didn't last, however. The Royal Commission on Broadcasting counted sixteen different CBC properties in Toronto in its 1957

Fig. 26-1. In 1938, two years after the founding of the CBC, Montreal architects Ross and Macdonald prepared this perspective of a proposed studio complex/medical arts building to serve as its English-language headquarters in Toronto. [Fonds Ross & Macdonald, Collection Centre Canadien d'Architecture/Canadian Centre for Architecture, Montreal.]

report, and twenty in Montreal. The space problem had been exacerbated with the advent of television broadcasting, and the commission concluded that it was only going to get worse. It urged the creation of new headquarters in both cities, not in their expensive, congested downtown cores, but in cheaper suburban areas within commuting distance. It would involve a huge capital outlay, but as the commissioners concluded, "We think all that we can do is take a deep breath and plunge into [it] …"

In Toronto, the CBC plunged quickly, optioning thirty-three acres north of Eglinton in suburban Don Mills, on the east side of the planned Don Valley Parkway. After a false start (spooked by the cost, it let the option expire in the fall of 1958), the CBC closed on the

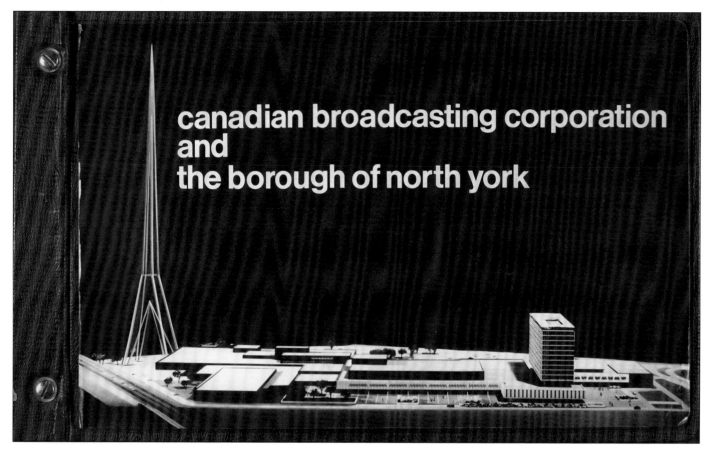

Fig. 26-2. In 1964, the CBC announced that it was months away from beginning construction on a sprawling broadcast facility at Eglinton and the Don Valley Parkway. Its modernist styling, complete with space-age transmission-tower, suited its high-tech function. The facility is shown here on the cover of a book prepared by the Borough of North York for the CBC in 1968. Its purpose was to extoll the advantages of a site that the CBC had long been ambivalent about. [Toronto Public Library.]

land in April 1960. Its new private competitor in the local television market, CFTO, began broadcasting from its suburban Agincourt studios in December 1960, but budget issues continued to delay construction for the CBC. It seemed decidedly ambivalent about the move in any event. In February 1964, even as it announced that it was "months away" from starting construction on a sprawling, $40-million complex on the Don Mills lands, complete with a space-age transmission tower (Fig. 26-2) CBC president J. Alphonse Ouimet was meeting with a Toronto delegation, led by Mayor Phil Givens, whose sole purpose was to get it to build downtown instead. The head of the CBC's English network, Herbert Walker, saw nothing strange in this: "As far as we're concerned, we're going ahead in Don Mills. There's no let-up in our preparations. But like any business in the same situation, we'll be willing to listen to alternative proposals right up until we start building."

City council had reason to believe it could affect the broadcaster's plans. The year before, the CBC had committed to building its French-language headquarters in east-end Montreal, an area that the Montreal city council wanted to see redeveloped. To make it happen, the city agreed to assemble a twenty-five-acre site using its expropriation powers, evicting five thousand people and demolishing hundreds of buildings before it was through. Ouimet was willing to deal in Toronto, too. He said that the CBC would locate downtown if council could provide a site that was equal in size and cost to its Don Mills parcel. The same month that the city delegation met with him, Toronto city council approved its own east-end urban renewal scheme for the St. Lawrence Market area, between Yonge and Jarvis. It was to be called the St. Lawrence Centre, a performing arts district covering several city blocks that was planned as the city's centennial project. There was a spot for the CBC, and the CBC was interested. City council, as it turned out, lost interest. It scaled back the plan drastically, eventually reducing it to a single theatre building, still unbuilt when the centennial year of 1967 rolled around (see *Unbuilt Toronto*, Chapter 30).

Not that anything was happening up at the Don Mills site. But that looked set to change. In June 1967, *Star* columnist Roy Shields reported that the CBC was "pretty well committed" to Don Mills after having looked at fifteen downtown locations without finding any of them suitable, and having found Toronto city council indifferent about helping out. Mayor William Dennison denied that he and council were indifferent to attracting the CBC, while admitting that the $5 million in municipal assistance it would probably take was a non-starter. The federal government, which had three cabinet ministers from Toronto, was keen to smooth over any hurt feelings. The day after Shields's column appeared, Secretary of State Judy Lamarsh telegraphed city council to assure them that no decision had been made, and that a downtown location was still a possibility.

The problem of finding one that was large enough and cheap enough seemed licked when CN and CP made it formally known, in the fall of 1967, that they were working on Metro Centre, a redevelopment proposal for 187 acres of surplus downtown rail land. With the hope of attracting the CBC, they were designating the block bounded by Simcoe and John, north and south of Front Street, as a telecommunications district. It would be located just to the north of a telecommunications tower that would eventually become the CN Tower. The CBC, ever coy, said it would study the matter, but by the time the Metro Centre plan was formally unveiled in December 1968, the CBC had officially signed on. President George Davidson made it clear that the CBC's involvement was limited to the telecommunications tower, however, which would be linked by cable to its production and head office facility in Don Mills.

Federal cutbacks and the costs of the Montreal project kept the CBC from moving forward until 1972. At a press conference on March 27 of that year, the federal energy minister, Donald Macdonald, announced that the CBC headquarters would go in Metro Centre after all, north of the broadcast tower as proposed. Although construction started on the CN Tower the next year, it would be several more before the CBC actually got its downtown land. Finally, in 1978, it paid CN $19.5 million for the 9.3-acre parcel bounded by Front, Wellington, John, and Simcoe.

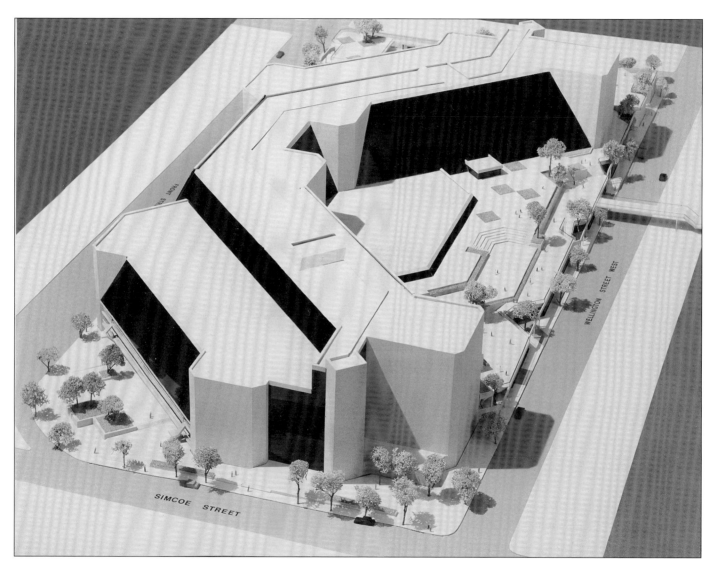

Fig. 26-3. This proposal for the CBC's English-language headquarters, *circa* 1974, covered 9.3 acres on Front Street. The CBC would later decide to use only a portion of the site, leasing the rest out for other development. [Toronto Public Library.]

Four years earlier, Bregman and Hamann had designed a scheme for this site. Plans from around this time show a facility arranged around a series of studios and rehearsal halls. They were aligned in a blunted V-shape pointing toward Front Street, serviced by central carpentry and paint shops in the centre of the "V," with direct access off Wellington. A diagonal interior public street led from the major pedestrian approach at Wellington and Simcoe to the main lobby, centred on Front. Visitors walking along it would be able to look in on both the radio and television studios (Fig. 26-3).

The problem was, as ever, finding the money to build it. But circumstances were set to change. As real-estate prices boomed in the 1980s, the value of the CBC's Front Street land boomed with them. In 1981, the land was already worth a reported $70 million, a figure that would more than double by the decade's end. The CBC realized that if it could build on only a portion of its land, it could use the value in the rest to help finance its building.

There was still an architectural stumbling block though: what to do with the sprawling studios and shops that had necessitated such a large parcel in the first place? Barton Myers Associates, who had now been retained as architectural consultants, had a clever solution. They proposed that the television studios could be placed on *top* of the building, connected by freight elevators to carpentry and shipping facilities in the basement. Not only would this do away with the need to span them to support the floors above, it would free up the floors below for public and office space. The result was that the building could now go up instead of out, allowing the CBC to occupy only 35 to 40 percent of the site.

The plan now was that a private developer could take out a long-term lease on the whole site, building hotels, offices, and commercial buildings on the eastern portion. At the same time, the developer would build the new broadcast centre on the western portion, leasing it back to the CBC. When the thirty-five-year term of that lease was up, the CBC would own the building outright, never having put a cent down to build it. In March 1985, the CBC put out a pre-qualification call for interested developers. An unusual respondent was the City of Scarborough, which took the opportunity to make the case that the CBC should simply sell its downtown holdings and use the money to build in Scarborough instead, at McCowan Road and Progress Avenue. In reaction, Toronto (which at one point had been urging the CBC to locate at Harbourfront) made the Front Street site even more attractive by significantly upping its permitted density.

In June 1986, the CBC invited six developers to come up with proposals. Three finalists were chosen, each with its own architects. Trizec Equities partnered with Zeidler Roberts, and Campeau Corporation was working with Moriyama and Teshima (Figs. 26-4, 26-5). A controversy arose when it was discovered that the other finalist, Cadillac Fairview, had chosen American architects Philip Johnson and John Burgee to work with the local firm of Bregman and Hamann. Arthur Erickson, who had designed the nearby Roy Thomson Hall, complained to the CBC and the federal government that it was an insult to the profession in Canada to bring in foreigners for such a culturally important commission. It didn't matter. Cadillac Fairview was chosen as the developer, based, according to CBC president Pierre Juneau, on its superior financial proposal.

Philip Johnson, who had been seminal in introducing North Americans to European modernism in the 1930s, when he was director of the architecture department at the Museum of Modern Art, had now become closely identified with postmodernism. His AT&T Building in Manhattan, capped with a broken pediment that many

Figs. 26-4 (above), 26-5 (right). In 1986, the CBC invited teams of developers and architects to submit proposals for its Front Street property. The broadcasting centre would occupy the western portion of the site, with commercial buildings to the east. The scheme developed by Zeidler Roberts (left), working with developer Trizec Equities, is shown in a watercolour rendering by Michael McCann. The proposal of Campeau Corporation/Moriyama Associates is shown at right. [Zeidler Partnership; Archives of Ontario, F 2187-1-96.]

found reminiscent of a piece of Chippendale furniture, had become one of the design school's poster buildings. For Toronto, he proposed pouring the historical detailing on even thicker. As he explained to the *Globe and Mail*: "I looked around. You have Victoriana in Toronto. There's a lot of Richardsonian Romanesque: Queen's Park is very good, I like that building. I decided that if the government buildings could be monumental, who's the CBC not to be? I was Post-Modernist in those days, so I decided to make it as monumental as we possibly could."

The rooftop studios came out looking like Athenian temples. To the CBC, it didn't scream "broadcasting facility." Even Johnson thought it looked off, but by 1988, the year before ground was broken, he was associated with a new architectural style, deconstructivism. And so, fifty years after it was first proposed, was the CBC's Toronto headquarters.

Chapter 27

OLYMPIC PROPOSALS
1954–2001/UNBUILT

IF THEY GAVE OUT MEDALS FOR TENACITY in trying to land the Summer Olympics, Toronto would have a serious shot at the podium. Had they been successful, Toronto's bids to hold the games in the 1970s, 1990s, and again in 2008 would have left a lasting physical legacy, in some cases radically changing the face of the city long after the cheering had died down.

Mayor Allan Lamport was an early proponent of Toronto as an Olympic city, virtually waging a one-man campaign for the 1960 games. With letters of support in hand from Premier Leslie Frost and Prime Minister Louis St. Laurent, Lamport travelled to Athens in May 1954 to make Toronto's case to the International Olympic Committee. Although lacking a stadium that could meet the IOC's eighty-thousand-seat minimum, the city proposed to create one by adding temporary bleachers to Exhibition Stadium. Back home, there was skepticism that Hogtown stood much of a chance against Rome (the

eventual winner), but that will never be known for sure. The next year, with Lamport no longer mayor, the city was out of the running when it failed to submit its bid application on time.

In 1968, Metropolitan Toronto put together another proposal, this time in an effort to convince the Canadian Olympic Committee to back its bid for the 1976 Olympics. Metro had just amended its official plan to include a concept that had been developed by the Toronto Harbour Commissioners, Harbour City (see *Unbuilt Toronto*, Chapter 7). Harbour City was an entire community built on artificial islands west of the island airport. In Metro's Olympic plan, it would serve as the Olympic village, the home away from home for the competing athletes. To the west, on fill placed just offshore from the CNE, Metro proposed an 80–100,000-seat circular stadium (Fig. 27-1).

As per IOC requirements, the stadium was not covered, but could be after the games were over, at which

Fig. 27-1. In 1968, Metro Toronto proposed to build a circular stadium in its bid to host the 1976 summer Olympics. To be constructed on fill in front of the CNE, it would be adjacent to a new aquatics centre to the west. In the foreground are two of the towers of an early version Harbour City, a proposed new community on artificial islands that would have served as the Olympic village. [Toronto Public Library.]

Fig. 27-2. In 1959, Kansas-based architect G. Ross Anderson proposed that a circular stadium be built on the lake in front of the CNE as part of a bid for the 1964 Olympics. [Clara Thomas Archives and Special Collections, York University, Toronto Telegram Collection, ASC06973.]

time its capacity would also be reduced to sixty thousand spectators. It would be approached by a ceremonial entrance on its east side, which would also contain a dais with the Olympic flame. To the west of the stadium, a raised walkway would lead to an aquatics centre. In its circular form and location, the stadium was reminiscent of a proposal put forward in 1959 by Toronto-born architect and part-time University of Kansas professor G. Ross Anderson. He had suggested it to council as part of a possible bid for the 1964 Olympics (Fig. 27-2).

The Canadian Olympic Committee chose Montreal over Toronto as Canada's candidate for the '76 Olympics, with Montreal going on to host them. But Toronto's Olympic dream was waiting to be rekindled. Paul Henderson, who had competed for Canada in yachting at the 1968 games, and had worked on Toronto's 1976 bid, set out to revive it. Inspired by the successful 1984 Los Angeles Olympics, Henderson and other local businesspeople formed the Toronto Ontario Olympic Council (TOOC) with the goal of bringing the games to Toronto in 1996. By August 1986, Toronto council was unanimously on board.

Although ground had yet to be broken for the city's new domed stadium (see Chapter 28), it was going to be too small to accommodate the track and field events, and didn't have enough seats to meet the IOC's requirements. In a plan approved by Metro in 1989, a new, larger venue would go on the site of Exhibition Stadium. It was given a waterfront presence by a plaza that was extended over Lake Shore Boulevard. As with earlier proposals, its eighty-thousand-seat Olympic capacity was intended to be reduced (to thirty thousand) after the games. Other new facilities proposed in the TOOC's plan were an Olympic aquatic centre and a rowing and canoeing basin by Ontario Place, a velodrome in Etobicoke's Centennial Park, and a second aquatic centre, given a futuristic

design by SkyDome architect Rod Robbie, at Ellesmere Road and Midland Avenue in Scarborough. The Canada Coliseum, a commercial arena then being considered for the Yonge and Highway 401 area, was pegged as the venue for basketball (see Fig. 19-4).

Despite all these sporting facilities, it was the Olympic village that would have had the greatest impact on the city's built form. The TOOC had originally proposed it for the Port Lands, fronting the eastern harbour (the east end of the proposed Ataratiri development was to be used for the media village. See Fig. 8-3). When council became worried about the loss of industrial land, the Olympic village was proposed for an even handier spot, just north of the major waterfront facilities, on surplus railway lands bounded by Spadina, Bathurst, Front, and Lake Shore. They were part of a massive tract owned by CN that stretched east of Spadina as well, taking in the CN Tower and the domed stadium site.

The tower was one of the few remnants of the 1968 Metro Centre development that would have seen the railway lands developed with a sea of high-rises (see *Unbuilt Toronto*, Chapter 6). But in 1986, the railway lands had been rezoned. Except for those buildings actually fronting Spadina itself, the development between Spadina and Bathurst was envisaged along the lines of the St. Lawrence neighbourhood, with a defined street wall on a traditional grid, and no building exceeding forty-five metres, or roughly fifteen storeys. City officials thought it

Fig. 27-3 (right). The railway lands between Spadina and Bathurst would have been redeveloped as a mid-rise athletes' village in Toronto's bid for the 1996 Olympics, as shown in this detail of an illustration by Rey Aguila. Bathurst Street is to the right. Spadina is just out of view, to the left. [Toronto Public Library.]

could take fifteen years for the area to develop (twenty-five years later, it is still not complete), but the Olympic village proposal seriously accelerated that timeline. Some 3,200 units of housing in twenty buildings spread across the western railway lands would now have to be ready by 1996. The official bid book released by the TOOC in January 1990 depicted that not-too-distant future (Fig. 27-3).

CN said that it was on board for the plan, but only if council confirmed that it could proceed under the permissions it had for office towers to the east, which were still subject to certain municipal conditions. The composition of council had changed in 1988, however. It was the height of a development boom, and a faction of NDP councillors had been voted in on an anti-development backlash. At their insistence, council had secured the provision that, after the games, the Olympic village would be converted to affordable housing, with 60 percent of it subsidized. It would be a significant legacy of the games, but councillors who had been elected to put an end to "let's make a deal" planning weren't prepared to make a deal on the rest of the railway lands to get it. They stood firm in insisting that the buildings on the eastern railway lands should be residential, to help alleviate Toronto's affordable housing shortage, and built at a much lower density.

On the day council was set to ratify a contract that the IOC required all prospective host cities to sign, CN confirmed that it would not make the western railway lands available for the Olympic village without a side deal on the remainder of its lands. With the NDP caucus sticking to its guns, a vote at that point would almost certainly have ended Toronto's Olympic quest. In an effort to stave off that result, council adjourned the matter for three days. When it reconvened, CN had backed down, some felt as a result of federal pressure on the crown corporation. By a count of 12–4, council voted to sign the Olympic contract on April 12, 1990.

But the bid's problems weren't over yet. An anti-poverty group, Bread Not Circuses, continued its efforts to make sure Toronto didn't get the games, shifting its focus fully now to lobbying the IOC. More than a few observers felt that their campaign, as well as the tortured road to council's endorsement, tipped the balance against Toronto, which placed third in the IOC's voting. When the 1996 games opened in Atlanta, Toronto's western railway lands were still undeveloped. In 1998, the city agreed to redistribute the density on them to allow towers, paving the way for the high-rises that now typify CityPlace.

That same year, Toronto was ready to try again for Olympic glory, this time with the 2008 games. David Crombie was chair of the bid committee. Not only was he a former mayor and federal member of parliament, but between 1988 and 1991 he had led a royal commission into the future of Toronto's waterfront. With Crombie at the helm, it was no coincidence that the Olympics master plan that was released in November 1999 seized on the games as a catalyst to waterfront redevelopment. The idea was fully supported by all three levels of government. The week before, the city, the province, and the federal government had created the Toronto Waterfront Revitalization Task Force under chair Robert Fung. It was mandated to integrate the 2008 Olympics requirements into its waterfront plans.

In the Olympics master plan prepared by the 2008 bid committee, the stadium was not proposed for the by-now traditional location in or near the CNE, but for the Port Lands, in the industrial quays crossed by Cherry Street. The area would also house the Olympic village and aquatic centre. The CNE would serve as the

Fig. 27-4. Carol Anne Letheran (seated, left), chief executive officer of the Canadian Olympic Association, gives the thumbs-up with Mayor Art Eggleton (seated, right) and members of the Olympic Task Force, April 12, 1990. The task force, made up of senior city bureaucrats, was charged with handling the '96 Olympics file for the city. Task Force chair Herb Pirk is standing to the far right. After a showdown over the Olympic village lands that nearly sank the bid, council had just voted to give its endorsement of the games. [City of Toronto Archives, Series 1281, 1990-121, Item 9.]

focus of the games on the western waterfront, featuring a velodrome and, as in the '96 bid, a plaza stretching over Lake Shore Boulevard, this time connecting with Ontario Place. It was just one of three new waterfront Olympic plazas, including one in front of the Port Lands stadium and another at the foot of Yonge Street.

It was an impressive plan. But as the IOC met in Moscow to choose which city would get the prize, bid organizers felt the need to up the ante. On July 13, 2001, hours before the committee was to make its decision, Toronto's bid committee announced that if Toronto got the games, the proposed Yonge Street Olympic plaza would instead be the site of a permanent World Olympic Youth Centre. It would be designed by Frank Gehry, and appeared in a rendering to be very similar to his famed Guggenheim Museum in Bilbao, Spain. The gambit failed. Beijing got the games and Toronto lost its waterfront Gehry. Four months later, however, the Olympic Spirit centre, an interactive Olympics museum, was announced for the proposed Torch building at the southeast corner of Dundas Square. Citing poor attendance, it closed in 2006, after only two years in operation. Perhaps Torontonians were having trouble feeling the love for a movement that never seemed to reciprocate it.

Chapter 28

ROGERS CENTRE
1983/BUILT TO DIFFERENT PLANS

ROGERS CENTRE IS PROBABLY THE second-most distinctive feature on the city's skyline. But its prominence in the city's psyche seems decidedly smaller. No one really seems to hate it, but no one really seems to love it, either. Even the retractable roof that was so exciting in 1989 was a paradox — the state of the art for an art that was on the way out. Perhaps that's fair enough. After all, Rogers Centre — once, and for many, still SkyDome — was the culmination of a dream that had begun back in the 60s.

In *Like No Other in the World*, his illustrated history of SkyDome, Mike Filey traces several of Toronto's failed stadium proposals, domed and otherwise. None would have been more beautiful than Memorial Stadium. It was to be built on reclaimed land on the new "Lake Front Boulevard" (ultimately Lake Shore Boulevard), between Strachan and Bathurst. Designed by Chapman, Oxley, and Bishop, it would have had an initial capacity of twelve thousand spectators, but could be expanded later to seat twenty-five thousand. The Bathurst line looping around it would mean that those spectators could take the streetcar right to its doors. In the municipal elections held on January 1, 1923, however, Torontonians made it clear that they weren't interested in going to Memorial Stadium in a streetcar or any other way, voting against the $225,000 expenditure necessary to build it (Fig. 28-1).

Echoes of its arcaded facade were visible in Maple Leaf Stadium, a privately built baseball field that Chapman, Oxley, and Bishop designed for the foot of Bathurst (see Fig. 5-2, upper right). It was the home of the Maple Leafs baseball team, who played there from 1926 until the year before its demolition in 1968. Football, meanwhile, was played in two public stadiums, first the University of Toronto's Varsity Stadium and — when the newly created Metropolitan Toronto failed to follow up on a 1954

PROPOSED MEMORIAL STADIVM
FOR THE
CITY OF TORONTO

COMMISSIONER OF PARKS.

Chapman Oxley & Bishop
Architects & Engineers
ROUS & MANN

Fig. 28-1. In the municipal elections of 1923, Torontonians voted against the construction of Memorial Stadium, planned by the city for what is now Lake Shore Boulevard, between Bathurst and Strachan. It was one of several failed stadium proposals over the years.
[City of Toronto Archives, Fonds 200, Series 372, Subseries 52, Item 1021.]

report recommending a new facility — at the expanded Exhibition Stadium after 1958.

The next decade saw a new benchmark in stadium design, with the opening of the Houston Astrodome in 1965, the first multi-purpose covered stadium in the world. In 1969, North York figured Metro Toronto could use one, too, and it knew where: North York, on the Downsview airport lands. North York mayor James Service travelled to Houston to inspect the Astrodome, to Montreal to discuss how that city had managed to snag a Major League baseball team, and to New York to meet with the commissioner of baseball about getting one for Toronto. "Yorkdome" — later the "Metrodome" — would have put the "multi" in multi-purpose sports facility, providing a venue not only for football and baseball, but for hockey, as well: potentially as the new home for the Leafs. Metro council followed up the next year by appointing a special committee in December 1970 to investigate the idea of a new stadium for Toronto. Its report, released in August 1971, confirmed the desirability of a domed stadium on the Downsview site. Although Metro council endorsed the concept, without the land from the feds or money from the province, it was left stranded on first base.

A coup and a storm changed all that. The coup came in 1976, when Toronto finally got its Major League baseball team. The Blue Jays, the American League's newest team, would play in the not-so-new Exhibition Stadium, which had been upgraded for them. The storm came five years later, during the 1982 Grey Cup game between the Toronto Argonauts and the Edmonton Eskimos. As icy rain pelted the crowds, reporters pressed Metro Chair Paul Godfrey about when Toronto was going to get a dome. Godfrey motioned to Premier William Davis a few rows down: "There's the guy that we have to get on side." Godfrey had been actively fighting for a new stadium since the Metrodome days, first as a North York alderman and then as a member of Metro's special

Fig. 28-2. Plans for the Trillium Dome were submitted to the province's stadium study committee in 1983. It would have been at the centre of a three-thousand-acre development at Highway 401 and Hurontario Street in Mississauga. [Jim Strasman, Strasman Architects.]

committee on stadiums. The two politicians talked after the game. There were no promises from Davis, but Godfrey said he could "see it in his eyes … I went out of there knowing we had lost the event but that I was about to win the biggest political battle in my life."

He was right. In June 1983, Davis announced the creation of a special committee to make recommendations on all aspects of a new stadium for the Greater Toronto Area. BC Place had opened as Canada's first covered stadium that year. Ontario was now playing catch-up. The stadium study committee was instructed to report back to the premier as soon as possible.

Retired Ontario Hydro head Hugh Macaulay was chair of the committee. It received almost two hundred submissions, including several specific stadium proposals. Perhaps the most comprehensive was the Trillium Dome (Fig. 28-2). Promoted by Mississauga-based developer Harold Shipp, and endorsed by the cities of Mississauga and Brampton and the Region of Peel, its planning, financial, and architectural prospectus covered five volumes. Shipp proposed constructing Trillium Dome on a 3,300-acre parcel at the northwest corner of Highway 401 and Hurontario Street. It would have been at the centre of a new mixed-use community, three of whose buildings — as shown conceptually by architect Jim Strasman — would serve as monumental gates to the stadium precinct. Although surrounded by concentric rings of parking, it was designed to allow direct access to Ontario's proposed GO-ALRT light-rail system (see Chapter 7). The giant trillium shown on the roof would have been visible from planes taking off and landing at nearby Toronto International Airport.

In February 1984, after a half-year of study, the Macaulay committee released its findings. From thirty-four potential stadium sites across the GTA, it recommended one at the southwest corner of Sheppard and the Allen — again, on the federal airport lands at Downsview. Its central location and easy access to the highway and rapid transit network (once the Spadina subway was extended) put it ahead of the two runners-up, the Woodbine racetrack site in north Etobicoke and Exhibition Place. The committee recommended that a crown corporation (which would be formed later that year as the Stadium Corporation of Ontario) build a sixty- to sixty-five-thousand-seat, multi-purpose stadium. It would be publicly financed, but with major private-sector contributions. A final recommendation was most exciting: the stadium should have a retractable roof.

The Downsview site turned out to be a non-starter when the federal government and de Havilland aircraft, which employed three thousand people there, were opposed to sharing it. At a press conference held on January 17, 1985, however, Davis announced that a new location had been secured, a parcel just west of the CN Tower. It was within walking distance of the GO and subway trains at Union Station, and, thanks to the office buildings in the area, there were already six thousand underground parking spots nearby that were available on evenings and weekends.

The land was owned by CN, which had pitched it to the Stadium Corporation the previous September as the site of its proposed "Tower Dome," designed by Crang and Boake. In the deal now proposed, CN, a federal agency, would contribute $20 million to service the land, plus an additional $10 million toward the project generally. For their part, Metro and the province also agreed to chip in $30 million each, with the province on the hook to guarantee the venture's loans. A group of thirteen private corporations, including Coca-Cola, CIBC, and McDonald's, had agreed to invest $5 million each, each receiving in return the use of a luxury SkyBox, and some also scoring exclusive concession rights at the stadium.

Fig. 28-3. In September 1984, Canadian National proposed the "Tower Dome," designed by architects Crang and Boake, for vacant land just to the west of the CN Tower. The province's Stadium Corporation, then looking for a spot to build a new domed stadium, liked what it saw. In the background, to the west of Roy Thomson Hall, the model shows the unrealized buildings designed by Arthur Erickson to complement his concert hall.
[Toronto Public Library.]

Fig. 28-4. This stadium design, by Bregman and Hamann, was one of four submitted through an invitational bidding process in 1985. As with the design ultimately chosen, when the roof was open, the playing field was completely uncovered, an important factor for the Stadium Corporation's technical review committee. [B+H Architects (photograph by Lenscape).]

Fig. 28-5. The domed stadium design of Webb Zerafa Menkes Housden came in with the lowest bid, but left only 60 percent of the playing field uncovered. [WZMH Architects.]

A model of the CN/Crang and Boake Tower Dome was shown to the press that day (Fig. 28-3). The sixty-thousand-seat stadium was in the circular configuration that had been recommended to the Stadium Corporation by an expert panel the month before. For illustrative purposes, it featured a rotating roof that allowed for 50 percent openness, although no decision had been made on what form the retractable roof should ultimately take. The roof's design, and ultimately the design of the stadium itself, would be driven by the Stadium Corporation's decision to seek competitive bids on a design-build contract.

A technical review committee chaired by architect Murray Beynon considered approximately twenty proposals, choosing four contractors in the summer of 1986 to submit detailed plans and bids. Crang and Boake were back on board, on a team with Eastern Construction Co. The Foundation Company of Canada submitted a design by Bregman and Hamann, and Webb Zerafa Menkes Housden prepared the design submitted in a bid by PCL Contractors Eastern Inc. (Figs. 28-4, 28-5). Finally, EllisDon submitted a design by architect Rod Robbie working with the engineering firm Adjeleian Allen Rubeli and with NORR Architects and Engineers.

Based on the technical review committee's adjusted costings, the bids by Eastern Construction/Crang and Boake and by EllisDon/Robbie were the two lowest, at $175.4 and $175.8 million respectively. The Stadium Corporation was hoping to get those even lower, but cost wasn't the only factor. Design was crucial. The roof of the Crang and Boake stadium folded into a fixed, bow-tie-shaped arch over the centre of the stadium's field, casting significant shadows. The Robbie/Adjeleian design, on the other hand, left 100 percent of the field and the vast majority of the seats fully exposed. The committee had a winner. On December 12, 1985, the Stadium Corporation's board ratified the choice.

Three-and-a-half years later, on June 3, 1989, SkyDome officially opened. As Torontonians had hoped, the world — or at least the Americans — took note that they had the first ballpark with a fully retractable roof. Writing in the *New York Times*, Paul Goldberger offered faint praise: "While watching a baseball game with the SkyDome's roof open is a lot better than seeing baseball played inside a fixed-dome stadium, there is still something missing. We are outdoors only in that there is no roof over our heads, but we never escape the feeling that we are in a vast work of engineering …"

It turned out that maybe SkyDome wasn't the best of both worlds — more like an attempt to optimize several: open and covered, baseball and football, public and private. The month that it opened, work began on Camden Yards in Baltimore, the first in a trend toward baseball stadiums that were more intimate, single-purpose, and open air, drawing their inspiration from the classic pre-war ballparks.

Even as SkyDome's cutting-edge caché was fading, its debt was growing. A facility that had originally been budgeted at $150 million had ended up costing almost $600 million. Adding features such as a hotel and health club along the way hadn't helped. Ontario's NDP government cut its losses in 1994, selling it for $151 million, writing off $321 million in the process. Four years later, SkyDome was seeking bankruptcy protection. It changed hands again in 1999 for $85 million, before Rogers Communications bought it in 2004 for a mere $25 million.

It wasn't an outcome its promoters were predicting back in the heady 1980s. But in an interview with the *Canadian Press* on its twentieth anniversary, Paul Beeston, president and CEO of the Jays, took a positive view:

I've read too much about this being a bad place, it's got no personality, it's just a mass of concrete. Fact of the matter is it's in downtown Toronto, the roof works 20 years later and you can visualize 20 years more here.… Is it Camden Yards or PNC Park? No. Does it have the history of Fenway Park or Wrigley Field? No. But it's ours, the roof works, we start our games at 7:07 or 1:07 and we play every day we're supposed to play.

In other words, it may not be a field of dreams, but all in all, not a bad batting average.

Chapter 29

ARTS AND LETTERS CATHEDRAL
1925/UNBUILT

SINCE ITS FOUNDING IN 1908, THE ARTS and Letters Club of Toronto has served as a meeting, performance, and exhibition space for practitioners in what are known within its walls as the five "LAMPS" fields: literature, architecture, music, painting, and stage (originally "sculpture").

In 1920, the club rented space from the St. George's Society at St. George's Hall on Elm Street, its address to this day (Fig. 29-1). It immediately undertook a major renovation of the 1890 building, including the creation of a baronial-style dining hall designed by Sproatt and Rolph, a firm whose named principals were both club members. Architect Jules Wegman, who had been a member since 1911, had even grander ideas. As Margaret McBurney recounts in her history of the club, for a February 1925 club dinner called "The Architects' Revenge," he drew up plans for the "Arts and Letters Cathedral," a tongue-in-cheek proposal to expand St.

George's Hall in a cruciform shape to the four ends of its block (Fig. 29-2).

Wegman's proposal made no bones about which of the LAMPS disciplines he considered most important. The Architects' Hall was not only the largest space in his cathedral, it was entered through an architects' court of honour, off the "Boulevard des Architects" (the renamed Bay Street). Members of the profession would also have had the option of entering the club through the architects' loggia, connected to the architects' garage (featuring a "Turkish lounge" for the architects' chauffeurs). Club founder Augustus Bridle was, in all fairness, also well accommodated, his personal entrance off Yonge leading to a suite of private rooms. Wegman even proposed a statue in his likeness at the cathedral's central crossing — conveniently removable when performances took place on the stage. Artists were given smaller quarters in their Artists' Hall to the north. Its entrance off an existing alley

Fig. 29-1. St. George's Hall at 14 Elm Street was built by the St. George's Society of Toronto in 1890. It is shown here in 1919, the year before it also became home to the Arts and Letters Club of Toronto. [Arts and Letters Club of Toronto (photograph by Arthur Goss).]

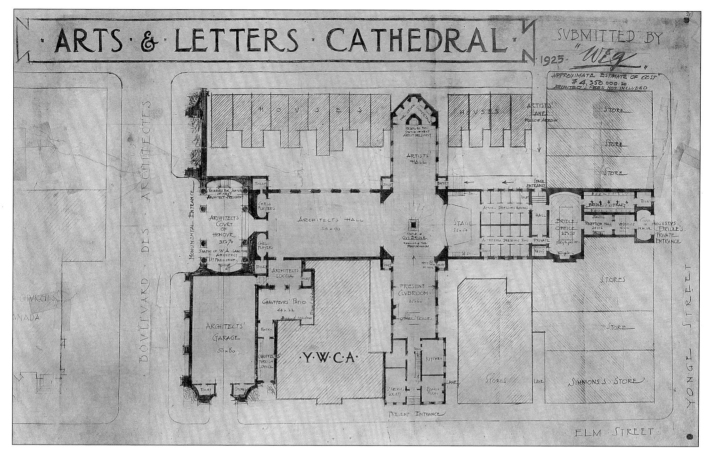

Fig. 29-2. The "Arts and Letters Cathedral," architect Jules Wegman's fanciful expansion proposal of 1925 for the Arts and Letters Club. [Arts and Letters Club of Toronto.]

(renamed Artists' Lane) was decidedly less imposing than that provided for the architects. The remaining LAMPS disciplines, identified as "other trades," were thrown together in the existing club room. Wegman noted that the whole thing was to cost approximately $4,350,000, "architects' fees not included."

The Arts and Letters Cathedral not only offers a glimpse into the spirit and camaraderie of the Arts and Letters Club in its early years, it provides insight into the wit and imagination of its important though relatively little-known designer. Jules Frederic Wegman emigrated from Switzerland to Chicago with his family at the age of ten. He followed his father into the architectural profession, working at the firm of Burnham and Root in the 1880s and 1890s. There he served as design assistant to John Wellborn Root, working with the architect

Fig. 29-3. Arthur Lismer's 1925 caricature of Jules Wegman, asleep at the Arts and Letters Club, dreaming of the Art Gallery of Toronto. [Arts and Letters Club of Toronto.]

on the grounds for the 1893 Chicago World's Fair. In 1905, he was invited to come to Toronto to work at the offices of Darling and Pearson, becoming a partner in that firm in 1924. He had worked on many of the firm's significant commissions, including the Canadian Bank of Commerce head office (see Chapter 14) and the Art Gallery of Toronto (see Chapter 22) by the time of his sudden death of a heart attack in 1931.

Suggestions in the Arts and Letters Cathedral to the contrary, an entry on Wegman in the *Journal of the Royal Architectural Institute of Canada* from 1945 states that the architect was "deeply interested in music, sculpture, painting and good literature." As for his own field of architecture, "all his work was created in an atmosphere of tobacco, a good cigar brought him inspiration." A good nap may also have done the same. A 1925 cartoon drawn at the Arts and Letters Club by fellow club member and Group of Seven painter Arthur Lismer (Fig. 29-3) identifies the sleeping Wegman as the architect for the newly expanded Art Gallery of Toronto (shown, cathedral-like, in Wegman's dreams). In a note beside a snail at the bottom of the page Lismer explains: "Why it wasn't finished in time."

Sources

Chapter 1: University Avenue Monuments

"$1,000 scrap price all Wolfe statue worth — connoisseur," *The Toronto Daily Star*, August 25, 1951.

"$1462 tax, duty on $5,000 statue of Gen. Wolfe," *The Toronto Daily Star*, August 15, 1951.

"$30,000 costs out of line, can move it for $200." *The Globe and Mail*, August 17, 1951.

Barker, Geoff. "Sydney International Exhibition 1879," *www. powerhousemuseum.com/collection/blog/index.php/2009/09/ sydney-international-exhibition-1879* (accessed June 6, 2011).

"Board backtracks, uproar blocks purchase of statue," *The Globe and Mail*, August 23, 1951.

"Chit Chat," *The Daily Telegraph* (Quebec City), November 24, 1893.

"Choose Beck memorial plan," *The Evening Telegram*, June 26, 1929.

City of Toronto Archives. Subseries 1, Files 16 and 17 (Memorial to Sir Adam Beck); Subseries 1, File 35 (Wolfe Monument); Subseries 1, File 286 (Beautification of University Avenue); Series 721, Files 31 and 32 (University Avenue Beautification, Parts 1 and 2).

City of Toronto, Council Minutes, 1929, Appendix "A," 200, 519, 1436, 2003, 2281; 1930, Appendix "A," p. 1657; 1932, Appendix "A," 563–64.

City of Toronto Planning and Development Department. *Toronto Civic Sculpture*. Toronto: July, 1985.

City of Toronto. *Proposed Memorial to Sir Adam Beck: Conditions of Competition for the Selection of a Design*. April 29, 1929.

Dendy, William. *Lost Toronto*. Toronto: McClelland & Stewart, 1993.

"Design accepted for memorial to Sir Adam Beck," *The Evening Telegram*, June 26, 1929.

Doughty, Arthur George. *The Cradle of New France*. London: Longmans, Green & Company, 1909.

du Toit, Allsopp, Hillier. *The Art of the Avenue: A University Avenue Public Art Study*. June 1989.

Faludi, E.G. and Austin Floyd. *Report to the Toronto City Planning Board: The Decorative Treatment of University Avenue*. October 3, 1950.

Glenbow Archives, Eric Harvie Fonds, Series 42, G-1-1248 (General James Wolfe Statue).

Hansard (Canada), April 13, 1871, 1082. (Vol. 2).

Hood, Sarah B. "Bombs away," *National Post*, December 1, 2007.

"Letter from Ottawa," *The Globe*, April 15, 1871.

Morris, William. *Letters Sent Home*. London: Frederick Warne & Co., 1875.

Musée de la civilisation du Québec. Accession number 88-3163, Marshall Wood statue (commentary).

Oxley, Loren A. "Retrospect — The first 75 Years." *Rotunda* 15, No. 2 (Summer 1982).

"Paying N.Y. man $5,000 for 1890 Wolfe statue for University Ave," *The Toronto Daily Star*, August 15, 1951.

"The Prince in Toronto," *The Daily Globe*, September 12, 1860.

"The Queen in effigy," *The Daily Telegraph*, August 6, 1880.

"The Queen's statue," (letter to the editor) *The Globe*, April 7, 1873.

"The Queen's statue," (letter to the editor) *The Globe*, April 16, 1873.

"Statue of Her Majesty," *The Globe*, October 4, 1871.

"A statue of the Queen," *The Morning Chronicle* (Halifax), August 5, 1873.

"Statue of Victoria blown up," *The Toronto Daily Star*, July 12, 1963.

"To use maple trees for University Avenue," *The Toronto Daily Star*, October 19, 1950.

Tumpane, Frank, "Bargain Basement Statue," *The Globe and Mail*, August 16, 1951.

Untitled, *The Globe*, April 28, 1892.

"Where they are is known; why they went, isn't," *The New York Times*, April 1, 2007.

"Wolfe statue would cost $38,000," *The Globe and Mail*, August 16, 1951.

Chapter 2: Government House/Whitney Block

"$400,000 mansion shunned by new lieutenant governor," *The Windsor Star*, April 29, 1963.

"500 guests attend opening of East Block," *The Toronto Daily Star*, March 27, 1928.

"Another new clause," *The Globe*, March 17, 1910.

"Approves boulevard approaching capital," *The Toronto Daily Star*, February 11, 1928.

Blizzard, Christina. "Ontario's vacant lot," *The Toronto Sun*, January 28, 2007.

Bradburn, Jamie, "Historicist: The Saga of Chorley Park," *Torontoist*, August 9, 2008 (*http://torontoist.com/2008/08/historicist.php*).

Brigdens, Ltd., *The East Block of the Ontario Parliament Buildings*. Toronto: Brigdens, Ltd., 1928.

"Cabinet rejects plans," *The Globe*, October 27, 1910.

"Call building 'Henry'? Minister is surprised," *The Toronto Daily Star*, February 9, 1928

"Chorley Park, North Rosedale," (advertisement) *The Globe*, June 17, 1911.

City of Toronto Archives. Fonds 1248, Series 1345, Files 8, 9 and 12.

"Competitive Designs for Ontario Government House." *Construction* 4, No. 6 (May 1911): 49.

"Contracts Department" *Contract Record and Engineering Review* 30, No. 50 (December 13, 1916), 1182.

"Contract given for East Block without tenders," *The Toronto Daily Star*, March 16, 1928.

Dale, Clare A. *The Palaces of Government*. Toronto: Ontario Legislative Library, 1993.

Dendy, William. *Lost Toronto*. Toronto: McClelland & Stewart, 1993.

"East Block: Ontario Parliament Buildings Toronto." *Construction* 21, No. 5. (May 1928).

"East Block opened Monday," *The Toronto Daily Star*, March 23, 1928.

"Extraordinary Conditions of Ontario Government House Competition." *Construction* 3, No. 12 (November 1910).

"Government House site," *The Globe*, October 28, 1910; April 11, 1911; April 27, 1911; May 19, 1911.

Greer, William N. et al. *Heritage Significance Study: Whitney Block & Tower, Queen's Park, Toronto*. May 31, 1996.

"Lyons is exonerated, Raney's report killed," *The Toronto Daily Star*, April 1, 1926.

"Mainly Constructional." *Contract Record and Engineering Review* 33, No. 9 (February 26, 1919).

Marshall, John, "Marble halls of Chorley Park under hammer," *The Windsor Daily Star*, December 4, 1937.

"Mr. Gage makes a generous offer," *The Globe*, June 10, 1911.

"Mr. McEwing's opinions," *The Toronto Daily Star*, February 11, 1910.

"The New East Block." In *The Toronto Year Book, 1929*. Toronto: Municipal Intelligence Bureau, 1929.

"The new East Block of the Parliament Buildings, Queen's Park, Toronto." In *The Toronto Year Book, 1926*. Toronto: Municipal Intelligence Bureau, 1926.

"A new government house," *The Globe*, February 26, 1910.

"Notes and Comments," *The Globe*, May 22, 1911.

"Ontario govt. block ready in about year," *The Toronto Daily Star*, July 31, 1925.

"Ontario offers prizes," *The Globe*, May 23, 1910.

"The plans of the new government house," *The Toronto Daily Star*, August 19, 1910.

"Premier Frost 'horrified,' Sigmund Samuel gives house for Lieutenant Governor," *The Toronto Daily Star*, November 19, 1959.

"Premier is predicting film making in Canada," *The Toronto Daily Star*, April 24, 1928.

"Province may build new $1,000,000 block," *The Toronto Daily Star*, May 15, 1930.

"Provincial Architect F.R. Heakes is dead," *The Toronto Daily Star*, October 1, 1930.

Radlak, Ted. "Sasaki Saved?" *Landscape Architecture* 92, No. 11 (November 2002): 79–85.

Reaume, J.O. *Report of the Minister of Public Works for the Province of Ontario for the Twelve Months Ending 31st October 1910.* Toronto: King's Printer for Ontario, 1911.

Reaume, J.O. *Report of the Minister of Public Works for the Province of Ontario for the Twelve Months Ending 31st October 1911.* Toronto: King's Printer for Ontario, 1912.

Sewell, John. *Doors Open Toronto.* Toronto: Alfred A. Knopf, 2002.

"The site of Government House," *The Globe*, August 23, 1910.

Chapter 3: 1910 Subway Plan/Radial Railways Plan

An Act respecting the City of Toronto. S.O. 1910, Chapter 135.

Armstrong, Christopher and H. V. Nelles. "Suburban Street Railway Strategies in Montreal, Toronto and Vancouver, 1896–1930." *Power and Place: Canadian Urban Development in the North American Context.* Edited by Gilbert A. Stetler and Alan F.J. Artibise. Vancouver: University of British Columbia Press, 1986.

Bow, James. "Early Subway Proposals." *Transit Toronto, www. transit.toronto.on.ca* (accessed January 22, 2011).

"Complete subway system with 2 cross-town lines planned by works dept," *Toronto World*, November 23, 1911.

Doucet, Michael J. "Politics, Space and Trolleys: Mass Transit in Early Twentieth-Century Toronto." In *Shaping the Urban Landscape: Aspects of Canadian City-Building Process.* Ottawa: Carleton University Press, 1982.

Due, John. F. *The Intercity Electric Railway Industry in Canada.* Toronto: University of Toronto Press, 1966.

Filey, Mike. *More Toronto Sketches.* Toronto: Dundurn Press, 1993.

Filey, Mike with Ted Wickson. *The TTC Story: The First Seventy-five Years.* Toronto: Dundurn Press, 1997.

Filey, Mike. *Toronto: The Way We Were.* Toronto: Dundurn Press, 2008.

Fleming, R.B. *The Railway King of Canada.* Vancouver: UBC Press, 1991.

Fogelson, Robert M. *Downtown: Its Rise and Fall, 1880–1950.* New Haven, CT: Yale University Press, 2001.

Harris, R.C. et al. *Report to the Civic Transportation Committee on Radial Railway Entrances and Rapid Transit for the City of Toronto*, Vols. 1 and 2. Toronto, 1915.

Jacobs and Davies Inc. and James Forgie. *Report on Transit* (Report to Toronto City Council, August 25, 1910).

"Report on Radial Railway Entrances and Rapid Transit for the City of Toronto." *Canadian Railway and Marine World* (January 1916).

"Report on Radial Railway Entrances and Semi-Rapid Transit for the City of Toronto." 29 *The Canadian Engineer* (December 30, 1915).

Stamp, Robert M. *Riding the Radials.* Erin, ON: The Boston Mills Press, 1989.

Werner, Hans. "The Subway Dreams of Horatio Hocken." *Canadian Heritage* 14, No. 1 (Spring 1988).

Chapter 4: War Memorials

"Alter cenotaph inscription," *The Toronto Daily Star*, November 3, 1925.

Archives of Ontario. RG 49-106 (Records of the War Memorial Committee of Ontario).

Baker, Victoria. *Emanuel Hahn and Elizabeth Wyn Wood: Tradition and Innovation in Canadian Sculpture.* Ottawa: National Gallery of Canada, 1997.

"Cenotaph hallowed mayor says," *The Globe and Mail*, November 8, 1965.

"Change words on cenotaph," *The Evening Telegram*, November 3, 1925.

City of Toronto Archives. Fonds 200, Series 487, Files 60, 63, and 64.

City of Toronto Board of Control Minutes, October 28, 1925.

City of Toronto Council Minutes, 1924, Appendix "A," 1603.

City of Toronto Council Minutes, November 2, 1925, p. 301.

City of Toronto Council Minutes, 1962, Appendix A, Board of Control Report No. 20, 1610.

City of Toronto Property Department. "Future Location of the Cenotaph (War of 1914–1918) now in front of the old City Hall." (Memorandum to Board of Control, July 9, 1962.).

"Cenotaph in memory of Ontario soldiers." *The Mail and Empire*, August 7, 1922.

Clark, Gregory. "Five years of peace and yet no war memorial." *The Toronto Star Weekly*, September 29, 1923.

Crerar, Adam. "Ontario and the Great War." *Canada and the First World War.* Edited by Robert Craig Brown and David Clark MacKenzie. Toronto: University of Toronto Press, 2005.

Filey, Mike. *Toronto Sketches 5*. Toronto: Dundurn Press, 1997.

"Good reason to be proud of city Queen tells 4,000 in Toronto," *The Toronto Star*, October 3, 1984.

"Great war memorial square featured in new city plan." *The Evening Telegram*, December 22, 1923.

Hill, Robert. *Biographical Dictionary of Architects in Canada, 1800–1950, www.dictionaryofarchitectsincanada.org* (Ferguson, William Moncrieff and Pomphrey, Thomas Canfield) (accessed April 3, 2011).

Jones, Donald J. "The architect soldier who built the '48th,'" *The Toronto Star, Saturday Magazine*, August 20, 1988.

Library and Archives Canada. "From Colony to Country," *www.collectionscanada.gc.ca/military* (accessed January 10, 2011).

"Local architects win city cenotaph award," *The Toronto Daily Star*, October 27, 1924.

Reddyhoff, Gillian. Author interview. March 2, 2010.

Rochon, Lisa. "Dishonourable Conduct," *The Globe and Mail*, June 16, 2004.

Shipley, Robert. *To Mark Our Place: A History of Canadian War Memorials*. Toronto: NC Press, 1987.

"Six of twenty designs being considered for war cenotaph in front of city hall," *The Evening Telegram*, October 27, 1924.

"Suggest province erect Cenotaph as a memorial," *The Mail and Empire*, January 6, 1923.

"Toronto Cenotaph Competition." *Journal, Royal Architectural Institute of Canada* 2, No. 1 (January–February 1925).

"Two sites in view for memorial hall," *The Mail and Empire*, August 14, 1922.

Warkentin, John. *Creating Memory: A Guide to Outdoor Public Sculpture in Toronto*. Toronto: Becker Associates/York University, 2010.

Weiss, Kevin. Author interview. February 25, 2010.

"Words on cenotaph stir up opposition," *The Toronto Daily Star*, November 2, 1925.

Chapter 5: Gardiner Expressway

"Agree to extend Lakeshore expressway across Queen," *The Globe and Mail*, May 19, 1954.

Belland, Lee, "New expressway route by-passes Fort York, 'costs now $1,000,000," *The Toronto Daily Star*, January 2, 1959.

Belland, Lee. "Pick hydro line, see year delay in expressway," *The Toronto Daily Star*, October 18, 1954.

"Campbell fails to get Fort York moved," *The Toronto Daily Star*, February 27, 1970.

"Ceasefire ends Fort York battle," *The Toronto Daily Star*, January 31, 1959.

City of Toronto Archives. Series 832, Files 37 (Helen Durie papers re: Stanley Barracks and Fort York).

City Planning Board of Toronto. *The Master Plan for the City of Toronto and Environs*. Toronto: 1943.

Colton, Timothy J. *Big Daddy: Frederick G. Gardiner and the Building of Metropolitan Toronto*. Toronto: University of Toronto Press, 1980.

"Decide shortly if expressway to be elevated," *The Globe and Mail*, July 7, 1956.

"Defer decision on relocating Old Fort York," *The Globe and Mail*, January 9, 1959.

"Expressway breaches Fort York," *The Globe and Mail*, February 4, 1958.

"Expressway delayed, Metro orders plans for northern route," *The Toronto Daily Star*, June 9, 1954.

"Fort York Threatened." *Ontario History* 50, No. 1 (Winter 1958).

"Fort York Wins a Modern Battle." *Ontario History* 51, No. 1 (Winter 1959).

French, William, "6-laner to soar along lakeshore," *The Globe and Mail*, May 4, 1954.

"Gardiner charm fails to convince historians," *The Toronto Daily Star*, June 19, 1958.

Haggart, Ronald, "Metropolitan Toronto,." *The Globe and Mail*, March 17, 1958.

Hill, Raymond, "Should move Fort York, will pay half, says Frost." *The Toronto Daily Star*, January 9, 1959.

"Inland expressway extra costs $11,000,000," *The Globe and Mail*, July 20, 1954.

"May halt expressway if Fort, CPR adamant," *The Globe and Mail*, June 19, 1958.

"May save fort from expressway bite," *The Toronto Daily Star*, February 3, 1958.

"May yet cut slice off Fort York site," *The Globe and Mail*, March 26, 1958.

McGuffin, William, "New route for expressway would save historic site, might cost Metro $2,000,000," *The Toronto Daily Star*, October 4, 1958.

"Metro chief capitulates with honor," *The Globe and Mail*, March 27, 1958.

"Metro urged to start part of speedway," *The Globe and Mail*, October 5, 1954.

"MPPs guard Ft. York," *The Telegram*, March 24, 1958.

"MPPs to look at Fort York, decide again," *The Toronto Daily Star*, March 25, 1958.

"Old fort to stay, Gardiner gives in, cost up to $1,000,000," *The Toronto Daily Star*, November 22, 1958.

"Old Fort York Saved," *Ontario History* 50, No. 2 (Spring 1958).

Otto, Stephen. "Once more unto the Breach: Defending Fort York in the 20th century." June 17, 1994.

"Park group approves expressway over fort," *The Globe and Mail*, February 21, 1958.

"Plan to move Fort York described as 'vandalism,'" *The Toronto Daily Star*, June 7, 1958.

"Plan to start expressway on April 1," *The Globe and Mail*, March 9, 1955.

"Second battle of Fort York," *Time* 72, No. 15 (October 13, 1958).

"Suggest Gardiner Freeway," *The Globe and Mail*, July 30, 1957.

"Title to Exhibition site binds city to maintain Old Fort York 'forever,'" *The Telegram*, October 16, 1958.

"'We can move fort on trailers,'" *The Toronto Daily Star*, January 21, 1959.

Westell, Anthony, "Fort York's future," *The Globe and Mail*, January 10, 1959.

"Would start in east till 'fort' row over," *The Toronto Daily Star*, December 27, 1958.

Young, Scott. "Let's move Fort York to shore." *The Globe and Mail*, June 3, 1958.

Chapter 6: Scarborough Expressway/Island Airport Bridge

B.A. Consulting Group Ltd. with van Nostrand Hanson DiCastri Architects. *Toronto City Centre Airport Fixed Link Options and Issues*. January 18, 1996.

Barber, John, "Island airport ain't gonna fly," *The Globe and Mail*, December 8, 2000.

Cowan, James, "Ottawa backs city on bridge," *The National Post*, December 5, 2003.

Dillon Consulting. *Fixed Link to the Toronto City Centre Airport. Environmental Assessment*. April, 1998.

Dillon Consulting. *Proposed Fixed Link Bridge to the TCCA: Draft EA Report, Toronto Port Authority*. June, 2003.

Filey, Mike. *Trillium and Toronto Island*. Toronto: Dundurn Press, 2010.

Hall, Joseph, "Report sees jet traffic for Island Airport," *The Toronto Star*, October 16, 2001.

Hume, Christopher, "Big island airport a city-killer: Jacobs," *The Toronto Star*, October 1, 2001.

James, Royson and Hichan Safieddine, "Bridge battle finally over," *The Toronto Star*, May 4, 2005.

"Keating St. extension to be opened Dec. 4," *The Globe and Mail*, December 9, 1955.

Lewington, Jennifer, "Ottawa pays $35 million to abort bridge," *The Globe and Mail*, May 4, 2005.

Lewington, Jennifer, "Port Authority to proceed with bridge to island," *The Globe and Mail*, October 2, 2003.

Lu, Vanessa, "Tunnel to island airport by 2011?" *The Toronto Star*, August 24, 2009.

Osbaldeston, Mark. *Unbuilt Toronto: A History of the City That Might Have Been*. Toronto: Dundurn Press, 2008.

Prittie, Jennifer, "Airport antics," *Eye Weekly*, October 3, 2005.

Prittie, Jennifer, "Red-tape rumble," *Eye Weekly*, December 12, 2005.

Re Merrens et al. and Municipality of Metropolitan Toronto. [1973] 2 Ontario Reports, 265.

Scarborough Planning Department. *The Scarborough Transportation Corridor Study*. Scarborough: 1984.

Sears, Val, "Scarborough Expressway plans zapped," *The Toronto Star*, September 23, 1973.

"Stage set for showdown over fixed link to island," *Daily Commercial News and Construction Record*, December 1, 2003.

Steuart G. et al. *Preliminary Review of the Scarborough Expressway*. Toronto: Metropolitan Toronto Transportation Plan Review, 1974.

Swainson, Gail, "Tear down east end Gardiner, report says." *The Toronto Star*, February 28, 1996.

Timson, Judy, "Spadina snarls Scarborough expressway plan," *The Toronto Star*, January 4, 1972.

Toronto Harbour Commissioners. *Toronto Harbour: The Passing Years*. Toronto: Toronto Harbour Commissioners, 1985.

Toronto Harbour Commissioners. *Toronto Waterfront Development 1912–1920*. Toronto: Toronto Harbour Commissioners, 1912.

"Unbuilt Toronto: The City That Could Have Been." Exhibition, Royal Ontario Museum. November 5, 2008–January 4, 2009 ("Fixed Link to Toronto City Centre Airport," exhibition panel).

Wilkes, Jim, "It's a go for Gardiner demolition," *The Toronto Star*, April 28, 2000.

Chapter 7: UTDC Rapid Transit/Network 2011

Best, Michael, "GO officials to back east end transit line," *The Toronto Star*, January 30, 1984.

Bow, James, "The Scarborough Rapid Transit Line," *Transit Toronto, www.transit toronto.on.ca* (accessed February 20, 2011).

Bow, James, "UTDC Kingston Transit Development Centre," *Transit Toronto, www.transit toronto.on.ca* (accessed February 20, 2011).

Bow, James. "Where Have All the Subways Gone?" *uTOpia: Towards a New Toronto*, Edited by Jason McBride and Alana Wilcox. Toronto: Coach House Books, 2005.

Bragg, William. "GO-Urban's bright future fades suddenly." *The Toronto Star*, November 14, 1974.

Campion-Smith, Bruce. "Eglinton subway project underway." *The Toronto Star*, August 26, 1994.

Campion-Smith, Bruce, "Tories derail Eglinton subway," *The Toronto Star*, July 22, 1995.

Coleman, Thomas, "Bonn found GO-Urban unable to beat trams, Lewis tells House." *The Globe and Mail*, November 20, 1974.

Coleman, Thomas, "GO-Urban magnetic train having trouble on curves," *The Globe and Mail*, November 7, 1974.

Coleman, Thomas, "Ontario cancels plans for magnetic trains," *The Globe and Mail*, November 14, 1974.

"Commuters split over GO Transit extension plan," *The Toronto Star*, October 8, 1982.

"Cost of ALRT increases," *Real Estate News*, April 6, 1984.

Dexter, Brian, "Go-Urban rail planners face tough job countering critics," *The Toronto Star*, January 4, 1974.

Dexter, Brian, "Where the 56 miles of Metro transit will go," *The Toronto Star*, November 23, 1972.

Foley, K.W. *Go-Urban and the Transit Demonstration Project* (Presentation to the Metropolitan Toronto Transportation Committee and the Toronto Transit Commission, April 9, 1974).

"Go-Urban plan magnetic fantasy Lewis declares," *The Toronto Star*, December 7, 1973.

"GO-Urban's magnet malfunction makes Tories target of ridicule," *The Globe and Mail*, November 8, 1974.

Gooderham, Mary, "Tories forgo light rapid transit plans," *The Globe and Mail*, June 11, 1985.

Hawker Siddeley Canada Ltd. *Technical Design Proposal for Intermediate Capacity Transit Demonstration System, Volume III*. Toronto, 1972.

Howard, Ross, "Hundreds of homes face expropriation on rapid rail route," *The Globe and Mail*, June 26, 1984.

Josey, Stan, "Snow assures skeptics electric rail on target," *The Toronto Star*, June 20, 1984.

Kirkland, Bruce, "Transit system bill now up 56%," *The Toronto Star*, May 3, 1974.

"Magnet trouble blamed for hitch in GO Urban test," *The Toronto Star*. November 7, 1974.

Marron, Kevin, "Snow says it may take 20 years to finish Hamilton-Toronto link," *The Globe and Mail*, June 14, 1984.

Municipality of Metropolitan Toronto and Toronto Transit Commission. *Network 2011: Final Report*. June, 1986.

Municipality of Metropolitan Toronto and Toronto Transit Commission. *Network 2011: A Rapid Transit Plan for Metropolitan Toronto*. May 27, 1985.

"Network 2011 — To Think What Could Have Been," *Transit Toronto, www.transittoronto.on.ca* (accessed February 29, 2011).

"Ontario's Transportation Fiasco," *Bus and Truck Transport*, March, 1977.

Polanyi, Margaret, "Rail, TTC expansion part of $5-billion plan to improve rapid transit," *The Globe and Mail*, April 6, 1990.

Quintner, David. "'Wonderful,' said Churchill — and that was 60 years ago," *The Toronto Star*, November 14, 1974.

Small, Peter, "Closing bill on Eglinton $42 million, TTC figures," *The Toronto Star*, August 3, 1995.

Smith, Michael, "Light rail flip-flop saves $300 million GO official says." *The Toronto Star*, June 15, 1985.

Smith, Michael, "New subway on Sheppard gets go-ahead from Metro," *The Toronto Star*, June 25, 1986.

Smith, Michael, "Spadina subway extension okayed," *The Toronto Star*, April 27, 1989.

Snow, James. Announcement of Inter-Regional Rapid Transit Strategy. October 7, 1982.

Snow, James. *Mr. Jim*. Hornby, ON: James W. Snow, 1990.

"Snow says GO line won't be scrapped," *The Toronto Star*, May 15, 1984.

Stead, Sylvia, "Rapid transit to link Hamilton, Oshawa," *The Globe and Mail*, October 8, 1982.

Strasman, Jim. Author interview. February 25, 2011.

Sutherland, D.A. et al. "Ontario's GO-ALRT Program: An overview." September 1984.

Sutton, Robert. "Federal plans led Ontario to drop light rail train," *The Toronto Star*, June 11, 1985.

"Tempers flare over GO rail line in Hamilton," *The Globe and Mail*, March 26, 1984.

Toronto Area Transit Operating Authority, GO Transit annual reports for the years ending March 31, 1983 and March 31, 1986.

Chapter 8: East of Bay Development/Ataratiri

Allen, David. "Bill Davis' leadership is questioned," *The Toronto Star*, April 21, 1973.

Archives of Ontario. C 315-3; RG 29-59; RG 15-2 (East of Bay Development).

Burns, Daniel. *Ataratiri: Second Annual Report to the Ministry of the Environment, August 1989–July 1990*. Toronto: City of Toronto Housing Department: September 28, 1990.

Caplice, Dennis P. and Greer, Tom. *St. Lawrence Square*. (Report to the Premier and Mayor, July, 1988).

Carriere, Vianney, "Government Bay-Yonge complex to be shelved, Davis announces," *The Globe and Mail*, March 30, 1973.

City of Toronto Housing Department. *Ataratiri (formerly St. Lawrence Square)* (Miscellaneous Reports, Vols. 1–3, 1988).

City of Toronto Planning and Development Department. *Ataratiri: Part II Official Plan Proposals*. September 11, 1991.

City of Toronto Property Department et al. *St. Lawrence Square: Stage One — Preliminary Concept and Proposal*. (Joint department head report to city council, July 12, 1988.)

"Davis cancels downtown superblock," *The Toronto Star*, March 30, 1973.

Krawczyk, Bob, TOBuilt (Mowat Block and Hearst Block), *www.tobuilt.ca* (accessed March 26, 2011).

Lewington, Jennifer, "Community set to rise on Don Lands," *The Globe and Mail*, March 28, 2006.

Manthorpe, Jonathan, "Ontario plans huge complex in area east of Queen's Park," *The Globe and Mail*, March 7, 1973.

McInnes, Craig. "Cost of saving urban project looks inviting — on paper," *The Globe and Mail*, March 18, 1992.

McInnes, Craig. "Jakobek still trying to scuttle housing project." *The Globe and Mail*, August 10, 1991.

McInnes, Craig, "Model community threatened by delays, cost hikes," *The Globe and Mail*, July 1, 1991.

Metropolitan Toronto and Region Conservation Authority. *Report on St. Lawrence Square Housing Project*. October, 1988.

"Province plans to cut losses in Ataratiri lands." *Building* 46, No. 1 (February/March 1996).

"Secret Queen's Park plan revealed," *The Toronto Citizen*, November 1, 1972.

Snow, James. *Mr. Jim*. Hornby, ON: James W. Snow, 1990.

Speirs, Rosemary. "Conservatives lose 2 'safe' seats to Liberals," *The Toronto Star*, March 16, 1973.

Speirs, Rosemary, "Queen's Park proposes downtown superblock," *The Toronto Star*, March 7, 1973.

Chapter 9: Yonge-Dundas Square

Alsculer, Karen B. et al. *Dundas Square Design Competition: Report of the Jury*. December 1, 1998.

City of Toronto. *Downtown Yonge Street Regeneration Program, Yonge Dundas Redevelopment Project*. December 1996.

City of Toronto. *Dundas Square Design Competition*. September 1998.

City of Toronto. *Request for Proposals: Yonge Dundas Redevelopment Project, Parcels B and C*. July 15, 1997.

City of Toronto. *Request for Qualifications: Yonge Dundas Redevelopment Project*. February 1997.

"Create improved centre area, civic commission to direct." *The Evening Telegram*, November 27, 1924.

"Dundas Square design competition narrowed to six finalist teams." (City of Toronto press release, October 15, 1998.)

Gillmor, Don, "The Longest Mall," *Toronto Life* 42, No. 2 (February 2008).

Goodfellow, Margaret and Phil Goodfellow. *A Guidebook to Contemporary Architecture in Toronto*. Vancouver: Douglas & McIntyre, 2010.

Gray, Jeff, "Square to open with a flair," *The Globe and Mail*, May 30, 2003.

"Great central public square our next civic improvement?" *The Evening Telegram*, July 27, 1924.

"Great war memorial square featured in new city plan," *The Evening Telegram*, December 22, 1923.

Kuitenbrouwer, Peter, "Problems plague redevelopment at Dundas Square site," *The National Post*, December 4, 2000.

Kuitenbrouwer, Peter, "Trees, but no theatre: PenEquity promised a 24-screen multiplex called Metropolis. What happened?" *The National Post*, September 14, 2002.

Marvin Hertzman Holdings Inc. v. Toronto (City). [1998] O.J. No. 3854 (December 28, 1998) (decision of the Ontario Court of Justice [General Division]).

"Mayor Lastman unveils winning design for Dundas Square." (City of Toronto press release, December 1, 1998.)

"Model shows plans to improve Toronto's streets," *The Evening Telegram*, January 15, 1924.

Munroe, Ian, "Metropolis centre to be unveiled this fall," *The National Post*, April 12, 2007.

Oleson David. Author interviews. May 21 and 27, 2010; August 5, 2010.

Soskolne, Ron. Author interview. August 11, 2010.

Toronto (City) Official Plan Amendment No. 92 (Re). [1998] O.M.B.D. No. 745 (June 5, 1998), (Ontario Municipal Board decision).

Young, Pamela, "Architects devise calm in urban storm," *The Globe and Mail*, January 2, 1999.

Chapter 10: John Howard Public Buildings

City of Toronto Culture. *The Textures of a Lost Toronto: John Howard's Documentary Art & Drawings, 1830s–1880s, www.toronto.ca/culture/howard* (accessed January 9, 2010).

Dendy, William. *Lost Toronto.* Toronto: McClelland & Stewart, 1993.

Firth, Edith G. "Howard, John George." In *Dictionary of Canadian Biography Online, www.biographi.ca* (accessed January 9, 2010).

John George Howard, 1803–1890: A Tribute. Catalogue of an exhibition held at the Market Gallery of the City of Toronto Archives, March 7–May 6, 1979.

Vattay, Sharon. *Defining Architecture in Nineteenth-Century Toronto: The Practices of John George Howard and Thomas Young.* Ph.D. Thesis, University of Toronto, 2001.

Chapter 11: Confederation Life Building

"Confederation Life Association Building Competition — Experts' Report." *The Canadian Architect and Builder* 2, No. 11 (November 1889).

"Confederation Life — Notice to Architects." *The Canadian Architect and Builder* 2, No. 6 (June 1889).

Dendy, William. *Lost Toronto.* Toronto: McClelland & Stewart, 1993.

Editorial. *The Canadian Architect and Builder* 2, No. 2 (February 1889).

Editorial. *The Canadian Architect and Builder* 2, No. 4 (April 1889).

Editorial. *The Canadian Architect and Builder* 2, No. 6 (June 1889).

Editorial. *The Canadian Architect and Builder* 2, No. 12 (December 1889).

"Fourth Premiated Design for the Confederation Life Association Building, Toronto, Ont." *The Canadian Architect and Builder* 3, No. 8 (August 1890).

Gillespie, Bernard. "Toronto Projects Reviewed." *Canadian Architect* 27, No. 4 (April 1982).

Hill, Robert. *Biographical Dictionary of Architects in Canada, 1800–1950.*

www.dictionaryofarchitectsincanada.org (James & James) (accessed January 5, 2011).

Hudson, Edna. *The Romanesque Head Office of Confederation Life Association.* Toronto: Toronto Region Architectural Conservancy, 1997.

McHugh, Patricia. *Toronto Architecture: A City Guide.* Toronto: Mercury Books, 1985.

Otto, Stephen. Author interview. February 19, 2010.

"Second Premiated Design — James and James, Architects, New York." *The Canadian Architect and Builder* 3, No. 3 (March 1890).

"Third Premiated Design for the Confederation Life Association Building, Toronto, Ont." *The Canadian Architect and Builder* 3, No. 6 (June 1890).

"Toronto Board of Trade Competition." *The Canadian Architect and Builder* 2, No. 3 (March, 1889).

Chapter 12: Toronto Hotels

"Again defer action on Pellatt's 'castle,'" *The Toronto Daily Star*, October 22, 1926.

An Act to Amend the Mechanics' Lien Act, Statues of Ontario 1932, Chapter 19.

"Appeal court's judgment paralyzes building here," *The Toronto Daily Star*, December 4, 1931.

Archives of Ontario. RG-432, File #3456 (Donald, Mason & Co., Barristers, Toronto: Re Queen's Park Plaza — Mechanic's Lien Action).

"Battle of the Palace Hotel," *The Evening Star*, July 10, 1899.

"Blame club project in Casa Loma closing," *The Toronto Daily Star*, June 20, 1928.

"Building Queen's Park Plaza," *The Telegram*, March 30, 1928.

"Building restriction is subject of request," *The Toronto Daily Star*, March 30, 1926.

"By the Way." *The Canadian Architect and Builder* 13, No. 1 (January 1900).

"Cannot conduct dance in Casa Loma tonight," *The Toronto Daily Star*, April 16, 1927.

"Casa Loma." *Construction* 18, No. 11 (November 1925).

"Casa Loma again closes its doors," *The Toronto Daily Star*, June 19, 1928.

"Casa Loma again to echo 'How much am I bid?' Cry," *The Toronto Daily Star*, January 17, 1930.

"Casa Loma question comes up to-morrow," *The Toronto Daily Star*, September 14, 1926.

"Casa Loma to get $1,000,000 addition," *The Toronto Daily Star*, January 10, 1928.

"Casa Loma Hotel re-opens August 1st," *The Toronto Daily Star*, June 28, 1929.

"Castle on the hill being transformed," *The Toronto Daily Star*, March 14, 1927.

"The city wins," *The Evening Star*, March 30, 1899.

Contract Record and Engineering Review 41, No. 24 (May 25, 1927).

"A crack at hogtown," *The Toronto Daily Star*, November 12, 1901.

Dendy, William. *Lost Toronto*. Toronto: McClelland & Stewart, 1993.

Dendy, William and William Kilbourn. *Toronto Observed*. Toronto: Oxford University Press, 1986.

"Early arrivals at the King Edward Hotel," *The Toronto Daily Star*, May 11, 1903.

"East to be guarded under sewage pact," *The Toronto Daily Star*, November 16, 1926.

"Famous Pellatt castle, show place of Toronto, to be apartment house," *The Toronto Star Weekly*, November 14, 1925.

"For the Palace Hotel," (letter to the editor), *The Toronto Daily Star*, January 8, 1901.

Hill, Robert (Hugh G. Holman) *Biographical Dictionary of Architects in Canada, 1800–1950*. www.dictionaryofarchitectsincanada.org (accessed November 6, 2010).

"An ideal site," *The Evening Star*, January 19, 1895.

"Ideas upon which no duty is paid," *The Toronto Daily Star*, May 1, 1901.

"Illustrations," *The Canadian Architect and Builder* 11, No. 10 (October 1898).

Inglis v. Queen's Park Plaza Co. Ltd., [1932] Ontario Reports, 110 (Ontario Court of Appeal).

"Large Private Hotel Proposed for Uptown Toronto Corner." *The Contract Record and Engineering Review* 40, No. 51 (December 22, 1926).

Litvak, Marilyn M. *Edward James Lennox: Builder of Toronto*. Toronto: Dundurn Press, 1995.

The London and Western Trust Co., et al. v. Sale, [1937] O.J. No. 109 (Ontario Court of Appeal).

"May run castle on hill as an apartment hotel," *The Toronto Daily Star*, May 3, 1927.

"New hotel rumor denied by CPR," *The Toronto Daily Star*, December 18, 1925.

"New role planned for 'Plaza' building," *The Toronto Daily Star*, January 18, 1935.

"New wing for Casa Loma, finances being arranged," *The Toronto Daily Star*, August 26, 1927.

"No promise yet," *The Evening Star*, July 3, 1896.

"Not pleased with the Palace Hotel," *The Toronto Daily Star*, February 23, 1901.

Oreskovich, Carlie. *Sir Henry Pellatt: The King of Casa Loma*. Toronto: McGraw-Hill Ryerson, 1982.

"Osgoode judgment triples liens filed," *The Toronto Daily Star*, December 18, 1931.

"A palace hotel," *The Evening Star*, January 28, 1898.

"Palace hotel," *The Evening Star*, January 18, 1899.

"Palace hotel in sight at last," *The Toronto Daily Star*, May 14, 1900.

"The Palace Hotel," *The Toronto Daily Star*, July 24, 1900.

"The Palace Hotel," *The Toronto Daily Star*, July 30, 1901.

"Perspective drawing of 'Casa Loma' — new style," *The Toronto Daily Star*, May 1, 1926.

"Plan renewing work on Bloor St. tower," *The Toronto Daily Star*, June 20, 1930.

Plummer, Kevin. "Depression Skyscraper Debacle." *Torontoist*, January 30, 2010. (*http://torontoist.com*).

"Proposed new wing to be built on Casa Loma," *The Toronto Daily Star*, June 3, 1927.

"Proposed Palace Hotel for Toronto," *The Canadian Architect and Builder* 8, No. 6 (June 1895).

"Queen's Hotel sale is being negotiated," *The Toronto Daily Star*, December 18, 1925.

"Queen's Park Plaza," *The Globe*, October 22, 1934.

"Queen's Park Plaza proposal rejected," *The Toronto Daily Star*, March 24, 1931.

Queen's Park Plaza, Canadian Centre for Architecture (prospectuses), M CAN ID 96-A182.

Re Casa Loma, [1927] 4 D.L.R. 645 (Ontario Supreme Court, Appellate Division, September 30, 1927).

"Receiver is appointed for King Edward." *The Financial Post*, December 17, 1932.

"Sale at Auction" (advertisement), *The Toronto Daily Star*, November 15, 1928.

"Spence assails Casa Loma plan as wet paradise," *The Toronto Daily Star*, July 6, 1927.

"Time limit on the new hotel," *The Evening Star*, February 27, 1900.

"To open Casa Loma for public to view," *The Toronto Daily Star*, August 25, 1926.

"'Twould be a place," *The Evening Star*, May 25, 1895.

"United Bond Company faces $129,115 deficit," *The Toronto Daily Star*, December 23, 1930.

Untitled drawing and caption, *The Toronto Daily Star*, June 17, 1927.

"Work on the Palace Hotel," *The Toronto Daily Star*, October 24, 1900.

Chapter 13: Bank of Toronto Head Office/Toronto-Dominion Centre

"A Canadian Architecture?" *Construction* 3, No. 6 (May 1910).

The Bank of Toronto (special reprint of a portion of the *The Bankers Magazine*, November, 1913). New York: Bankers Publishing, 1913.

"The Bank of Toronto, Toronto, Ont." *Construction* 6, No. 9 (September,1913).

Dendy, William. *Lost Toronto*. Toronto: McClelland & Stewart, 1993.

Editorial. *Construction* 3, No. 8 (July 1910).

Editorial. *Construction* 3, No. 10 (September 1910).

Editorial. *Construction* 6, No. 9 (September 1913).

Krinsky, Carol Herselle. *Gordon Bunshaft of Skidmore, Owings and Merrill*. New York and Cambridge: The Architectural History Foundation and The MIT Press, 1988.

Lambert, Phyllis. Author interview. May 14, 2009.

Lambert, Phyllis. "Punching Through the Clouds: Notes on the Place of the Toronto-Dominion Centre in the North American *Oeuvre* of Mies." *The Presence of Mies*. Edited by Detlef Mertens. Princeton: Princeton Architectural Press, 1994.

Lobko, Joe, "Bank's Vaulting Ambition," *The Toronto Star*, May 20, 2004.

McArthur, Glenn. *A Progressive Traditionalist: John M. Lyle, Architect*. Toronto: Coach House Books, 2009.

"New bank to be only 3 storeys," *The Toronto Daily Star*, June 9, 1910.

Stoffman, Daniel. *The Cadillac Fairview Story*. Toronto: The Cadillac Fairview Corporation, 2004.

"Union Station planned for Toronto." *The Canadian Engineer* (June 7, 1907).

"A vigorous plea for Canadian architects," *The Toronto Daily Star*, June 15, 1910.

Chapter 14: Canadian Bank of Commerce Building/Commerce Court

"$50,000,000 addition on King W. planned by Bank of Commerce," *The Toronto Daily Star*, February 20, 1956.

Buck, Derek. "Commerce Court: Restoration on a Grand Scale." *Canadian Interiors* 13, No. 4 (April 1976).

The Canadian Bank of Commerce Annual Reports, 1908–1914, Vol. III. Toronto, 1914.

CIBC Archives. Accession 89.43. Architectural Plans, Drawings and Photographs — Premises Department.

Dendy, William. *Lost Toronto*. Toronto: McClelland & Stewart, 1993.

Dendy, William and William Kilbourn. *Toronto Observed*. Toronto: Oxford University Press, 1986.

Govan, James. "Samuel Herbert Maw" (obituary). *Journal, Royal Architectural Institute of Canada* 29, No. 11 (November 1952).

"The Head Office Building" *The Caduceus, Staff Magazine of The Canadian Bank of Commerce* 6, No. 2 (July 1925).

"Imperial Bank will erect new head office building," *The Toronto Daily Star*, August 24, 1934.

McHugh, Patricia. *Toronto Architecture: A City Guide*. Toronto: Mercury Books, 1985.

"The New Canadian Bank of Commerce Building, Toronto." *Journal, Royal Architectural Institute of Canada* 8, No. 1 (January 1931).

"New Bank of Commerce Head Office," *The Telegram*, January 12, 1928.

"No Trace Found of Legendary Grave." *The News* [CIBC employee newsletter] 2, No. 6 (July/August, 1969).

Otto, Stephen. "A City Reaching for New Heights." *Spacing* (Spring/Summer 2009).

Ross, Victor and Arthur St. L. Trigge. *The History of the Canadian Bank of Commerce*, Vols. 1 and 2. Toronto: The Canadian Bank of Commerce, 1920, 1922.

Smith, Kenneth R. "Bank of Commerce building doomed in redevelopment plan," *The Globe and Mail*, November 23, 1965.

Smith, Kenneth R. "Secrecy shrouding bank high-rise plan," *The Globe and Mail*, April 10, 1968.

Toronto Historical Board. *Heritage Property Report: Canadian Bank of Commerce Building and Commerce Court, 25 King Street West and 199 Bay Street*. Toronto: March 1991.

Trigge, Arthur St. L. *The History of the Canadian Bank of Commerce*, Vol. 3. Toronto: The Canadian Bank of Commerce, 1934.

"Twenty-Five and Still Tops." *Current Account, Personnel Magazine of The Canadian Bank of Commerce* 5, No. 9 (January 1956).

"The Why and Wherefore of the New Head Office Building." *The Caduceus* 11, No. 1. (April 1930).

Wickens, Max. "Stella Vanzant, dead since 1814, could delay bank tower," *The Toronto Star*, August 6, 1968.

Chapter 15: Canadian National Building

"26-storey building local possibility," *The Toronto Daily Star*, January 9, 1925.

"26-storey building recently forecast to cost $5,000,000," *The Toronto Daily Star*, May 23, 1925.

"Begin new skyscraper," *The Toronto Daily Star*, May 26, 1925.

Canada v. Dominion Building Corp., [1928] S.C.R. 65. (Supreme Court of Canada decision).

Canada v. Dominion Building Corp., [1932] S.C.R. 511. (Supreme Court of Canada decision).

Canada v. Dominion Building Corp., [1935] S.C.R. 338. (Supreme Court of Canada decision).

"Canadian National City Ticket Office" (advertisement), *The Toronto Daily Star*, December 9, 1927.

"C.N.R. chief here to interview big shippers," *The Toronto Daily Star*, July 3, 1925.

"C.N.R. renovates King-Yonge place," *The Toronto Daily Star*, June 4, 1927.

"C.N.R. to proceed with skyscraper, King and Yonge," *The Toronto Daily Star*, January 23, 1925.

Dominion Building Corp. v. Canada, [1933] Ex.C.R. 164 (Exchequer Court of Canada decision).

"A dream that won't come true," *The Toronto Daily Star*, February 5, 1927.

"Drop Skyscraper plan for King and Yonge, the C.N.R. to move back," *The Toronto Daily Star*, December 11, 1926.

"Graham has ordered probe into debts of nationals," *The Toronto Daily Star*, September 12, 1925.

"Grant reference to courts after government defeated, Canada now faces big suit," *The Toronto Daily Star*, February 11, 1927.

Greenaway, C.R. "The race of the skyscrapers," *The Toronto Star Weekly*, June 13, 1925.

"Nationals will move office in fortnight," *The Toronto Daily Star*, September 2, 1925.

"New C.N.R. offices will be highest yet," *The Toronto Daily Star*, March 23, 1923.

"Pass order to raze King and Yonge site," *The Toronto Daily Star*, July 31, 1925.

"Predict C.N.R. coming back to King-Yonge," *The Toronto Daily Star*, May 10, 1926.

R. v. Dom. Bldg. Corp., [1933] 3 D.L.R. 577.

"Says C.N.R. reason skyscraper plan was dropped here," *The Toronto Daily Star*, December 13, 1926.

"Senator again makes charge of dishonesty," *The Toronto Daily Star*, September 14, 1925.

"Skyscraper projected for King-Yonge canyon," *The Toronto Daily Star*, May 20, 1927.

"The two party leaders and the railway problem," *The Toronto Daily Star*, September 11, 1925.

"Ticket office of C.N.R. now at King and Toronto," *The Toronto Daily Star*, September 21, 1925.

"T.L. Church and the new skyscraper," *The Toronto Daily Star*, June 27, 1925.

"To start demolishing C.N.R. building soon," *The Toronto Daily Star*, January 9, 1925.

"Will continue plans for new skyscraper," *The Toronto Daily Star*, November 6, 1925.

Chapter 16: Toronto's New Skyline

"18-storey Toronto building entirely refaced," *The Contract Record and Engineering Review* 44, No. 49 (December 3, 1980).

"The Atlas Building, Toronto." *The Contract Record and Engineering Review* 42, No. 27 (July 4, 1928).

Boothman, Barry E.C. "High Finance/Low Strategy: Corporate Collapse in the Canadian Pulp and Paper Industry, 1919–1932." *The Business History Review* 74, No. 4 (Winter 2000).

"City gets Dominion Bldg., What about us? — tenants," *The Toronto Daily Star*, February 21, 1946.

"C.P.R. Building sheds terra cotta coating," *The Toronto Daily Star*, August 23, 1929.

Dendy, William and William Kilbourn. *Toronto Observed*. Toronto: Oxford University Press, 1986.

Filey, Mike. *Toronto Sketches*. Toronto: Dundurn Press, 2003.

"Holt Gundy buys King St. properties," *The Toronto Daily Star*, October 21, 1927.

"Holt Gundy will replace Union Bank," *The Telegram*, December 31, 1927.

Hudson, Edna. *The Romanesque Head Office of Confederation*

Life Association. Toronto: Toronto Region Architectural Conservancy, 1997.

"Imperial Bank will erect new head office building," *The Toronto Daily Star*, August 24, 1934.

"King and Bay building plan for 28 floors," *The Toronto Daily Star*, November 23, 1927.

"King-Bay skyscraper project is abandoned, ground sold to bank," *The Toronto Daily Star*, January 25, 1928.

"King Edward Sale," *The Financial Post*, April 6, 1918.

Krawczyk, Bob. "T.O. Built," *www.tobuilt.ca* (accessed February 27, 2010).

Litvak, Marilyn M. *Edward James Lennox: Builder of Toronto*. Toronto: Dundurn Press, 1995.

McHugh, Patricia. *Toronto Architecture: A City Guide*. Toronto: Mercury Books, 1985.

"Metropolitan Building" (advertisement), *The Toronto Daily Star*, April 20, 1925.

"The Metropolitan Building, Toronto." *Construction* 18, No. 7 (July 1925).

Morawetz, Tim. *Art Deco Architecture in Toronto*. Toronto: Glue, Inc., 2009.

"Nathanson buys King-York corner," *The Toronto Daily Star*, November 29, 1927.

"New C.P.R. hotel not chateau style," *The Toronto Daily Star*, May 20, 1927.

"New Ford Hotel opens January 19," The Montreal *Gazette*, January 13, 1930.

"New office building for Bay Street," *The Toronto Daily Star*, February 18, 1927.

Osbaldeston, Mark. *Unbuilt Toronto: The City That Might Have Been*. Toronto: Dundurn Press, 2008.

"Ready to start right away on hotel annex." *The Toronto Daily Star*, August 31, 1912.

"Revised plan of new 'Commerce and Transportation' building." *The Toronto Daily Star*, June 3, 1927.

"Richard Ford building chain of Ford Hotels," *Hotel Monthly* 35, No. 410 (May 1927).

"'The Royal York,' Toronto." *The Contract Record and Engineering Review* 41, No. 27 (July 13, 1927).

"Skyscraper plans are growing apace," *The Toronto Daily Star*, December 1, 1927.

"A survey of Canadian construction." *Contract Record and Engineering Review* 43, No. 2 (January 9, 1929).

"Three new issues," *The Toronto Daily Star*, August 6, 1924.

"Toronto's down-town area is it will be when projected developments are completed," *The Telegram*, January 16, 1928.

Untitled, *Toronto Telegram*, February 9, 1927 (illustration of Atlas Building, with caption).

Chapter 17: Simpson Tower/North American Life Building

"1871 — Simpson's from Coast to Coast — 1928" (advertisement). In *Toronto Year Book, 1928*. Toronto: Municipal Information Bureau, 1928.

Burton, C.L. *A Sense of Urgency: Memoirs of a Canadian Merchant*. Toronto: Clarke, Irwin and Company Ltd., 1952.

Burton, G. Allan. *A Store of Memories*. Toronto: McClelland & Stewart, 1986.

Carr, Angela. *Toronto Architect Edmund Burke*. Montreal: McGill-Queen's University Press, 1995.

Dennison, Merrill. *This Is Simpson's*. Toronto: Simpson's, 1947.

"Huge Department Store Project in Toronto." *Contract Record and Engineering Review* 42, No. 16 (April 18, 1928).

"New Simpson tower to soar 400 feet up," *The Toronto Daily Star*, October 9, 1964.

"New North American Life Building," *The Evening Telegram*, September 27, 1932.

"North American Life Building," *Contract Record and Engineering Review* 46, No. 42 (October 19, 1932).

"North American Life moves to new building," *The Evening Telegram*, September 27, 1932.

"Plans of first unit, N.A. Life are now complete," *The Evening Telegram*, August 18, 1931.

Plummer, Kevin. "North American Edifice Complex." *Torontoist*, February 10, 2010 (*http://torontoist.com*).

"Progress on North American Life Building." *Contract Record and Engineering Review* 46, No. 28 (July 13, 1932).

"Proposed home of the North American Life," *The Evening Telegram*, August 11, 1931.

Robert Simpson Co. buys Queen St. West property," *The Toronto Daily Star*, June 19, 1936.

Schaffer, Kristen. *Daniel H. Burnham: Visionary Architect and Planner*. New York: Rizzoli, 2003.

"Simpson Co. plans arcade along front of building," *The Toronto Daily Star*, March 22, 1929.

"Simpson's salutes the new Toronto city hall" (advertisement), *The Toronto Daily Star*, September 11, 1965.

"Start work on new Bay block," *The Evening Telegram*, July 26, 1929.

Vining, Charles, "Simpson's great new store joins Bay Street to Yonge," *The Toronto Daily Star*, April 11, 1928.

Chapter 18: Bank of Montreal Building

"15-storey bank building to arise at Bay and King," *The Toronto Daily Star*, December 5, 1938.

"Bank building steel coming, lane closed," *The Toronto Daily Star*, August 8, 1939.

Bank of Montreal Archives. 2002-316 ai/di. Folder 51, BMO Toronto, New Building, Sequence of Important Events, 1936–1948; 2004-368; Various Internal Memoranda, ID 2448, Acc. No. 2004-368.

"Bank of Montreal Building." *Journal, Royal Architectural Institute of Canada* 26, No. 3 (March 1946).

"Building in August reached $1,027, 635," *The Toronto Daily Star*, September 5, 1939.

"Finish skyscraper plan for $3,000,000 bank tower," *The Toronto Daily Star*, February 21, 1930.

"Lost for half a century, sculpture found in garden," *The Toronto Daily Star*, June 19, 1939.

McKelvey, Margaret E. and Merilyn McKelvey. *Toronto: Carved in Stone*. Toronto: Fitzhenry and Whiteside, 1984.

Morris, R. Schofield. "Bank of Montreal Building, Toronto." *Royal Architectural Institute of Canada Journal* 26, No. 11 (November 1949).

"New bank building started, ready for tenants in year," *The Toronto Daily Star*, July 17, 1939.

"New Bk. of Montreal opens, most-up-to-date in Canada," *The Toronto Daily Star*, September 1, 1949.

"Old Mail building now all but gone," *The Toronto Daily Star*, April 6, 1939.

"The return to an old stall," *The Monetary Times*, July 30, 1938.

"Vault walls would halt smartest of burglars," *The Toronto Daily Star*, September 1, 1939.

Chapter 19: Wittington Place/Sapphire Tower

Appleby, Timothy, "Court orders sale of Stinson site." *The Globe and Mail*, August 18, 2007.

Berridge, Joe. Author interview. September 7, 2010.

Best, Michael, "Mammoth $750 million development planned for Yonge-Highway 401 site," *The Toronto Star*, April 9, 1987.

Best, Michael, "Weston project 'world-class' Lastman says," *The Toronto Star*, April 10, 1987.

Canadian Centre for Architecture. Wittington Place Competition Fonds, 1989.

City of Toronto Archives. Fonds 282, Series 1336, File 480.

City of Toronto. Report 9, Clause 13, considered by City Council on December 5, 6, and 7, 2005 (Official Plan Amendment and Rezoning Application – 56-66 Temperance Street).

Dunnell, Milt. "Lastman's dream: North York Maple Leafs." *The Toronto Star*, January 7, 1989.

Goddard, John, "The Harry vs. The Donald in downtown high-rise rivalry," *The Toronto Star*, April 17, 2004.

Goddard, John, "One King reaches new heights. Developer has plans to trump Trump." *The Toronto Star*, March 27, 2004.

Hill, Robert. "The Westnor Collection: A Summary." (Report prepared for the Canadian Centre for Architecture, September, 2002.)

Josey, Stan, "Big projects bring boom mayor says," *The Toronto Star*, January 16, 1992.

Kidd, Kenneth, "Trumping the Donald," *The Toronto Star*, March 13, 2005.

Krivel, Peter, "Improvements to the 401 proposed by developers," *The Toronto Star*, July 14, 1994.

Lewington, Jennifer, "Sapphire Tower rejected, shorter buildings approved," *The Globe and Mail*, November 16, 2005.

Mays, John Bentley, "Spirit of ingenuity in the sky," *The Globe and Mail*, January 7, 2005.

Mays, John Bentley, "Will Temperance Street finally get its jewel?" *The Globe and Mail*, February 16, 2007.

McGill University Archives. Moshe Safdie Fonds.

Nickle, David, "Committee goes ahead with plans for interchange," *The North York Mirror*, July 3, 1994.

Nickle, David, "NY could see $30 million upgrade," *The North York Mirror*, June 18–19, 1994.

Nickle, David, "Official plan amendment requested with proposal of multi-use complex," *The North York Mirror*, January 19, 1992.

Nickle, David, "Westnor must scale down plans for Yonge/401 area," *The North York Mirror*, July 1–2, 1995.

"Shiny blue cylinders make Sapphire Tower," *The Toronto Star*, December 4, 2004.

Small, Peter, "North York to review downtown project," *The Toronto Star*, July 6, 1995.

Soskolne, Ron. Author interview. January 8, 2011.

Starkman, Randy, "Donohue's courting NBA franchises," *The Toronto Star*, January 18, 1989.

Stein, David Lewis, "Sewers may back up on North York's dreams," *The Toronto Star*, March 22, 1989.

Tossell, Ivor, "High-rise angst: Is Stinson's tower next?" *The Globe and Mail*, November 12, 2005.

Turner, Peter. Author interviews. April 2010 and March 2011.

Wells, Jennifer. "Stinson's tower of big dreams tumbling down," *The Toronto Star*, August 10, 2007.

Westnor Ltd. v. North York (City). 1 M.P.L.R. (3d) 131 (Ontario Municipal Board decision dated September 29, 1997).

"Wittington project gets green light," *The Globe and Mail*, October 1, 1997.

Chapter 20: John Maryon Tower

"140-storey offices plan for College St.," *The Toronto Daily Star*, October 16, 1971.

"Eaton's has not approved 140-storey Yonge tower," *The Toronto Daily Star*, October 19, 1971.

Purdie, James, "World's tallest building proposed for Eaton's College St. store site," *The Globe and Mail*, October 16, 1971.

"Tallest of 'em all," *The Evening Telegram*, October 21, 1971.

"Will Toronto enter 'world's tallest' sweepstake?" *Canadian Building* 21, No. 12 (December 1971).

"World's highest building planned," *The Evening Telegram*, October 18, 1971.

Chapter 21: Toronto Reference Library

"2-year freeze called senseless." *The Toronto Star*, September 17, 1973.

"45-ft. law used by city to curb size of library." *The Toronto Star*, December 20, 1973.

"Andrew Carnegie is bubbling with cheer." *The Toronto Daily Star*, April 27, 1906.

Beckman, Margaret, et al. *The Best Gift: A Record of the Carnegie Libraries in Ontario*. Toronto: Dundurn Press, 1984.

"Board votes new study of $30 million library," *The Toronto Star*, January 4, 1974.

Bruce, Lorne. *Free Books for All: The Public Library Movement in Ontario, 1850–1930*. Toronto: Dundurn Press, 1994.

Cassels, W.G. Report to Metropolitan Executive Committee Re. Proposed Metropolitan Toronto Library, 1973.

Caufield, Jon. *The Tiny Perfect Mayor*. Toronto: James Lorimer and Co., 1974.

City of Toronto By-laws No. 348-73 and No. 114-74.

City of Toronto (Planning Board). Metro Central Library. Application to Committee on Buildings and Development for Re-zoning and Request for Exemption from By-law 348-73. April 11, 1974.

City of Toronto (Planning Board). *Progress Report to City of Toronto Executive Committee Re. Metropolitan Central Library*. April 1, 1974.

"Competition for the Public Library Building at Toronto." *The Canadian Architect and Builder* 18, No. 215 (November 1905).

Dendy, William and William Kilbourn. *Toronto Observed*. Toronto: Oxford University Press, 1986.

Filey, Mike. *Toronto Sketches 9*. Toronto: Dundurn Press, 2006.

"Laird of Skibo visits Toronto," *The Globe*, April 28, 1906.

"Lawyer quits board in $30-million library fight," *The Toronto Star*, December 11, 1973.

"Library architects," *The Toronto Daily Star*, May 12, 1906.

"The library plans," *The Toronto Daily Star*, April 6, 1906.

Lind, Loren, "Redesigned reference library wins approval of city council," *The Globe and Mail*, April 18, 1974.

"A long wrangle over library site," *The Globe*, November 25, 1906.

MacGray, Ken, "Architects irked that aldermen dare to criticize," *The Toronto Star*, January 8, 1974.

McHugh, Patricia. *Toronto Architecture: A City Guide*. Toronto: Mercury Books, 1985.

"Metro Council approves plan for new library," *The Toronto Star*, December 12, 1973.

Moriyama, Raymond, et al. *Metropolitan Toronto Central Library Programme and Site Selection Study*. (Report prepared for the Metropolitan Toronto Library Board, 1971.)

"New library plan could be scrapped," *The Toronto Star*, March 5, 1974.

"The new public library," *The Globe*, May 14, 1906.

"Our illustrations." *The Canadian Architect and Builder* 19, No. 6 (June 1906).

Penman, Margaret. *A Century of Service: Toronto Public Library, 1883–1983*. Toronto: Toronto Public Library Board, 1983.

"Plans not right yet," *The Toronto Daily Star*, April 20, 1906.

Plummer, Kevin, "Historicist: Andrew Carnegie's Toronto Legacy," *Torontoist*, October 25, 2008 (*http://torontoist.com*).

"Public library plans," *The Globe*, April 24, 1906.

Sewell, John, "New library plans need a trip back to drawing board," *The Globe and Mail*, December 3, 1973.

Stoffman, Daniel, "Metro executive wants $30 million library plan scaled down," *The Toronto Star*, November 20, 1973.

Stoffman, Daniel, "New library's $30 million price means a fight," *The Toronto Star*, December 10, 1973.

Stoffman, Daniel, "$30 million library to let you 'sit under a tree and read,'" *The Toronto Star*, November 20, 1973.

Toronto Library Board Minutes, January 27, 1903–May 17, 1906.

Toronto Library Board. Programme of a Competition for the Selection of an Architect for the Public Reference Library Building in the City of Toronto. Toronto, 1905.

Toronto Public Library. "Toronto's Carnegie Libraries." *www. torontopubliclibrary.ca* (accessed February 22, 2010).

"Will build new library," *The Globe*, May 12, 1906.

Chapter 22: Royal Ontario Museum/Art Gallery of Ontario

An Act respecting The Art Gallery of Toronto. S.O. 1966, Chap. 8.

An Act respecting The Art Museum of Toronto. S.O. 1903, Chap. 129.

An Act respecting the City of Toronto. S.O. 1911, Chap. 119.

Art Gallery of Ontario. *Art Gallery of Ontario: Selected Works*. Toronto: Art Gallery of Ontario, 1990.

Art Gallery of Ontario. *Stage Three: Architectural Proposals by Competition Finalists*. Toronto: Art Gallery of Ontario, 1987.

Browne, Kelvin. *Bold Visions: The Architecture of the Royal Ontario Museum*. Toronto: Royal Ontario Museum, 2008.

"C/A Cost Dossier: Metro Toronto Police Station No. 52." *The Canadian Architect* 22, No. 9 (September 1977).

Carr, Angela. "Architecture of Art Galleries in Canada." In *The Canadian Encyclopedia*. *www.thecanadianencyclopedia.com* (accessed December 10, 2010).

Currelly, Charles Trick. *I Brought the Ages Home*. Toronto: The Ryerson Press, 1956.

Dendy, William and William Kilbourn. *Toronto Observed*. Toronto: Oxford University Press, 1986.

Dickson, Lovat. *The Museum Makers*. Toronto: Royal Ontario Museum, 1986.

Kimmel, David. "Toronto Gets a Gallery: The Origins and Development of the City's Permanent Public Art Museum." *Ontario History* 84, No. 3 (September 1992).

Kimmel, David. "Walker, Sir Byron Edmund." In *Dictionary of Canadian Biography Online*, *www.biographi.ca* (accessed December 17, 2010).

Knelman, Martin. "The Architectural Ballad of Barton Myers," *The Toronto Star*, May 4, 2008.

"Large Structure of Unusual Architectural Distinction for Royal Ontario Museum." *The Contract Record and Engineering Review* 46, No. 26 (June 29, 1932).

Oxley, Loren A. "Retrospect — The first 75 Years." *Rotunda* 15, No. 2 (Summer 1982).

Reid Dennis. "A Century of Building the Art Gallery of Ontario." *Frank Gehry: Toronto*. Edited by Dennis Reid. Toronto: Art Gallery of Ontario, 2006.

Richards, Larry. "Reframing the AGO." *Canadian Architect* 32, No. 4 (April 1987).

Teather, Lynne J. *The Royal Ontario Museum: A Prehistory, 1830–1914*. Toronto: Canada University Press, 2005.

"Toronto Art Gallery." *Construction* 19, No. 4 (April 1926).

Walker, Harold C. et al. "Fifty Years and the Future." *Journal, Royal Architectural Institute of Canada* 27, No. 1 (June,1950).

Chapter 23: Trinity College/Innis College

"Announce plans for new college," *The Varsity*, January 29, 1964.

"Award '69." *Canadian Architect*.

Brown, Craig. *History of the Faculty of Arts and Science* (working title — unpublished manuscript).

Burns, John. "Province balks at cost of Innis College plans," *The Globe and Mail*, February 21, 1968.

"College for 900 students to open next fall," *The Globe and Mail*, January 28, 1964.

Dendy, William. *Lost Toronto*. Toronto: McClelland & Stewart, 1993.

Friedland, Martin L. *The University of Toronto: A History*. Toronto: University of Toronto Press, 2002.

"Friends and neighbours welcome Innis to its new home," *U of T Bulletin*, October 19, 1973.

"Innis asks limit of 800 students," *U of T Staff Bulletin*, October 15, 1970.

"Innis College may fold," *The Toronto Daily Star*, July 18, 1968.

"Innis College plan costly, province won't finance it," *The Toronto Daily Star*, February 20, 1968.

Massey, Hart. *Innis College: Architectural Feasibility Study*. Ottawa: Hart Massey Architect, 1966.

Owen, Graham W. "Projects for Trinity College, Toronto." *The Journal of Canadian Art History* 4, No. 1 (Spring 1977).

"Plan buildings for Innis College," *The Globe and Mail*, June 6, 1972.

Reed, T.A., ed. *A History of the University of Trinity College.* Toronto: University of Toronto Press, 1952.

Richards, Larry Wayne. *University of Toronto: The Campus Guide.* New York: Princeton Architectural Press, 2009.

Ryerson University Archives and Special Collections, RG 204-3, 204-6, 204-7, 204-19 (Campus Planning Department).

"Seven years later, Innis to get 22-story tower," *The Globe and Mail*, September 10, 1966.

Thompson, David, "How to learn economics in a rowboat," *The Toronto Daily Star*, August 24, 1964.

Trinity College. *Trinity College, Queen's Park Toronto* (undated fundraising booklet, *circa* 1920).

University of Toronto Archives. A1970-0016 (Innis College plans).

Vallee, Brian, "College opens new building — on a shoestring," *The Toronto Daily Star*, January 10, 1976.

Chapter 24: Palace Pier/Metronome

"3 a.m. crowd watches it burn." *The Toronto Daily Star*, January 7, 1963.

Adams, James. "Metronome could get public funds: hopes raised for proposed music museum, concert hall on old Canadian Malting site," *The Globe and Mail*, April 26, 2002.

Adams, James, "Metronome seeking funds, even though lease lapsed," *The Globe and Mail*, April 26, 2002.

Aulakh, Raveena, "History museum won't have home at water's edge," *The Toronto Star*, September 2, 2009.

Bragg, Rebecca, "Waterfront music complex gets backing of task force," *The Toronto Star*, July 20, 1999.City of Toronto. Clause embodied in Report No. 7 of the Economic Development and Parks Committee, as adopted by Council of the City of Toronto at its Special Meeting held on July 30, 31 and August 1, 2002.

"Determined to proceed with amusement pier," *The Toronto Daily Star*, May 8, 1927.

"Dominion Palace may be finished by end of June," *The Financial Post*, February 12, 1931.

Filey, Mike, "Glory days of the Palace Pier," *The Toronto Sun*, January 20, 2002.

Filey, Mike. *I Remember Sunnyside* (revised edition). Toronto: Dundurn Press, 1996.

Filey, Mike, "On the Sunnyside," *The Toronto Sun*, January 6, 2006.

"Fire may have beat wreckers to one-time roller rink," *The Globe and Mail*, January 8, 1963.

"Harbor Board approves new Sunnyside pier," *The Toronto Daily Star*, July 5, 1927.

Harris, John. Author interviews (June 16, 2010; January 6, 2011).

Hill, Robert (Craig, James Henry). *Biographical Dictionary of Architects in Canada, 1800–1950,* www.dictionaryofarchitectsincanada.org.

Maloney, Paul, "Hush! Empty silos may become a big tomb," *The Toronto Star*, November 13, 1996.

"May foreclose on Palace Pier," *The Financial Post*, June 5, 1937.

Mays, John Bentley, "History could fill an old silo with new life, *The Globe and Mail*, August 21, 1993.

McNamara, Helen, "When the big bands played the Palace Pier," *The Telegram*, January 8, 1963.

"Metronome" (special section), *The National Post*, November 18, 2000.

Metronome Canada Inc. corporate files: various documents, including lease with City of Toronto dated March 30, 1999, response to 1993 request for expressions of interest and response to 1996 request for proposals.

Mills, Carys, "City looks to develop former Canada Malting site," *The Globe and Mail*, September 15, 2010.

"Palace Pier." In *The Toronto Year Book, 1931.* Toronto: The Municipal Intelligence Bureau, 1931.

"Palace Pier jinxed from its start," *The Toronto Daily Star*, January 7, 1963.

"Pier for Toronto amusement area." *Contract Record and Engineering Review* 41, No. 27 (July 13, 1927).

Toronto Harbour Commissioners. *Toronto Waterfront Development 1912–1920.* Toronto: Toronto Harbour Commissioners, 1912.

Chapter 25: Spadina Gardens/Union Station Arena

"An open letter to the citizens of Toronto," (Full-page ad, Maple Leaf Gardens, Limited) *The Toronto Star*, July 14, 1997.

"Approve removal of bars to arena," *The Mail and Empire*, February 18, 1931.

Archives of Ontario. F229-282. Maple Leaf Gardens Arena: General Matters; Mortgage; Plans and Blueprints, Draft agreements, etc.

"Arena is authorized but time limit set," *The Toronto Daily Star*, February 27, 1931.

"Arena planned for old Knox College Site," *The Toronto Daily Star*, January 9, 1931.

Brazao, Dale, "Leafs turn up heat," *The Toronto Star*, April 18, 1997.

Brazao, Dale and Donovan Vincent, "A tale of two arenas has the city in a spin," *The Toronto Star*, April 17, 1997.

Christine, James and Robert MacLeod. "Raptors flee Eaton Centre," *The Globe and Mail*, October 12, 1994.

DeMara, Bruce et al. "Leafs' arena put on a fast track," *The Toronto Star*, April 30, 1997.

DeMara, Bruce and Paul Moloney, "Arena deal is dead," *The Toronto Star*, June 25, 1997.

DeMara, Bruce, "Leafs' Arena plan dead," *The Toronto Star*, July 19, 1997.

DeMara, Bruce. "Leafs' rink for Ex okayed." *The Toronto Star*, December 11, 1997.

DeMara, Bruce and Paul Moloney, "Maple Leaf station deal now in peril," *The Toronto Star*, June 20, 1997.

"Gardens' expansion facing long delay," *The Toronto Daily Star*, May 16, 1963.

Hornby, Lance. *The Story of Maple Leaf Gardens*. Champaign, IL: Sports Pub. Inc., 1998.

Hume, Christopher, "Time not on new arena's side," *The Toronto Star*, February 13, 1998.

Israelson, David, "A fast guide to takeover," *The Toronto Daily Star*, April 23, 1997.

Israelson, David, "Gardens director looming large," *The Toronto Star*, April 23, 1997.

Israelson, David, "Leafs' study of rail lands so much hot air," *The Toronto Star*, April 17, 1997.

Israelson, David, "Leafs vs. Raptors: It's a battle of words," *The Toronto Star*, April 19, 1997.

Kilgour, David. *Maple Leaf Gardens: Memories and Dreams, 1931–1999*. Toronto: Maple Leaf Sports and Entertainment Ltd., 1999.

"Maple Leaf Gardens would build extension over two sidewalks," *The Globe and Mail*, May 16, 1963.

"Maple Leaf Gardens, Limited," (advertisement) *The Toronto Daily Star*, March 5, 1931.

Maple Leaf Gardens, Limited. *A Sports & Entertainment Centre at Union Station*. Toronto: June 18, 1997.

"Maple Leaf hockey club not interested in Knox site," *The Toronto Daily Star*, January 9, 1931.

Moloney, Paul, "Historical board rejects Union Station rink entrance," *The Toronto Star*, May 19, 1997.

Moloney, Paul, "Leafs' arena site puts councillors into top gear," *The Toronto Star*, April 29, 1997.

Moloney, Paul, "Soaring costs for new arena worry the Leafs," *The Toronto Star*, June 14, 1997.

Moloney, Paul, "Union Station sale needs federal okay," *The Toronto Star*, May 30, 1997.

Moloney, Paul and Bruce DeMara, "Price of arena will cripple us Leafs say," *The Toronto Star*, June 21, 1997.

Moloney, Paul et al., "Last-ditch bid to revive arena deal." *The Toronto Star*, June 26, 1997.

"New $1,500,000 arena seats 20,000 patrons," *The Toronto Daily Star*, February 24, 1931.

"New $1,500,000 arena to be built on site of old Knox College," *The Globe*, January 9, 1931.

Obodiac, Stan. *Maple Leaf Gardens: Fifty Years of History*. Toronto: Van Nostrand Reinhold Ltd., 1981.

Ormsby, Mary, "Raptors speed up arena work," *The Toronto Star*, May 3, 1997.

"Plan $1,500,000 sports arena on old Knox College site," *The Mail and Empire*, January 9, 1931.

"Report favourably on 'Spadina' Arena," *The Toronto Daily Star*, February 26, 1931.

"Smythe asks speed in granting permit for hockey arena," *The Globe*, February 13, 1931.

Smythe, Thomas Stafford with Kevin Shea. *Centre Ice*. Bolton, ON: Fenn Publishing, 2000.

"Sponsors of arena ask for exemptions," *The Mail and Empire*. February 13, 1931.

Swainson, Gail, "Ex is it, Stavro promises," *The Toronto Daily Star*, December 2, 1997.

"Votes for Catholic women and police board changes pass council; arena is killed," *The Globe*, March 10, 1931.

Chapter 26: Canadian Broadcasting Centre

"Aid likely for Metro redevelopment," *The Globe and Mail*, December 20, 1968.

Adams, James, "Dismantling a cultural landmark," *The Globe and Mail*, July 17, 2002.

Best, Michael, "These are the contestants … this is the prize … in the CBC sweepstakes," *The Toronto Daily Star*, February 3, 1964.

Borough of North York. *Canadian Broadcasting Corporation and the Borough of North York*. 1968.

Bragg, William, "Scarborough has 'great hope' for CBC centre, controller says," *The Toronto Star*, October 25, 1985.

Bregman and Hamann. *Bregman and Hamann — Spaces For People.* 1980.

Brown, Louise, "'Desperate' CBC pushes for a home," *The Toronto Star*, November 8, 1987.

Canada (Dominion Bureau of Statistics). *Canada 1945: The Official Handbook of Present Conditions and Recent Progress.* Ottawa: Dominion Bureau of Statistics, 1945.

Canadian Broadcasting Corporation. Annual Reports, 1939–1940. Ottawa: King's Printer, 1940.

Canadian Broadcasting Corporation. *The Broadcast Centre Development Pre-Qualification Call*, March 4, 1985.

Canadian Broadcasting Corporation. *Canadian Broadcasting Corporation: A Brief History.* Ottawa: CBC Public Relations, 1976.

Canadian Broadcasting Corporation. *The Toronto Broadcast Centre.* Toronto, 197–.

"CBC abandons option on land in Don Mills," *The Enterprise*, September 4, 1958.

"CBC buys Jarvis Street site for headquarters in Toronto," *The Globe and Mail*, December 2, 1944.

"CBC centre proposed in Front St. complex," *The Toronto Daily Star*, September 13, 1967.

"CBC plan to build office-studios here," The Montreal *Gazette*, January 9, 1939.

"CBC shelves plans to better main facilities," *The Financial Post*, November 4, 1939.

City of Scarborough. *City of Scarborough Broadcast Centre Proposal.* 1985.

"Controllers will ask Judy to save $50 million CBC centre for city," *The Toronto Daily Star*, June 23, 1967.

Corelli, Adam. "'We interrupt this programming …' If its new Broadcast Centre is such a bargain, why won't the CBC discuss the numbers?" *Saturday Night* (September 1994).

Corriveau, Jeanne, "Réinventer le 'Faubourg à m'lasse," *Le Devoir*, December 13, 2008.

Emmerson, Jim, "Just one hurdle left to clear for CBC centre," *The Toronto Star*, June 14, 1986.

Ferguson, Jock, "Architects upset over use of U.S. firm," *The Globe and Mail*, July 29, 1987.

Filey Mike. *Toronto Sketches 7.* Toronto: Dundurn Press, 2003.

"Front St. railyard suggested for CBC," *The Telegram*, June 24, 1967.

Fulford, Robert. *Accidental City.* Toronto: Macfarlane Walter & Ross, 1995.

Hoy, Claire, "Metro Centre will start soon — or so officials say," *The Toronto Daily Star*, December, 19, 1970.

"Ici la maison de Radio-Canada," *www.archives.radio-canada.ca/arts_culture/medias/dossiers/1069/* (accessed April 1, 2011).

Lasker, David, "Broadcasting a new style," *The Globe and Mail*, September 10, 1992.

Lasker, David, "Form and content, Broadcast centre bares its bones," *The Globe and Mail*, October 31, 1991.

Miller, David, "CBC plans to build $150 million HQ near Massey Hall," *The Toronto Star*, December 5, 1977.

Miller, Jack, "CBC's eyesore of a centre becomes a site for sore eyes," *The Toronto Star*, July 20, 1985.

"Mr. Erickson's pout" (editorial), *The Globe and Mail*, June 30, 1987.

"The Ontario Region: An Overview." In *Introducing CBC's 50th Anniversary, A Resource Kit.* Toronto: Canadian Broadcasting Corporation,1986.

Osbaldeston, Mark. *Unbuilt Toronto: A History of the City That Might Have Been.* Toronto: Dundurn Press, 2008.

"Plans are studied by CBC for studios in Toronto," *The Globe and Mail*, January 9, 1939.

"Promise Toronto CBC plum if the price is right," *The Toronto Daily Star*, February 6, 1964.

Royal Commission on Broadcasting, *Report.* Ottawa: The Queen's Printer, 1957.

"Radio Building is Bought by Commission." *Daily Commercial News and Building Record* XVI, No. 62 (March 29, 1939).

Sears, Val, "Super HQ planned," *The Toronto Star*, July 16, 1981.

Shields, Roy, "$50-million 'CBC city' goes to Don Mills," *The Toronto Daily Star*, June 22, 1964.

Shields, Roy, "Who said what over the CBC move," *The Toronto Daily Star*, June 23, 1964.

[untitled] *The Toronto Star*, March 27, 1972 (front page).

Chapter 27: Olympic Proposals

Byers, Jim. "CN squeezing city on huge project councillors say," *The Toronto Star*, August 22, 1989.

Byers, Jim, "Games housing set for approval," *The Toronto Star*, September 21, 1989.

Byers, Jim, "Going for gold! Metro approves Toronto's bid for Olympics," *The Toronto Star*, August 10, 1989.

Byers, Jim, "Olympic Spirit set to close; Downtown attraction poorly attended, needs millions to stay open CEO says," *The Toronto Star*, July 20, 2006.

Byers, Jim and Bruce De Mara, "Games plan," *The Toronto Star*, November 10, 1999.

Canadian Olympic Association. *Toronto's Proposal to Host the Games of the XXVIth Olympiad*. January, 1990.

Christie, James, "Games' legacy: state-of-the-art venues," *The Globe and Mail*, September 7, 1990.

Christie, James, "Toronto nears starting gate for Olympic bid," *The Globe and Mail*, June 26, 2000.

City of Toronto By-law No. 1997-0614.

City of Toronto Housing Department and Jerome Markson Architects. *Bathurst-Spadina/St. Lawrence: A Discussion of the Comparison of Neighbourhood Density*. September, 1990.

City of Toronto Planning and Development Department. *The Railway Lands Review: Proposals*. March, 1991.

Infantry, Ashante, "Cromibe carries torch for Olympics in Toronto," *The Toronto Star*, February 24, 1998.

Filey, Mike. *Like No Other in the World*. Toronto: Sun Controlled Ventures, 1989.

Filey, Mike. *Toronto Sketches 7*. Toronto: Dundurn Press, 2003.

Glover, Robert. "The Railway Lands." *East/West: A Guide to Where People Live in Downtown Toronto*. Edited by Nancy Byrtus et al. Toronto: Coach House Books, 2000.

Fung, Robert A. et. al. *Our Toronto Waterfront: Gateway to the New Canada*. Toronto: Toronto Waterfront Revitalization Task Force, 2000.

"Games would mean new homes, official says," *The Toronto Star*, March 23, 1990.

Hunt, Jim, "Putting note of realism into Olympic dream," *The Toronto Daily Star*, January 20, 1954.

Kidd, Bruce, "The Toronto Olympic Commitment: Towards a Social Contract for the Olympic Games." *Olympika: The International Journal of Olympic Studies* 1 (1992).

"Lamport would go to Greece for Olympics," *The Toronto Daily Star*, March 11, 1954.

Municipality of Metropolitan Toronto. *An Invitation to Stage the Games of the XXIst Olympiad in Metropolitan Toronto*. 1968.

Pigg, Susan, "A stylish Olympic 'bid book,'" *The Toronto Star*, January 19, 1990.

Pigg, Susan, "Will Olympics dash last hopes of reformers?" *The Toronto Star*, April 4, 1990.

"Planned pool complex 'boost to Games bid,'" *The Globe and Mail*, November 21, 1989.

Polanyi, Margaret, "Toronto council approves bid for 1996 Summer Olympics," *The Globe and Mail*, September 22, 1989.

Polanyi, Margaret, "Million-dollar worries unlikely to stop Toronto in bid for '96 Olympics," *The Globe and Mail*, January 29, 1990.

Polanyi, Margaret, "Toronto to decide next week on site to tout in Games bid," *The Globe and Mail*, September 16, 1989.

Stackhouse, John "Race for the Gold." *Report on Business (Globe and Mail)* (September 1990).

Theobald, Steven, "Olympic Spirit Centre put in game plan," *The Toronto Star*, November 28, 2001.

Toronto 2008 Olympic and Paralympic Games: Master Plan. November 1999.

Van Rijn, Nicolaas, "World youth centre vowed if vote is won," *The Toronto Star*, July 13, 2001.

Chapter 28: Rogers Centre

"Award of Excellence (Project: New Massey Hall & Massey Hall Park, Toronto). *Canadian Architect Yearbook*, 1977.

Borough of North York. Extract From Clause 15 From Report No. 38 of the Board of Control dated September 24, 1969.

Christie, Alan, "CN Tower site picked for 62,000-seat dome," *The Toronto Star*, January 18, 1985.

Christie, Alan, "Did the Dome contract go to the best bidder?" *The Toronto Star*, February 24, 1986.

City of Toronto Archives. Series 1020, File 449.

CN Real Estate and Crang and Boake Architects. *CN Tower Dome Proposal to the Ontario Stadium Corporation*. Toronto: CN Real Estate and Crang and Boake Architects. September, 1984.

David, Shi. "Rogers Centre celebrates 20 year history," June 3, 2009, *www.citytv.com*.

Filey, Mike. *Like No Other in the World*. Toronto: Sun Controlled Ventures, 1989.

Diamond, Jack and Sarah Pearce. "The Domed Stadium, Toronto." *The Canadian Architect* 32, No. 5 (May 1987).

Goldberger, Paul, "Double header in Toronto: batter up, top down," *The New York Times*, July 16, 1989.

Haliechuk, Rick, "Stadium will be perfect circle with seating for up to 62,000," *The Toronto Star*, January 18, 1985.

Hart, Matthew. "Edifice Rex." *Toronto*. (May 1989).

Lott, John, "Godfrey's dream come true," *The National Post*, November 30, 2004.

Macaulay, H.L. et al. *The Stadium Study Committee Report*. Toronto: The Stadium Study Committee, 1984.

"Oriole Park at Camden Yards history." *www.baltimore.orioles. mlb.com/bal/ballpark/information/index.jsp?content=history* (accessed February 12, 2011).

"Proposed Memorial Stadium for Toronto," *The Toronto Daily Star*, April 15, 1922.

"Proposed new War Memorial Stadium," *The Toronto Telegram*, April 15, 1922.

Spears, Tom, "Dream of a Metro dome began with Paul Godfrey 15 years ago," *The Toronto Star*, January 17, 1985.

Stein, David Lewis, "Will best site win in derby for dome?" *The Toronto Star*, October 24, 1984.

Technical Evaluation Committee (M. Beynon et al.). *Executive Summary of Evaluation of Various Proposals for Retractable Stadium Roofs*. December, 1984.

Toughill, Kelly. "'82 Grey Cup game clinched Dome Godfrey says." *The Toronto Star*, April 24, 1987.

Trillium Dome Corporation. *Submission to the Stadium Study Committee by the Trillium Dome Corporation*. September 30, 1983.

Chapter 29: Arts and Letters Cathedral

Hill, Robert. *Biographical Dictionary of Architects in Canada, 1800–1950*. *www.dictionaryofarchitectsincanada.org* (Jules Frederic Wegman) (accessed April 1, 2010).

James, Scott. *"Pungent Personalities": Arts and Letters Club Drawings by Arthur Lismer, 1922–43* (catalogue of an exhibition held at the Thomas Fisher Rare Book Library, May 23–September 1, 2006). Toronto, 2006.

"Jules Frederic Wegman." *Royal Architectural Institute of Canada, Journal* 21 (December 1945).

McBurney, Margaret. *The Great Adventure: 100 Years at the Arts and Letters Club*. Toronto: The Arts and Letters Club of Toronto, 2007.

Monroe, Harriet. *John Wellborn Root: A Study of His Life and Work*. Park Forest, IL: Prairie School Press, 1966.

"Toronto Architect Passes Suddenly," *The Toronto Daily Star*, May 1, 1931.

INDEX

ALSO BY MARK OSBALDESTON

Unbuilt Toronto

A History of the City That Might Have Been

978-1550028355

$26.99

Unbuilt Toronto explores never-realized building projects in and around Toronto, from the city's founding to the twenty-first century. Delving into unfulfilled and largely forgotten visions for grand public buildings, landmark skyscrapers, highways, subways, and arts and recreation venues, it outlines such ambitious schemes as St. Alban's Cathedral, the Queen subway line, and early city plans that would have resulted in a Paris-by-the-Lake. Featuring 147 photographs and illustrations, many never before published, *Unbuilt Toronto* casts a different light on a city you thought you knew.

OF RELATED INTEREST

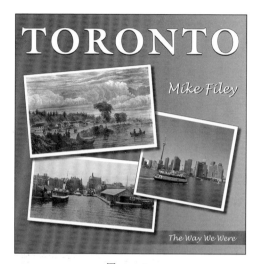

Toronto
The Way We Were
by Mike Filey
978-1550028423
$45.00

For the Record
The First Women in Canadian Architecture
Edited by Joan Grierson
978-1550028201
$28.99

For decades, Toronto historian Mike Filey has regaled readers with stories of the city's past through its landmarks, neighbourhoods, streetscapes, social customs, pleasure palaces, politics, sporting events, celebrities, and defining moments. Now, in one lavishly illustrated volume, he serves up the best of his meditations on everything from the Royal York Hotel, the Flatiron Building, and the Necropolis to Massey Hall, the Palais Royale, and the Canadian National Exhibition, with streetcar jaunts through Cabbagetown, the Annex, Rosedale, and Little Italy, and trips down memory lane with Mary Pickford, Glenn Miller, Bob Hope, and Ed Mirvish.

When Marjorie Hill graduated in 1920 as Canada's "first girl architect," she was entering a profession that had been established in Canada just thirty years earlier. *For the Record*, the first history of women architects in Canada, provides a fascinating introduction to early women architects, presented within the context of developments in both Europe and North America.

Profiles of the women who graduated from the School of Architecture at the University of Toronto between 1920 and 1960 are illustrated with photographs of their work and include archival material that has never before been published. The book also provides current information on schools of architecture in Canada and includes a list of other resources to encourage young women who are thinking of pursuing careers in architecture.

DUNDURN
www.dundurn.com

What did you think of this book?
Visit www.dundurn.com for reviews, videos, updates, and more!